CONCISE NINTH EDITION

YOUR COLLEGE EXPERIENCE

Strategies for Success

John N. Gardner

President, John N. Gardner Institute for Excellence in Undergraduate Education

Distinguished Professor Emeritus, Library and Information Science
Senior Fellow, National Resource Center for The First-Year Experience and
Students in Transition
University of South Carolina, Columbia

A. Jerome Jewler

Distinguished Professor Emeritus, School of Journalism and
Mass Communications, College of Mass Communications
and Information Studies
University of South Carolina, Columbia

Betsy O. Barefoot

Vice President and Senior Scholar

John N. Gardner Institute for Excellence
in Undergraduate Education
Brevard, North Carolina

Bedford / St. Martin's
Boston • New York

D1530640

THOMAS
THURMOND

For Bedford/St. Martin's

Executive Editor: Carrie Brandon
Developmental Editors: Julie Kelly and Martha Bustin
Production Editor: Kerri A. Cardone
Senior Production Supervisor: Dennis J. Conroy
Marketing Manager: Christina Shea
Editorial Assistant: Nicholas Murphy
Copyeditor: Robin Hogan
Senior Art Director: Anna Palchik
Text Design: Jerilyn Bockorick
Cover Art and Design: Billy Boardman
Composition: Nesbitt Graphics, Inc.
Printing and Binding: RR Donnelley and Sons

President: Joan E. Feinberg
Editorial Director: Denise B. Wydra
Editor in Chief: Karen S. Henry
Director of Marketing: Karen R. Soeltz
Director of Production: Susan W. Brown
Associate Director, Editorial Production: Elise S. Kaiser
Managing Editor: Elizabeth M. Schaaf

Library of Congress Control Number: 2010928944

Manufactured in the United States of America.

5 4 3 2 1 0
f   e d c b a

For information, write: Bedford/St. Martin's, 75 Arlington Street, Boston, MA 02116 (617-399-4000)

ISBN: 978-0-312-63798-9 (Student Edition)

ISBN: 978-0-312-63799-6 (Instructor's Annotated Edition)

Dear Student,

When we were in our first year of college, first-year seminars were, by and large, non-existent. Colleges and universities just allowed new students to "sink or swim." As a result, some students made it through their first year successfully, some barely survived, and some simply dropped out.

Today, most colleges and universities offer college success courses to provide essential help to students in navigating their way through the first year. You are likely reading *Your College Experience*, Concise Ninth Edition, because you are enrolled in your institution's college success course. Although this book may seem different from your other textbooks, we believe it may be the most important book you read this year because it's about improving your chances for success in college and beyond. But before you start reading, you probably have some questions about the book and the course. Here are some of the most common questions we hear from students across the country.

- **Why should I take this course?** Research conducted by colleges and universities has found that first-year students are far more likely to be successful if they participate in courses and programs designed to teach them how to succeed in college. This course is intentionally designed to help you avoid some of the pitfalls—both academic and personal—that trip up many beginning students.

- **Aren't all the topics in this book common sense?** In college, topics such as time management and money management become even more important when you're living away from home. Even if you're living with your family, or have a family of your own, college will challenge you to manage your time, feel comfortable interacting with professors, and study effectively. So while some of this may be common sense, this book will provide new insights and information to help you make decisions that lead to success.

- **What am I going to get out of this course?** This course will provide a supportive environment where you will be able to share your successes and your frustrations, get to know others who are beginning college, develop a lasting relationship with your instructor, and begin making plans for life after college.

As college professors with many years of experience working with first-year students, we're well aware that starting college can be challenging. But we also know that if you apply the ideas in this book to your everyday life, you will be more likely to enjoy your time in college, graduate, and achieve your life goals. Welcome to college!

John N. Gardner
A. Jerome Jewler
Betsy O. Barefoot

John N. Gardner brings unparalleled experience to this authoritative text for first-year seminar courses. John is the recipient of his institution's highest award for teaching excellence. He has twenty-five years of experience directing and teaching in the most respected and most widely emulated first-year seminar in the country, the University 101 course at the University of South Carolina. John is universally recognized as one of the country's leading educators for his role in initiating and orchestrating an international reform movement to improve the beginning college experience, a concept he coined as "the first-year experience." He is the founding executive director/president of two influential higher education centers that support campuses in their efforts to improve the learning and retention of beginning college students: the National Resource Center for The First-Year Experience and Students in Transition at the University of South Carolina (www.sc.edu/fye), and the John N. Gardner Institute for Excellence in Undergraduate Education (www .jngi.org), based in Brevard, N.C. The experiential basis for all of his work is his own miserable first year of college on academic probation, an experience he hopes to prevent for this book's readers. Today, as a much happier adult, John is married to fellow author of this book, Betsy Barefoot.

A. Jerome Jewler is a best-selling author, educator, and friend to students. He is a distinguished professor emeritus of the College of Mass Communications and Information Studies as well as former co-director of the University 101 first-year seminar, including its faculty development component, at the University of South Carolina, Columbia. He has been a special mentor to advertising students, has taught a doctoral seminar on teaching mass communication courses, and has helped hundreds of new students—as well as upper-class students—determine their academic and life goals. As University 101 co-director, he planned and conducted training workshops for first-year seminar instructors. He is a recipient of the Mortar Board award for teaching excellence, was recognized as USC Advisor of the Year, and nationally as the Distinguished Advertising Educator in 2000. In retirement, he guides public school children on tours of natural history, cultural history, and science and technology at the South Carolina State Museum. He also volunteers at the Richland County Public Library in Columbia and is an active member of NAMI (National Alliance on Mental Illness), Mid-Carolina branch. He is also the author of *Climates of the Mind, A Bipolar Memory Including The Therapy Journals.*

Betsy O. Barefoot is a writer, researcher, and teacher whose special area of scholarship is the first year of college. During her tenure at the University of South Carolina from 1988 to 1999, she served as co-director for research and publications at the National Resource Center for The First-Year Experience and Students in Transition. She taught University 101, in addition to special-topics graduate courses on the first-year experience and the principles of college teaching. She conducts first-year seminar faculty training workshops around the U.S. and in other countries and is frequently called on to evaluate first-year seminar outcomes. Betsy currently serves as vice president and senior scholar of the John N. Gardner Institute for Excellence in Undergraduate Education, in Brevard, N.C. In this role she led a major national research project to identify institutions of excellence in the first college year. She currently works with both two- and four-year campuses in evaluating all components of the first year.

Icon KEY...

On the cover and throughout the text we have used icons to represent the different topical areas covered in this book. While some connections are likely obvious to you, you might find others a bit more obscure. Check out the key below to learn some interesting facts about these items.

1 Exploring Your Purpose for Attending College	The mortarboard is an item of academic headwear and is traditionally worn by participants in graduation ceremonies. It is named for its similarity in appearance to a tool used by bricklayers to hold mortar.
2 Managing Your Time	The first mechanical alarm clock, capable of striking an alarm at any time specified by the user, was invented in 1559 by Taqi al-Din, of the Ottoman Empire.
3 Understanding Emotional Intelligence	The two masks associated with drama clearly show the range of human emotions. They are the symbols of two ancient Greek Muses: Thalia was the Muse of comedy (the laughing face), while Melpomene was the Muse of tragedy (the weeping face).
4 Discovering How You Learn	Although Thomas Edison is often credited with the invention of the light bulb, the first patent for an incandescent light bulb was granted to Joseph Wilson Swan in 1878, about a year before Edison. In cartoons, comic strips, and other images, a light bulb over a person's head means that he or she has an idea or a new insight.
5 Thinking Critically: The Basis of a College Education	Created in 1974 by Hungarian sculptor and professor of architecture Ernö Rubik, the Rubik's Cube is considered the world's best-selling toy. Solving the puzzle requires deep critical thinking skills.
6 Being Engaged in Learning: Listening, Taking Notes, and Participating in Class	Because of their durability, composition books are often used in long-term academic projects, not only for note taking but also for peer review or journaling.
7 Reading to Learn: Learning to Remember	The common folk wisdom that an elephant never forgets is based on observations that elephants follow the same paths and even hand down memories of directions and places across generations.
8 Improving Your Performance on Exams and Tests	The most commonly used index in the U.S. educational system uses five letter grades: A, B, C, D, and F. The grade A+ is a novelty in American education.

Brief
CONTENTS

CONTENTS

1 Exploring Your Purpose for Attending College   1

2 Managing Your Time   17

5 Thinking Critically: The Basis of a College Education   63

6 Being Engaged in Learning: Listening, Taking Notes, and Participating in Class 79

7 Reading to Learn: Learning to Remember 99

PREFACE FOR INSTRUCTORS

Anyone who teaches beginning college students today knows how much they have changed in recent years. They are increasingly job-focused, technologically adept, concerned about the future, and unevenly prepared for college. Engaging and retaining today's students is a challenge at all levels, but particularly in the first year. Since the early 1980s, college and university educators have recognized that the college success course or first-year seminar is a powerful tool in an overall plan to improve student success. But as students themselves change, so should these courses and course textbooks.

The Concise ninth edition of *Your College Experience* responds to the dynamic nature of college success courses and to changing student needs. While the book continues to address ongoing issues such as learning strategies, critical thinking, and time management, we have added material on matters of increasing importance. The Concise ninth edition, which you hold in your hands, has been re-tooled to focus on academic topics, and so there is expanded coverage of writing, speaking, the library, research, and information literacy. A new chapter has been added on emotional intelligence, to help students manage the emotional ups and downs that so often threaten academic success. Because any book that seeks to support students in their academic success must also support their efforts to stay in college, a new chapter on money discusses managing money, building credit, and financing college.

For schools and instructors who want a book that takes a broader view of college success, the complete ninth edition also includes chapters on relationships, wellness, and choosing a career (ISBN 13: 978-0-312-68774-8). Essentially the same material is also published in a more modular and streamlined format, in *Step-by-Step to College and Career Success*, Fourth Edition (ISBN 13: 978-0-312-63801-6).

What remains the same since the inception of the college success course over the past twenty-five years is our level of commitment to and deep understanding of our students. Although this concise edition of *Your College Experience*, has been significantly revised, it is still based on our collective knowledge and experience in teaching first-year students, as well as on feedback from generations of users. It is grounded in the growing body of research on student success and retention and includes many valuable contributions from leading experts in the field. Our contributors were chosen for their knowledge and currency in their fields as well as their own deep commitments to their students and to the discipline. More than that, however, it is a text born from our devotion to students and to their success. Simply put, we do not like to see students fail. We are confident that if students both read and heed the information herein, they will be more likely to become engaged in the college experience, to learn more, and to persist to graduation.

We have written this text for students of any age in both two-and four-year residential and commuter institutions. Our writing style is intended to convey both respect and admiration for students while recognizing their continued need for challenge and support. We have addressed every topic that our experience, our research, and our reviewers tell us is a concern for students at any type of college or university, with any kind of educational background.

Whether you are considering this textbook for use in your first-year seminar or already have made a decision to adopt it, we thank you for your interest, and we trust that you will find it to be a valuable teaching aid. We also hope this book will guide you and your campus in understanding the broad range of issues that can affect student success.

NEW TO THE CONCISE NINTH EDITION

An expanded academic focus. The Concise ninth edition includes added coverage of writing, speaking, the library, research, and information literacy, providing students with tools and strategies for building the critical academic skills needed to succeed in college.

A new chapter devoted to Emotional Intelligence. Recognizing that the ability to identify behavior and understand and get along with people is central to success in school, this new chapter discusses what emotional intelligence is, why everyone should understand it, and why it matters in college. Written by Catherine Anderson of Gallaudet University, prominent scholar and certified master trainer in emotional intelligence assessment, this chapter discusses why EI skills—such as stress management, adaptability, and interpersonal skills—are crucial to student success.

A new chapter on money management. This chapter outlines important strategies that students can employ both in college and in their lives after college, from how to create a budget and cut costs, to how to obtain and keep financial aid.

A completely revised critical thinking chapter. In an effort to make this complex but crucial topic easier to teach and learn, we've completely revised this chapter, shifting the emphasis to a more comprehensible, student-centered exploration of the meanings, value, and practical application of critical thinking.

New end-of-chapter exercises help students assess what they have learned. Every chapter ends with a collection of exercises. Short-answer questions ask students to reflect on chapter material and its relevance to their academic and personal lives both now and in the future. A one-minute paper prompt is a quick and easy assessment tool that will help alert you when students don't understand what was said or discussed in class. Fully revised Building Your Portfolio exercises help students assemble a collection of their own work.

More real models that let students see principles in action. Because many students learn best by example, full-sized replicas—more than in any competing book—show realistic examples of annotating a textbook, multiple styles of note taking, and other strategies for academic success.

A striking and thoughtful new design. As you page through the Concise ninth edition of *Your College Experience* you'll notice reference material is easier to find, critical thinking exercises and activities are highlighted, and photographs and artifacts of student life have been included to grab students' attention.

INSTRUCTOR RESOURCES AND SUPPLEMENTS

- **Instructor's Annotated Edition.** A valuable tool for new and experienced instructors alike, the IAE includes the full text of the student edition with abundant marginal annotations, chapter specific exercises, and helpful suggestions for teaching, fully updated and revised by the authors. ISBN 13: 978-0-312-63799-6.

- **Instructor's Manual and Test Bank,** by Julie Alexander-Hamilton of the John N. Gardner Institute for Excellence in Undergraduate Education, includes chapter objectives, teaching suggestions, additional exercises, test questions, a list of common concerns of first-year students, an introduction to the first-year experience course, a sample lesson plan for each chapter, and various case studies relevant to the topics covered. Available in print: ISBN-13: 978-0-312-63800-9. Also available online.

- **Computerized Test Bank** includes a mix of fresh, carefully crafted multiple-choice, fill-in-the-blank, and short-answer questions. The questions appear in Microsoft Word format and in easy-to-use test bank software that allows instructors to easily add, edit, re-sequence, and print questions and answers. Instructors can also export questions into a variety of formats, including WebCT and Blackboard. ISBN 13: 978-0-312-67691-9.

- *Ideas and Conversations: A Collection of Interviews about Teaching College Success,* a film directed by Peter Berkow and produced by Bedford/ St. Martin's, is a collection of interviews with instructors and administrators involved in the College Success course. Meet your colleagues and hear their tips for teaching this course and getting students engaged. The film is available on DVD: ISBN 13: 978-0-312-66878-5, or on the instructor's resources portion of our Web site.

- *French Fries Are Not Vegetables and Other College Lessons: A Documentary on the First Year of College* follows five students through their first year in college as they make the life transition associated with attending institutions of higher education. This raw and real-life film looks at these transitions from the student's perspective. Also included are sixteen short and topical lecture launchers that you can use if you prefer to spread the film out over several class sessions. Available on DVD: ISBN 13: 978-0-312-65073-5. Free to all adopters.

- **Custom with Care program.** Bedford/St. Martin's Custom Publishing offers the highest quality books and media, created in consultation with publishing professionals committed to the discipline. Make *Your College Experience*, Concise Ninth Edition, more closely fit your course and goals by integrating your own materials, including only the parts of the text you intend to use in your course, or both. Contact your local Bedford/ St. Martin's sales representative for more information.

- **Trade UP.** Bring more value and choice to your students' first-year experience by packaging *Your College Experience*, Concise Ninth Edition, with one of a thousand titles from Macmillan publishers at a fifty percent discount off the regular price. See the inside back cover or contact your local Bedford/St. Martin's sales representative for more information.

STUDENT RESOURCES

- *Your College Experience* free Companion Web site **bedfordstmartins.com/ gardner** offers a variety of rich learning resources designed to enhance the student experience. These resources include a collection of videos illustrating important concepts, skills, and situations that students will need to understand and master in order to become successful at college. Each video ends with accompanying questions to encourage further contemplation and discussion. Other features include downloadable podcasts offering quick advice on note-taking, money management, succeeding on tests, and many more topics; a "Where to Go for Help" links library directing students to further online resources for support; and much more.

- *CourseSmart e-Book for Your College Experience*, Concise Ninth Edition. We have partnered with CourseSmart to offer a downloadable or online version of *Your College Experience*, Concise Ninth Edition at about half the price of the print book. To learn more about this low-cost alternative go to www.coursesmart.com. ISBN-13: 978-0-312-67562-2.

- *The Bedford/St. Martin's Planner* includes everything that students need to plan and use their time effectively, with advice on preparing schedules and to-do lists and blank schedules and calendars (monthly and weekly) for planning. Integrated into the planner are quick tips on fixing common grammar errors, taking notes, and succeeding on tests; an address book; and an annotated list of useful Web sites. The planner fits easily into a backpack or purse, so students can take it anywhere. To order *The Bedford/St. Martin's Planner* packaged **free** with the text, use ISBN-13: 978-0-312-57778-0. To order the planner **stand-alone** use ISBN-13 978-0-312-57447-5.

- *Bedford/St. Martin's Insider's Guides*. These concise and student-friendly booklets on topics critical to college success are a perfect complement to your textbook and course. Bundle one with any Bedford/St. Martin's textbook at no additional cost. Topics include:

  - **NEW** *Insider's Guide to Global Citizenship*
  - **NEW** *Insider's Guide to Personal Responsibility*
  - **NEW** *Insider's Guide to College Etiquette*
  - *Insider's Guide to Credit Cards*
  - *Insider's Guide to Beating Test Anxiety*
  - *Insider's Guide to Time Management*
  - *Insider's Guide to Getting Involved on Campus*
  - *Insider's Guide to Community College*

For more information on ordering one of these guides **free** with the text go to **bedfordstmartins.com/gardner/catalog**.

- *Writing Journal.* Designed to give students an opportunity to use writing as a way to explore their thoughts and feelings, this writing journal includes a generous supply of inspirational quotes placed throughout the pages, tips for journaling, and suggested journal topics. To order the *Writing Journal* packaged **free** with the text, use ISBN-13: 978-0-312-57777-3. To order the journal **stand-alone** use ISBN 13: 978-0-312-59027-7.

ACKNOWLEDGMENTS

Special thanks to the reviewers of this edition whose wisdom and suggestions guided the creation of this edition of the text:

Darby Johnsen, Oklahoma City Community College

Steve Lindgren, Minnesota State Community and Technical College

Deborah Lanza, Sussex County Community College

Miranda Miller, Gillette College

SusAnn Key, Midwestern State University

Pamela R. Moss, Midwestern State University

We also thank reviewers of the previous edition. They have helped to shape the text you see today.

Rachel A Beech, Arizona State University-Polytechnic

Paula Bradberry, Arkansas State University

Stella Fox, Nassau Community College

Khalida I. Haqq, Mercer County Community College

Elizabeth Hicks, Central Connecticut State University

Darby Johnsen, Oklahoma City Community College

Debra Olsen, Madison Area Technical College

As we look to the future, we are excited about the numerous improvements to this text that our creative Bedford/St. Martin's team has made and will continue to make. Special thanks to Joan Feinberg, President of Bedford/St. Martins; Denise Wydra, Editorial Director; Karen Henry, Editor in Chief; Carrie Brandon, Executive Editor; Julie Kelly and Martha Bustin, Development Editors; Casey Carroll, Humanities Specialist; Jim Camp, Senior Specialist; Nicholas Murphy, Editorial Assistant; Elise Kaiser, Associate Director, Editorial Production; and Kerri Cardone, Production Editor.

Most of all, we thank you, the users of our book, for you are the true inspiration for our work.

CONTRIBUTORS

Although this text speaks with the voices of its three authors, it represents contributions from many others. We gratefully acknowledge those contributions and thank these individuals, whose special expertise has made it possible to introduce new students to their college experience through the holistic approach we deeply believe in.

Dr. Catherine Andersen is Associate Provost for Enrollment at Gallaudet University. Prior to this appointment, she was Gallaudet's interim dean of Enrollment Management and General Studies as well as Director of the First Year Experience for ten years. She is a Teagle Assessment Scholar (a national group that assists liberal arts colleges and universities in assessing student outcomes), is affiliated with the John N. Gardner Institute for Excellence in Undergraduate Education, and is a certified master trainer in Emotional Intelligence assessment. Dr. Andersen received a B.S from Ohio University, an M.S. from Hofstra University, and a Ph.D. from Indiana University. Dr. Andersen contributed her valuable and considerable expertise to the writing of the new chapter 3: "Understanding Emotional Intelligence."

Throughout her career of more than thirty years, **Natala Kleather (Tally) Hart** has served students with limited opportunities for higher education. Her work includes service in financial aid offices at several four-year public institutions: University of California, San Diego, Purdue University, Indiana University and Ohio State University; public service as the head of the Indiana State Scholarship and Loan Commission; and service to institutions of higher education at the College Board. She has contributed widely to college student financial literacy initiatives to improve student retention and completion. Her current role is founding head of the Economic Access Initiative at Ohio State, developing and evaluating mechanisms to encourage college-going among low-income 4th through 10th grade Ohio students and enrollment in graduate and professional programs for first-generation college students. Ms. Hart contributed her valuable and considerable expertise to the writing of the new chapter 12: "Managing Your Money."

Kate Trombitas is the Assistant Director of Ohio State University's Student Wellness Center where she serves as a financial specialist for undergraduate, graduate, and professional students. She holds a bachelor's degree in business administration from Ohio State's Fisher College of Business, and a master's degree in communications, also from Ohio State. Ms. Trombitas contributed her valuable and considerable expertise to the writing of the new chapter 12: "Managing Your Money."

Dr. Reynol Junco is an Associate Professor and the Director of Disability Services in the Department of Academic Development and Counseling at Lock Haven University of Pennsylvania. He holds a doctoral degree in Counselor Education with a focus on College Student Development from The Pennsylvania State University and a Master's degree in Clinical Psychology, also from Penn State. He is a licensed professional counselor in the state of Pennsylvania, and he has taught first-year seminars for over eight years. Dr. Junco's research focuses on using emerging technologies to help engage and support college students. Dr. Junco developed and wrote the "Wired Windows" features in this book.

 Julie Alexander-Hamilton is the Associate Vice President for Assessment Administration at the John N. Gardner Institute for Excellence in Undergraduate Education. She actively engages with colleges and universities as they prepare for and conduct an intensive self study of the first year of college. She holds a M.A. in College Student Development and a B.S. in Psychology from Appalachian State University. While at Appalachian, she taught the three-credit hour first-year seminar and was involved in faculty development and support, peer leader recruitment and training, and planning and implementing Appalachian's residential summer bridge program. Ms. Alexander-Hamilton developed and wrote the end-of-chapter review exercises and activities in this book.

We would also like to acknowledge and thank the numerous colleagues who have contributed to this book in its previous editions:

Chapters 2, 6, 7, 8: Jeanne L. Higbee, University of Minnesota, Twin Cities

Chapter 4: Tom Carskadon, Mississippi State University

Chapter 7: Mary Ellen O'Leary, University of South Carolina at Columbia

Chapter 8: Christel Taylor, University of Wisconsin at Waukesha

Chapter 9: Constance Staley, University of Colorado at Colorado Springs

Chapter 9: R. Stephen Staley, Colorado Technical University

Chapter 10: Charles Curran, University of South Carolina at Columbia

Chapter 10: Rose Parkman Marshall, University of South Carolina at Columbia

Chapter 10: Margit Watts, University of Hawaii, Manoa

Chapter 11: Juan J. Flores, Folsom Lake College

1 Exploring Your Purpose for Attending College

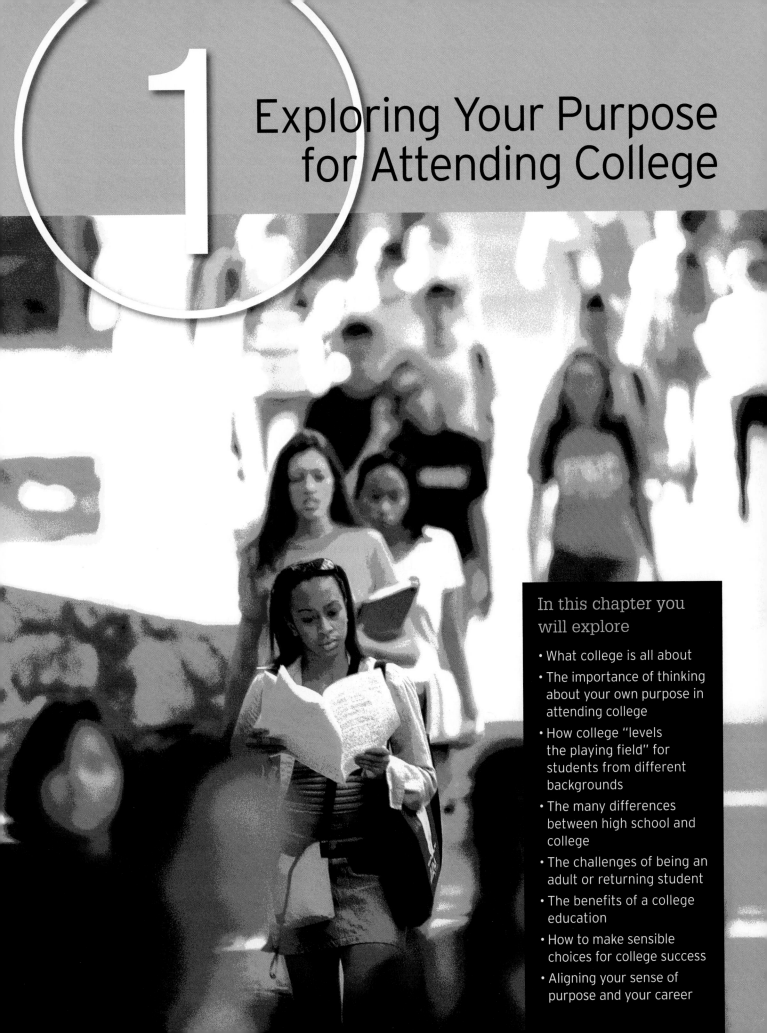

In this chapter you will explore

- What college is all about
- The importance of thinking about your own purpose in attending college
- How college "levels the playing field" for students from different backgrounds
- The many differences between high school and college
- The challenges of being an adult or returning student
- The benefits of a college education
- How to make sensible choices for college success
- Aligning your sense of purpose and your career

IN 1900 fewer than 2 percent of Americans of traditional college age attended college. Today, new technologies and the information explosion are changing the workplace so drastically that in order to support themselves and their families adequately, most people will need some education beyond high school. College is so important that more than 67 percent of high school graduates (approximately 18 million students) attend. Because higher education can be essential to your future earning power and your overall well-being, we are committed to providing a set of strategies you can use to do your best. That's what this book is all about.

As you're settling into your new college routine, we want to welcome you to the world of higher education. The fact that you are reading this textbook probably means you are enrolled in a first-year seminar or "college success" course designed to introduce you to college and help you make the most of it. In this chapter, we'll discuss how you fit into the whole idea of college. We'll consider why the United States has more colleges and universities than any other country in the world. We'll also help you explore the purposes of college—many that your college might define for you. But even more important, we'll help you define your purposes for being here and offer many strategies to help you succeed.

The College Experience

So, what is the college experience? Depending on who you are, your life circumstances, and why you decided to enroll, college can mean different things. College is often portrayed in books and films as a place where young people live away from home in ivy-covered residence halls. We frequently see college depicted as a place with a major focus on big-time sports, heavy drinking, and partying. And, yes, there is some of that at some colleges. But most students today don't move away from home, don't live on campus, and don't see much ivy. College is really far more than any single image you might carry around in your head.

YOUR TURN ▶

So far, is life at your college or university what you expected or hoped for? Why or why not?

There are many ways to define *college*. For starters, college is an established process designed to further formal education so that students who attend and graduate will be prepared for certain roles in society. These days, those roles are found especially in what has become known as "the information economy." This means most college graduates are going to be earning their living by creating, managing, and using information. Because the amount of available information expands all the time, your college classes can't possibly teach you all you need to know for years to come. The most important skill you will need to learn in college is how to keep learning throughout your life.

WHY COLLEGE IS IMPORTANT TO OUR SOCIETY

American society values higher education, which explains why the United States has so many colleges and universities—more than 4,400. College is the primary way in which people achieve upward social mobility, or the ability to attain a higher standard of living. In earlier centuries a high standard of living was almost always a function of family background. Either you were born into power and money or you spent your life working for others who had power and money. But in most countries today, earning a college degree helps to level the playing field for everyone. A college degree can minimize or eliminate differences due to background, race, ethnicity, family income level, national origin, immigration status, family lineage, and personal

connections. Simply put, college participation is about ensuring that more people have the opportunity to be evaluated on the basis of merit rather than family status, money, or other forms of privilege. It makes achieving the American dream possible.

College is also important because it is society's primary means of preparing citizens for leadership roles. Without a college degree, it is difficult to be a leader in a community, company, profession, or the military.

Another purpose of a four-year college degree is to prepare students for continuing their education in a graduate or professional school. If you want to become a medical doctor, dentist, lawyer, or college professor, a four-year college degree is just the beginning.

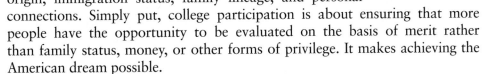

YOUR TURN ▶

When you hear the phrase "American dream," what do you think of? How would you describe to someone else the meaning of these words?

WHY COLLEGE IS IMPORTANT FOR YOU

College is about thinking, and it will help you understand how to become a "critical thinker"—someone who doesn't believe everything he or she hears or reads but instead looks for evidence before forming an opinion. Developing critical-thinking skills will empower you to make sound decisions throughout your life.

Although college is often thought of as a time when traditional-age students become young adults, we realize that many of you are already adults. Whatever your age, college can be a time when you take some risks, learn new things, and meet new and different people—all in a relatively safe environment. It's OK to experiment in college, within limits, because that's what college is designed for.

College will provide you with many opportunities for developing a variety of social networks, both formal and informal. These will help you make friends and develop alliances with faculty members and fellow students who share your interests and goals. Social networking Web sites (such as Facebook and MySpace) provide a way to enrich your real-life social networks in college. College definitely can and should be fun, and we hope it will be for you. You will meet new people, go to athletic events and parties, build camaraderie with new friends, and feel a sense of school spirit. Many college graduates relive memories of college days throughout their lives, fanatically root for their institution's athletic teams, return for homecoming and class reunions, and encourage their own children to attend their alma mater. In fact, you might be a legacy student—someone whose parents or grandparents attended the same institution.

In addition to being fun, college is a lot of work. Being a college student means spending hours studying each week, late nights, taking high-stakes exams, and possibly working harder than you ever have. For many students, college becomes much like a job, with defined duties, expectations, and obligations.

But most important, college will be a set of experiences that will help you to further define and achieve your own purpose. You might feel that you know exactly what you want to do with your life—where you want to go from here. Or, like many students, you might be struggling to find where you fit in life and work. It is possible that as you discover more about yourself and your abilities, your purpose for coming to college will change. In fact, the vast majority of college students change their academic major at least once during the college years, and some students find they need to transfer to another institution to meet their academic goals.

How would you describe your reasons for being in college and at this particular college? Perhaps you, like the vast majority of college students, see college as the pathway to a good job. Maybe you are in college to train or retrain for an occupation, or maybe you have recently experienced an upheaval in your life. Perhaps you are here to fulfill a lifelong dream of getting an education. Or maybe you are bored or in a rut and see college as a way out of it. Many students enter college without a purpose that has been clearly thought out. They have just been swept along by life's events, and now here they are.

Your college or university might require you to select a major during or before your first year, even before you have figured out your own purpose for college. Some institutions will allow you to be "undecided" or to select "no preference" for a year or two. Even if you are ready to select a major, it's a good idea to keep an open mind. There are so many avenues to pursue while you're in college—many that you might not have even considered. Or you might learn that the career you always dreamed of isn't what you thought it would be. Use your first year to explore and think about your purpose for college and how that might connect with the rest of your life.

YOUR TURN ▶

How would you describe your reasons for coming to college at this time in your life? Do you think your reasons will change during your college career? Why or why not?

Aligning Your Sense of Purpose and Your Career

If you are in are in college to prepare yourself for a career, here are some additional questions to ask yourself:

- Am I here to find out who I am and to study a subject that I am truly passionate about, regardless of whether it leads to a career?
- Am I here to engage in an academic program that provides an array of possibilities when I graduate?
- Am I here to prepare myself for a graduate program or immediate employment?
- Am I here to obtain specific training in a field that I am committed to?
- Am I here to gain specific skills for a job I already have?

Remember these following six simple, one-word questions. They can help you to prepare for a career and obtain that important first job:

Wired WINDOW

USING THE INTERNET TO LEARN ABOUT YOUR COLLEGE OR UNIVERSITY

The Internet offers a number of ways to get connected online. As you might already know, social networking Web sites such as Facebook and MySpace are a great way to connect with your friends. Through Facebook you can find new schoolmates with similar interests, join clubs or interest groups, and find friends in your classes. Keep in mind that the information you post on Facebook is available to everyone in your networks, including anyone with an e-mail address from your institution, unless you adjust your privacy settings. While most students use Facebook and MySpace appropriately, some students have faced conduct (and sometimes legal) sanctions for pictures and information they posted online. Therefore, it is important that you review your profile to make sure you are including only information you want the public to know about you. Ask yourself whether you want every Facebook user at your college or university to know personal information such as your residence hall room number or your cell phone number.

Another way in which you can learn about your specific college or university is by taking advantage of official and unofficial online campus resources. Your institution's Web site is one official resource that is useful for finding a range of information, from how to get help with your writing to when the term break begins. Unofficial resources include Web sites that rate professors and student-run wikis that have been created to help you find answers to common questions about your college or university.

Thinking Critically

A popular Web site for rating professors is RateMyProfessor.com. Keep in mind that ratings on such Web sites are not reviewed for accuracy, so use them only as a starting point to learn about a professor. Go to RateMyProfessor.com and search for one of your professors. What do the comments suggest about this professor's teaching style? How do the comments reflect on the students who wrote them? Use the information you gathered from reading the reviews to consider what you might do to be successful in a class taught by the professor you picked.

Why? Why do you want to be a _____ ? Knowing your goals and values will help you pursue your career with passion and an understanding of what motivates you. When you speak with an interviewer, avoid clichés such as "I'm a people person" or "I like to work with people." Sooner or later, most people have to work with people. And your interviewer has heard this way too often. Instead, be sure that you have crystallized your actual reasons for following your chosen career path. An interviewer will want to know why you are interested in the job, why it feels right for you at this time in your life, and whether you are committed to this career for the future.

Who? Who at your college or university or in your community can help you make career decisions? Network with people who can help you find out what work you want to do. Right now, those people might be instructors in your major, an academic advisor, and perhaps someone at your campus career center. Later, network with others who can help you attain your goal. Someone will almost always know someone else for you to talk to.

How? How will you develop the technical and communications skills required for working effectively? Don't be a technophobe. Learn how to do PowerPoint presentations, build web pages, and create Excel spreadsheets. Take a speech course. Work on improving your writing. Even if you think your future job doesn't require these skills, you'll be more marketable with them.

What? What opportunities are available in your preferred career fields? Be aware of the range of job options an employer presents, as well as such threats as a company's decision to **outsource** certain jobs—that is, contracting with an external organization to perform particular functions at a lower cost. Clearly understand the employment requirements for the career field you have chosen. Know what training you will need to remain and move up in your chosen profession.

Where? Where will your preferred career path take you? Will you be required to travel or live in a certain part of the country or the world? Or will job success require that you stay in one location? Although job requirements may change over the course of your lifetime, try to achieve a balance between your personal values and preferences and the predictable requirements of the career you are pursuing.

When? When will you need to start looking for your first job? Certain professions, such as teaching, tend to hire new employees at certain times of the year, generally spring or summer. Determine whether seasonal hiring is common for your preferred career.

CONNECTING YOUR MAJOR AND YOUR INTERESTS WITH YOUR CAREER

Some students are sure about their major when they enter college, but many others are at a loss. Either way, it's OK. At some point, you might ask yourself: Why am I in college? Although it sounds like an easy question to answer, it's not. Many students would immediately respond, "So I can get a good job or education for a specific career." Yet most majors do not lead to a specific career path or job. You actually can enter most career paths from any number of academic majors. Marketing, a common undergraduate business major, is a field that recruits from a wide variety of majors, including advertising, communications, and psychology. Sociology majors find jobs in law enforcement, teaching, and public service.

Today, English majors are designing web pages, philosophy majors are developing logic codes for operating systems, and history majors are sales representatives and business managers. You do not have to major in science to gain admittance to medical school. Of course, you do have to take the required science and math courses, but medical schools seek applicants with diverse backgrounds. Only a few technical or professional fields, such as accounting, nursing, and engineering, are tied to specific majors.

Exploring your interests is the best way to choose an academic major. If you're still not sure, take the advice of Patrick Combs, author of *Major in Success*, who recommends that you major in a subject about which you are really passionate. Most advisors would agree.

YOUR TURN ▶

Would you describe your major as something you're really passionate about? Why or why not? If your answer is "no," why are you pursuing this particular major?

Some students will find they're not ready to select an academic major in the first year. You can use your first year and even your second year to explore your interests and find out how they might connect to various academic programs. Over time, you might make different choices than you would have during your first year.

You can major in almost anything. As this chapter emphasizes, it is how you integrate your classes with your extracurricular activities and work experience that prepares you for a successful transition to your career. Try a major you think you'll like, and see what develops. But keep an open mind, and don't pin all your hopes on finding a career in that major alone. Your major and your career ultimately have to fit your overall life goals, purposes, values, and beliefs.

KEY COMPETENCIES

While employers expect skills and related work experience from today's college graduates, they also have begun to focus on additional key competencies that are critical for success in today's economy:

- **Integrity.** Your employment will depend on your being able to act in an ethical manner at work and in the community.
- **Innovation.** You should also be able to evaluate, synthesize, and create knowledge that will lead to new products and services. Employers seek individuals who are willing to take some risks and explore innovative and better ways to deliver products and services.

- **Initiative.** A great employee is able to recognize the need to take action, such as helping a team member, approaching a new client, or taking on assignments without being asked. Employers don't want employees who will wait passively for a supervisor to provide work assignments; they want people who will see what has to be done and do it.

- **Commitment.** Both employers and graduate schools look for a candidate's commitment to learning. They want you to express what you really love to study and are willing to learn on your own initiative. The best foundation for this competency is to be engaged in an academic program in which you wake up every morning eager to go to class.

Other Outcomes of College

Although a college degree clearly will make you more professionally marketable, the college experience can enrich your life in many other ways. We hope you will take advantage of the many opportunities you'll have to learn the skills of leadership, experience diversity, explore other countries and cultures, clarify your beliefs and values, and make decisions about the rest of your life—not just what you want to do but also, more important, how you want to live.

When you made the decision to come to college, you probably didn't think about all of the positive ways in which college could affect the rest of your life. Your reasons for coming might have been more personal and more immediate. There are all sorts of reasons, circumstances, events, and pressures that bring students to college; and when you put different people with different motivations and purposes together, it creates an interesting environment for learning.

We know without a doubt that college will make your life different from the life you would have had if you had never been a college student. Consider the following list. You will note that the first item is that college graduates earn more money. (Look at Table 1.1 to see about how much more.) However, note that these differences go far beyond making more money. When compared to non-college graduates, those who graduate from college are more likely to:

- earn more money
- have a more stable job history
- earn more promotions
- have fewer children
- be more involved in their children's school lives
- have more discretionary time and money
- become leaders in their communities and employment settings
- stay married longer to the same person
- be elected to public office
- participate in and enjoy the arts

TABLE 1.1 ▶ Median* Earnings by Educational Attainment for Year-Round, Full-Time Workers Age 25+

Doctoral degree	$80,860
Master's degree	$63,856
Bachelor's degree	$50,856
Associate degree	$38,272
High school graduate	$30,732
Less than high school diploma	$22,152

*These are median earnings, meaning half the group earned less and half earned more. These figures are annual amounts based on weekly data through the second quarter of 2007.

Source: U.S. Department of Labor, Bureau of Labor Statistics, Current Population Survey, 2008. (http://www.bls.gov/emp/emptab7.htm)

When compared to nongraduates, college graduates are less likely to:

- be imprisoned
- become dependent on alcohol or drugs
- be duped, conned, or swindled
- be involuntarily unemployed
- use tobacco products

Making the Transition

If you just graduated from high school, you will find some distinct differences between high school and college. For instance, you will probably be part of a more diverse student body, not just in terms of race but also in terms of age, religion, political opinions, and life experiences. If you attend a large college or university, you might feel like a number—not as special as you felt in high school. You will have more potential friends to choose from, but familiar assumptions about people based on where they live, where they go to church, or what high school they attend might not apply to the new people you're meeting.

You will be able to choose from many more types of courses, but managing your time is sure to be more complex because your classes will meet on various days and times, and you will have additional commitments, including work, family, activities, and sports. Your college classes might have many more students in them and meet for longer class periods. Tests are given less frequently in college—sometimes only twice a term—and you will most likely be required to do more writing in college. You will be encouraged to do original research and to investigate differing points of view on a topic. You will be expected to study outside of class, prepare assignments, do assigned reading, and be ready for in-class discussions. Your instructors might rely far less on textbooks and far more on lectures than your high school teachers did. Your instructors will rarely monitor your progress; you're on your own. But you will have more freedom to express views that are different from those of your instructors. They will usually have private offices and keep regular office hours in order to be available for you.

> ### YOUR TURN ▶
>
> In what ways are you already finding that college is different from high school? Did you anticipate these differences? Why or why not?

CHALLENGES AND OPPORTUNITIES FOR ADULT AND RETURNING STUDENTS

If you're a "returning" student—someone who might have experienced some college before—or if you are an adult living and working off campus, you might also find that college presents new challenges and opportunities. For instance, college might feel liberating, like a new beginning or a stimulating challenge or like a path to a career. However, working full-time and attending college at night, on weekends, or both can mean extra stress, especially with a family at home.

Adult students often experience a daunting lack of freedom because of many important conflicting responsibilities. Working, caring for a family, and meeting your other commitments will compete for the time and attention it takes to do your best or even to simply stay in college. You might wonder how you will ever get through college and still manage to care for your family. You might worry that they won't understand why you have to spend time in class and studying.

> ### YOUR TURN ▶
>
> As an adult or returning student, what challenges in college have you already faced? To whom can you turn for help? How might you avoid such challenges in the future?

In spite of your concerns, you should know that many college professors value working with adult students because, unlike eighteen-year-olds, your life experiences have shown you how important an education can be. Adult students tend to have intrinsic motivation that comes with maturity and experience, and that motivation will compensate for any initial difficulties you might have. You will bring a unique and rich perspective to what you're learning in your classes, a perspective that most eighteen-year-olds lack.

FIRST-YEAR MOTIVATION AND COMMITMENT

What attitudes and behaviors will help you to achieve your goals and be successful in college? If you are fresh out of high school, it will be important for you to learn to deal with newfound freedom. Your college professors are not going to tell you what, how, or when to study. If you live on campus, your parents won't be able to wake you in the morning, see that you eat properly and get enough sleep, monitor whether or how well you do your homework, or remind you to allow enough time to get to class. In almost every aspect of your life, you will have to assume primary responsibility for your own attitudes and behaviors.

If you are an adult student, you might find yourself with less freedom: You might have a difficult daily commute and have to arrange and pay for child care. You might have to juggle work and school responsibilities and still find time for family and other duties. As you walk around campus, you might feel uncertain about your ability to keep up with academic work. You also might find it difficult to relate to younger students, some of whom don't seem to take academic work seriously.

Whatever challenges you are facing, what will motivate you to be successful? And what about the enormous investment of time and money that getting a college degree requires? Are you convinced that the investment will pay off? Have you selected a major, or is this on your list of things to do after you arrive? Do you know where to go when you need help with a personal or financial problem? If you are a minority student on your campus, are you concerned about how you will be treated?

Thoughts like these are very common. Although your classmates might not say it out loud, many of them share your concerns, doubts, and fears. This course will be a safe place for you to talk about all of these issues with people who care about you and your success in college.

YOUR TURN ▶

On a scale of 1 to 5, with 5 being high, rate your own level of motivation for college. What do you think accounts for your current motivation level? If you don't think you are motivated, what strategies can you think of that would help motivate you?

What is Your Purpose in College?

Consider these differences in the way a student might feel about college:

I belong in college versus What on earth am I doing here? Where would you fall between these opposite attitudes? You might find that your exact position shifts depending on what's going on in your academic and personal life at any given time. But no matter how you feel on a particular day, as you begin college you will need to spend time sorting out your own sense of purpose and level of motivation. The clearer you are about why you're in college, the easier it will be to stay motivated, even when times are tough.

To build a clearer sense of purpose, look around you and get to know other students who work hard to be successful. Identify students who have the same major or the same career interests, and learn about the courses they have taken, work experiences they have had, and their plans for the future. Look for courses that are relevant to your interests—but don't stop there. Seek relevance in those required general education courses that might seem to be a waste of time or energy at first. Remember that general education courses are designed to give you the kinds of knowledge and skills you need for the rest of your life. Visit your career center, your library, and the Internet to investigate your interests and learn how to develop and apply them in college and beyond. A great Web site to help you research your career interests is the U.S. Department of Labor's Bureau of Labor Statistics (http://www.bls.gov), which includes information about average wages for each career by region, job growth statistics, and unemployment rates.

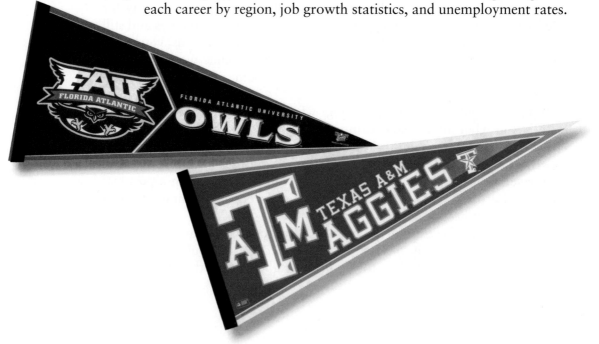

Talk to your residence hall advisors as well as your professors, academic advisors, and campus chaplains. College is designed to give you all the tools you need to find and achieve your purpose. It's all available—but finding it is up to you.

A FORMULA FOR SUCCESS

- **Keep up with your weekly schedule, and do your work on time.** Get a paper calendar or an electronic one, and use it consistently to keep track of assignments and appointments.

- **Be on time for class.** If you are frequently late, you give your instructors and fellow students the unspoken message that you don't think the class is important.

- **If you are a full-time student, limit the hours you work. If you must work, look for a job on campus.** Students who work a reasonable number of hours per week (about fifteen) and especially those who work on campus are more likely to do well in college.

- **Improve your study habits.** Find the most effective methods for reading textbooks, listening, taking notes, studying, and using information resources.

- **Use the academic skills center, library, and campus career center.** These essential services are there to help you be a better student and plan for your future.

- **Learn to think critically.** If you don't carefully examine and evaluate what you see, read, and hear, you're not really learning.

- **Strive to improve your writing and speaking.** The more you speak in public and write, the easier these skills will become.

- **Speak up in class.** Research indicates that you will usually remember more about what goes on in class when you get involved.

- **Learn from criticism.** Criticism can be helpful to your learning. If you get a low grade, meet with your instructor to discuss how you can improve.

- **Study with a group.** Research shows that students who study in groups often earn the highest grades and have the fewest academic problems.

- **Become engaged in campus activities.** Visit the student activities office; join a club or organization that interests you; participate in community service.

- **Meet with your instructors outside of class.** Instructors generally have office hours; successful students use them.

- **Find a competent and caring academic advisor or counselor.** If your personality and that of your advisor clash, ask the department office to find another advisor for you.

- **Take your health seriously.** How much you sleep, what you eat, whether you exercise, and how well you deal with stress will affect your college success.

- **Have realistic expectations.** If you are disappointed in your grades, remember that college is a new experience and your grades will probably improve if you continue to apply yourself.

Where to go FOR HELP...

ON CAMPUS ▶

To find the college support services you need, ask your academic advisor or counselor or consult your college catalog, phone book, and college Web site. Or call or visit student services (or student affairs) offices. Most of these services are free. In subsequent chapters, we will include a "Where to Go for Help" feature that is specific to the chapter topic.

Academic Advisement Center Help in choosing courses; information on degree requirements; help in finding a major.

Academic Skills Center Tutoring; help in study and memory skills; help in studying for exams.

Adult Reentry Center Programs for returning students; supportive contacts with other adult students; information about services such as child care.

Career Center Career library; interest assessments; counseling; help in finding a major; job and internship listings; co-op listings; interviews with prospective employers; help with résumés and interview skills.

Chaplains Worship services; fellowship; personal counseling.

Commuter Services List of off-campus housing; roommate lists; orientation to community; maps; public transportation guides; child-care listings.

Computer Center Minicourses; handouts on campus computer resources.

Counseling Center Confidential counseling for personal concerns; stress management programs.

Services for Students with Disabilities Assistance in overcoming physical barriers or learning disabilities.

Financial Aid and Scholarship Office Information on financial aid programs, scholarships, and grants.

Health Center Help in personal nutrition, weight control, exercise, and sexuality; information on substance abuse programs and other health issues; often includes a pharmacy.

Housing Office Help in locating on- or off-campus housing.

Legal Services Legal aid for students; if your campus has a law school, possible assistance by senior law students.

Math Center Help with math skills.

Fitness Center Facilities and equipment for exercise and recreational sports.

Writing Center Help with writing assignments.

MY INSTITUTION'S RESOURCES ▶

_____

_____

_____

_____

_____

_____

_____

_____

_____

_____

_____

_____

_____

_____

_____

_____

_____

_____

_____

_____

_____

Now that you have read and discussed this chapter, consider how you can apply what you have learned to your academic and personal life. The following prompts will help you reflect on chapter material and its relevance to you both now and in the future.

1. Review the "Other Outcomes of College" section of this chapter. While landing a lucrative career is probably high on your list of goals after college, take a look at the other possible outcomes of obtaining a college degree. List five outcomes from this section that you can relate to the most. If you think of an outcome that is not noted in the chapter, add it to your top five. Why are these outcomes important to you?

2. College students often feel the stress of trying to balance their personal and academic lives. The ups and downs of life are inevitable, but we can control our choices and attitudes. As a first-year student, you will want to begin developing a personal strategy for bouncing back after a particularly difficult time. Your strategy should include at least three steps you can take to get back on track and move forward.

One-Minute PAPER...

Chapter 1 explores how deciding to go to college, experiencing college life, and finding your own path can be a unique journey. Sometimes things that seem simple have more depth if they are given some thought. Take a minute (or several) to think about and note what you found most useful or meaningful during this class. Did anything that was covered in this chapter leave you with more questions than answers?

Building Your PORTFOLIO...

WHAT'S IN IT FOR ME? SKILLS MATRIX

How might the courses in which you are enrolled right now affect your future? Although it might be hard to imagine that there is a direct connection to your career or lifestyle after college, the classes and experiences you are now engaged in can play an important role in your future.

Developing a Skills Matrix will help you reflect on your college experiences and track the skills that will eventually help you land a great summer job, the hard-to-get internship, a scholarship, and one day, a career.

1. Using Microsoft Excel, develop a skills matrix like the one on page 16 to identify courses and out-of-class experiences that enhance the following skills: communications, creativity, critical thinking, leadership, research, social responsibility, and teamwork.

2. Add any additional skills categories or courses you would like to track.

3. Indicate what you did in your courses or activities that helped you learn one of these skills. Be specific about the assignment, project, or activity that helped you learn.

4. Save your skills matrix on your computer, flash drive, or external hard drive.

5. Update your matrix often. Add new skills categories, courses, and activities. Change the title to indicate the appropriate time period (e.g., Skills Learned in my First Two Years of College).

6. Start an electronic collection of your college work. Save papers, projects, and other relevant material in one location on your computer or on an external storage device. Be sure to back up your work to avoid digital disasters!

Skills Learned During First Term in College	My Courses and Activities					
	English	**Math**	**History**	**French**	**First-Year Seminar**	**Campus Activities**
Communication	Improved my writing skills			E-mailed French students	Had to give three oral presentations	Participated in Toastmasters
Creativity	Writing original poetry					Designed float for homecoming
Critical Thinking			Class members debated Afghan war			
Leadership					Led a group project on college sports	Participated in Emerging Leaders
Research					Conducted research on memory	
Social Responsibility					Participated in Habitat for Humanity Project	Tutored 2nd graders in reading
Teamwork		Had to study in a study group				Participated in intramural soccer

2 Managing Your Time

In this chapter you will explore

- How to take control of your time and your life
- How to use goals and objectives to guide your planning
- How to prioritize your use of time
- How to combat procrastination
- How to use a planner and other tools
- How to organize your day, your week, your school term
- The value of a to-do list
- How to avoid distractions

How do you approach time?

you approach time? You might find that you view this important resource differently than your classmates. For example, if you're a natural organizer, you probably enter all due dates for assignments on your calendar, cell phone, or PDA as soon as you receive each syllabus. If you take a more laid-back approach to life, you might prefer to be more flexible and go with the flow rather than following a daily or weekly schedule.

Most fundamentally, how you manage time reflects what you value. For instance, when you value friendships above everything else, your academic work can take a back seat to social activities. What you value most and how that relates to the way you spend your time often change in college.

Time management involves:

- Knowing your goals
- Setting priorities to meet your goals
- Anticipating the unexpected
- Taking control of your time
- Making a commitment to punctuality
- Carrying out your plans

Taking Control of Your Time

The first step to effective time management is recognizing that you can be in control. How often do you find yourself saying, "I don't have time"? Once a week? Once a day? Several times a day? The next time you find yourself saying this, stop and ask yourself whether it is really true. Do you really not have time, or have you made a choice, consciously or unconsciously, not to make time for that particular task or activity?

When we say that we don't have time, we imply that we don't have a choice. But we do have a choice. We have control over many of the commitments we choose to make. And we also have control over many small decisions that affect our time-management success, such as what time we get up in the morning, how much sleep we get, what we eat, how much time we spend studying, and whether we get exercise.

Being in control means that you make your own decisions. Two of the most often cited differences between high school and college are increased **autonomy**, or independence, and greater responsibility. If you are not a recent high school graduate, you have most likely already experienced a higher level of independence, but returning to school creates responsibilities above and beyond those you already have.

Whether you are beginning college immediately after high school or are continuing your education after a break, make sure that the way you spend your time aligns with your most important values. For instance, if you value becoming an expert in a particular academic area, you'll want to learn everything you can in that field by taking related classes and participating in internships. If you value learning about many things and are postponing a specific decision about your major, you might want to spend your time exploring many different areas of interest and taking as many different types of courses as possible.

OVERCOMING PROCRASTINATION

Procrastination is a serious problem that trips up many otherwise capable people. In the book *Procrastination: Why You Do It, What to Do About It*, psychologists Jane Burka and Lenora Yuen summarize a number of research studies about procrastination.[1] According to these authors, even students who are highly motivated often fear failure, and some students even fear success (although that might seem counterintuitive). Some students procrastinate because they are perfectionists; not doing a task might be easier than having to live up to your own very high expectations—or those of your parents, teachers, or peers. Others procrastinate because they find an assigned task boring or irrelevant or consider it "busy work," believing that they can learn the material just as effectively without doing the homework.

When you're in college, procrastinating can signal that it's time to reassess your goals and objectives; maybe you are not ready to make a commitment to academic priorities at this point in your life. Only you can decide, but a counselor or academic advisor can help you sort it out.

Here are some strategies for beating procrastination:

- Remind yourself of the possible consequences if you do not get down to work, then get started.
- Create a to-do list. Check off things as you get them done. Use the list to focus on the things that aren't getting done. Move them to the top of the next day's list, and make up your mind to do them.
- Break big jobs into smaller steps. Tackle short, easy-to-accomplish tasks first.
- Promise yourself a reward for finishing the task, such as watching your favorite TV show or going out with friends. For more substantial tasks, give yourself bigger and better rewards.
- Find a place to study that's comfortable and doesn't allow for distractions and interruptions.
- Don't talk on the phone, send e-mail or text messages, or surf the web during planned study sessions. If you study in your room, close your door.

If these ideas don't sufficiently motivate you to get to work, you might want to reexamine your purposes, values, and priorities: Why am I in college here and now? Why am I in this course? What is really important to me? Are these values important enough to forgo some short-term fun or laziness in order to get down to work? Are my academic goals really my own, or were they imposed on me by family members, my employer, or societal expectations? If you are not willing to stop procrastinating and get to work on the tasks at hand, perhaps you should reconsider why you are in college and if this is the right time to pursue higher education.

---

[1]Jane B. Burka and Lenora M. Yuen. *Procrastination: Why You Do It, What to Do About It* (Reading, MA: Addison-Wesley, 1983).

Researchers at Carleton University in Canada have found that college students who procrastinate in their studies also avoid confronting other tasks and problems and are more likely to develop unhealthy habits, such as higher levels of alcohol consumption, smoking, insomnia, a poor diet, or lack of exercise.[2] If you cannot get procrastination under control, it is in your best interest to seek help at your campus counseling service.

SETTING PRIORITIES

To help combat the urge to procrastinate, think about how to prioritize your tasks, goals, and values. For example, studying in order to get a good grade on tomorrow's test might have to take priority over attending a job fair today. However, don't ignore long-term goals in order to meet short-term goals. With good time management you can study during the week prior to the test so that you can attend the job fair the day before. Skilled time managers often establish priorities by maintaining a to-do list (discussed in more detail later in this chapter), ranking the items on the list to determine schedules and deadlines for each task.

Another aspect of setting priorities while in college is finding an appropriate way to balance your academic schedule with the rest of your life. Social activities are an important part of the college experience. Time alone and time to think are also essential to your overall well-being.

For many students, the greatest challenge of prioritizing will be balancing school with work and family obligations that are equally important and are not optional. Good advance planning will help you meet these challenges. But you will also need to talk with your family members and your employer to make sure that they understand your academic responsibilities. Most professors will

[2]Timothy A. Pychyl and Fuschia M. Sirois. *Procrastination: Costs to Health and Well-being.* Presentation at the APA Convention, August 22, 2002, Chicago.

work with you when conflicts arise, but if you have problems that can't be resolved easily, be sure to seek support from your college's counseling center.

YOUR TURN ▶

What are your most pressing obligations, other than your studies, that will have to fit into your time-management plan? Are any of them more important to you than doing well in college? Why or why not?

STAYING FOCUSED

Many of the decisions you make today are reversible. You can change your major, your career, and even your life goals. But it is important to take control of your life by establishing your own goals for the future, setting your priorities, and managing your time accordingly.

To begin, make a plan that starts with your priorities: attending classes, studying, working, and spending time with the people who are important to you. Then think about the necessities of life: sleeping, eating, exercising, and relaxing. Leave time for fun things such as talking with friends, checking out Facebook, watching TV, and going out. But finish what *needs* to be done before you move from work to pleasure. And don't forget about personal time. If you live in a residence hall or share an apartment with other students, talk with your roommates about how you can coordinate your class schedules so that each of you has some privacy. If you live with your family, particularly if you are a parent, work together to create special family times as well as quiet study times.

YOUR TURN ▶

List your current priorities in order of importance. What does your list suggest about why you consider some things more important? Less important? Have you put any items in the wrong place? What should you change, and why?

Getting Organized

In college, as in life, you will quickly learn that managing time is important to success. Almost all successful people use some sort of calendar or planner, either paper or electronic, to help them keep up with their appointments, assignments or tasks, and other important activities and commitments.

USE A PLANNER

Your college might sell a calendar in the campus bookstore designed specifically for your school, with important dates and deadlines already provided. Or you might prefer to use an online calendar or the calendar that comes on your computer, cell phone, or PDA. Regardless of the format you prefer (electronic or hard copy), it's a good idea to begin the term by completing a term assignment preview (Figure 2.1).

	Monday	Tuesday	Wednesday	Thursday	Friday
Week 1			First day of Classes!	Read Ch. 1–2 English	Discuss Ch. 1–2 History in Class Work 2–5
Week 2	English Quiz Ch. 1–2 Work 4–7	Psych Quiz Ch. 1	English Essay #1 Due Work 4–7	History Quiz Ch. 1–2	Discuss Ch. 3–4 English in Class Work 2–5
Week 3	English Quiz Ch. 3–4 Work 4–7	Psych Quiz Ch. 2 Read Bio Ch. 1–2	English Essay Due Work 4–7	Be Ready for Bio Lab Experiment	Discuss English pp. 151–214 Work 2–5
Week 4	Work 4–7	Read English pp. 214–275	English Essay Due Work 4–7 Discuss pp. 214–275	Read English pp. 276–311	Discuss English 276–311 Work 2–5

	Monday	Tuesday	Wednesday	Thursday	Friday
Week 5	Work 4–7	Psych Quiz Ch. 3–4	English Essay Due Work 4–7	Bio Lab Experiment	Prepare Psych Experiment Work 2–5
Week 6	Work 4–7	Present Psych Experiment	English Essay Due Work 4–7	Bio Lab Experiment	Work 2–5
Week 7	Work 4–7	Study for English Mid-Term	English Mid-Term!! Work 4–7	Bio Lab Experiment	Study Psych Mid-Term Work 2–5
Week 8	Study for Psych Mid-Term Work 4–7	Psych Mid-Term!!	Study for History Mid-Term Work 4–7	Bio Lab Experiment Study for History Mid-Term	History Mid-Term!! Work 2–5

▲ FIGURE 2.1

Term Assignment Preview. Using the course syllabi provided
by your instructors, create your own term calendar. You can find blank templates on
the book's Web site at **bedfordstmartins.com/gardner**. Remember, for longer assignments, such as term papers,
divide the task into smaller parts and establish your own deadline for each part of the assignment, such as
deadlines for choosing a topic, completing your library research, developing an outline of the paper, writing a first
draft, and so on.

To create a term assignment preview, begin by entering all of your commitments for each week: classes, assignment due dates, work hours, family commitments, and so on. Examine your toughest weeks during the term. If paper deadlines and test dates fall during the same week, make time to finish some assignments early. Note this in your cell phone, PDA, or calendar. If you use an electronic calendar, set a reminder for these important deadlines and dates. Break large assignments (term papers, for example) into smaller steps, such as choosing a topic, doing research, creating an outline, learning necessary computer skills, writing a first draft, and so on. Add deadlines for each of the smaller portions of the project.

Next, enter important dates and notes from the preview sheets into your calendar or planner and continue to enter all due dates as soon as you know them. Write down meeting times and locations, scheduled social events (including phone numbers in case you need to cancel), study time for each class you're taking, and so forth. Keep a backup copy on paper in case you lose your phone, you can't access the Internet, or your PDA or computer crashes. It's also a good idea to carry your calendar or planner with you. Your first term of college is the time to get into the habit of using a planner to help you maintain control of your schedule. Check your notes daily at the same time of day for the current week as well as the coming week. It takes just a moment to be certain that you aren't forgetting something important.

YOUR TURN ▶

What kind of planner do you currently use, if any? Does your method of planning work for you? Why or why not?

CHART A WEEKLY TIMETABLE

Now that you have created a term preview, the weekly timetable model in Figure 2.2 can help you tentatively plan how to spend your hours in a typical week. Here are some tips for creating a weekly schedule:

- As you create your schedule, try to reserve at least two hours of study time for each hour spent in class. This means that if you take a typical full-time class load of fifteen credits, for example, you should plan to study an additional 30 hours per week. If you are also working, reconsider how many hours per week it will be reasonable for you to be employed above and beyond this commitment, or consider reducing your credit load.

- Decide whether you study more effectively in the day or in the evening, or a combination of both. Determine whether you are capable of getting up very early in the morning to study or how late you can stay up at night and still wake up for morning classes.

- Not all assignments are equal. Estimate how much time you will need for each one, and begin your work early. A good time manager frequently finishes assignments before actual due dates to allow for emergencies.

	Sunday	Monday	Tuesday	Wednesday	Thursday	Friday	Saturday
6:00							
7:00							
8:00		←	BREAKFAST	→			
9:00	SLEEP IN!	Review English	PSYCH 101	Review English	PSYCH 101	Review English	
10:00		English 101	Review PSYCH	English 101	Review PSYCH	English 101	ENJOY!
11:00		LUNCH		LUNCH			
12:00	PICNIC	HISTORY 101	LUNCH	HISTORY 101	LUNCH	HISTORY 101	
1:00	W/JANE,						
2:00	ALEX,	BIO 101		BIO 101	BIO 101 LAB	WORK	
3:00	MICHELLE, etc.				↓	↓	BE LAZY!
4:00		WORK		WORK			
5:00						↓	GO
6:00	STUDY ENGLISH	DINNER	DINNER	DINNER	DINNER	DINNER	OUT
7:00	HISTORY	↓	STUDY ENGLISH	↓	STUDY ENGLISH		WITH
8:00		STUDY HISTORY	HISTORY		HISTORY		FRIENDS
9:00		STUDY PSYCH	BIO	STUDY PSYCH			
10:00							
11:00							

▲ FIGURE 2.2

Weekly Timetable. Using your term calendar, create your own weekly timetable. You can find blank templates on the book's Web site at **bedfordstmartins.com/gardner**. As you complete your timetable, keep in mind the suggestions in this chapter. Do you want your classes back to back or with breaks in between? How early in the morning are you willing to start classes? Do you prefer—or do work or family commitments require you—to take evening classes? Are there times of day when you are more alert? Less alert? How many days per week do you want to attend classes? At some institutions you can go to school full-time by attending classes exclusively on Saturday. Plan how you will spend your time for the coming week. Track all of your activities for a full week by entering into your schedule everything you do and how much time each task requires. Use this record to help you estimate the time you will need for similar activities in the future.

Keep track of how much time it takes you to complete different kinds of tasks. For example, depending on your skills and interests, it might take longer to read a chapter in a biology text than to read one in a literature text. Keeping track of your time will help you estimate how much time to allocate for similar tasks in the future.

YOUR TURN ▶

What are the best and worst times for you to study? Why? Have you found a particular time when it's easier for you to concentrate or be creative?

MAINTAIN A TO-DO LIST

Once you have plotted your future commitments, you can stay on top of your obligations with a to-do list, which is especially handy for last-minute reminders. It can help you keep track of errands you need to run, appointments you need to make, e-mail messages you need to send, and so on—anything you're prone to forget. You can keep this list on your cell phone or in your notebook, or you can post it on your bulletin board. Some people start a new list every day or once a week. Others keep a running list, and throw a page away only when everything on the list is done (see Figure 2.3). Whichever method you prefer, use your to-do list to keep track of all the tasks you need to remember, not just academics.

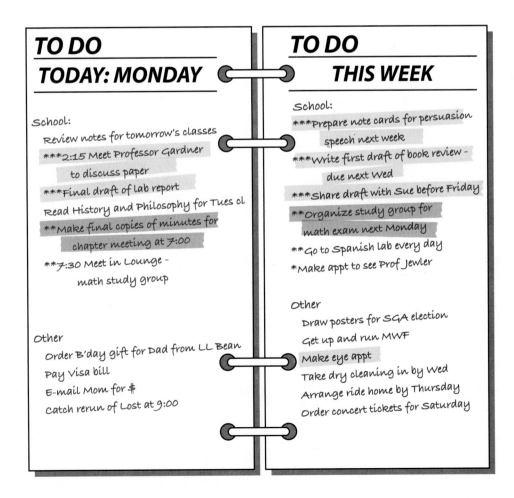

TO DO
TODAY: MONDAY

School:
Review notes for tomorrow's classes
***2:15 Meet Professor Gardner
    to discuss paper
***Final draft of lab report
Read History and Philosophy for Tues cl
**Make final copies of minutes for
    chapter meeting at 7:00
**7:30 Meet in Lounge –
    math study group

Other
Order B'day gift for Dad from LL Bean
Pay Visa bill
E-mail Mom for $
Catch rerun of Lost at 9:00

TO DO
THIS WEEK

School:
***Prepare note cards for persuasion
    speech next week
***Write first draft of book review –
    due next Wed
***Share draft with Sue before Friday
**Organize study group for
    math exam next Monday
**Go to Spanish lab every day
*Make appt to see Prof Jewler

Other
Draw posters for SGA election
Get up and run MWF
Make eye appt
Take dry cleaning in by Wed
Arrange ride home by Thursday
Order concert tickets for Saturday

◀ FIGURE 2.3
Daily and Weekly To-Do Lists

Making Sure Your Schedule Works for You

How might you wisely use time between classes? This might be your first opportunity to take classes that do not meet five days a week. Would you prefer spreading your classes over five or six days of the week, or would you like to go to class just two or three days a week or even once a week for a longer class period? Your attention span and other commitments should influence your decision.

CREATE A WORKABLE CLASS SCHEDULE

If you live on campus, you might want to create a schedule that situates you near a dining hall at mealtimes or allows you to spend breaks between classes

Wired WINDOW

GETTING THINGS DONE

A popular process to help you with time management and procrastination is the Getting Things Done (GTD) system created by David Allen. GTD is very popular with people who are heavy users of computers and technology, since it offers simple, straightforward, and easy-to-accomplish ways to help get your life in order. Although engaging in the GTD process does not require a computer or other technology tool, many Web sites and applications are dedicated to supporting the GTD process.

The basic premise behind GTD is that we are bombarded by things we have to do. These things are always tugging at us, even when we aren't consciously thinking about them. The constant tug, whether conscious or unconscious, causes us undue stress and negatively affects our thinking process. While the complete GTD system addresses both physical and mental items, let's focus on the application of GTD to your to-do list. (To learn more about the GTD system, visit http://www.43folders.com/2004/09/08/getting -started-with-getting-things-done.)

Here is the process:

1. Identify all of the things that demand your attention (these include courses, projects, work, family, etc.).
2. Allow yourself the freedom to forget about the things that aren't important.

3. Create a reliable and portable to-do list. (You can use whatever works best for you. Some examples include a small notepad that you carry with you, an application on your computer or cell phone, or a three-ring binder.) It is helpful to organize this list by contexts (such as home, school, computer, phone calls, errands, etc.).
4. Write down everything on your to-do list in the form of a *next task*. (For instance, when you need to write a term paper for your philosophy class, you might want to list the next task as "Choose a topic for Philosophy term paper.")
5. Do the things on your list when you are in the right context. (For example, send an e-mail to your professor when you are at your computer.)
6. Start at the beginning and go through the process again.

Think Critically

Try out the GTD system of keeping a to-do list. If you would like a technology-based tool that will help you implement the system, try Chandler (http:// chandlerproject.org), a free application that is available for all computer operating systems. After a few days of using the GTD system, ask yourself: Is this method of keeping a to-do list right for me? Why or why not? Are there ways in which I can improve this system to fit with my personality style?

ORGANIZE YOUR DAYS

Being a good student does not necessarily mean studying day and night and doing little else. Keep the following points in mind as you organize your day:

- **Set realistic goals for your study time.** Assess how long it takes to read a chapter in different types of textbooks and how long it takes you to review your notes from different instructors, and schedule your time accordingly. Give yourself adequate time to review and then test your knowledge when preparing for exams.

- **Use waiting time to review** (on the bus, before class, before appointments). Prevent forgetting what you have learned by allowing time to review as soon as is reasonable after class. (Reviewing immediately after class might be possible but not reasonable if you are too burned out to concentrate!)

- **Know your best times of day to study.** Schedule other activities, such as laundry, e-mail, or spending time with friends, for times when it will be difficult to concentrate.

- **Restrict repetitive, distracting, and time-consuming tasks** such as checking your e-mail, Facebook, or cell phone to a certain time, not every hour.

- **Avoid multitasking.** Even though you might actually be quite good at it, or at least think that you are, the reality is (and research shows) that you will be able to study most effectively and retain the most information if you concentrate on one task at a time.

- **Be flexible.** You cannot anticipate every disruption to your plans. Build extra time into your schedule so that unexpected interruptions do not prevent you from meeting your goals.

at the library. Or you might need breaks in your schedule for relaxation, catching up with friends, or spending time in a student lounge, college union, or campus center.

If you're a commuter student or if you must carry a heavy workload to afford going to school, you might prefer to schedule your classes in blocks without breaks. However, while taking back-to-back classes allows you to cut travel time by attending school one or two days a week and might provide for more flexible scheduling of a job or family commitments, it can also have significant drawbacks.

If you become ill on a class day, you could fall behind in all of your classes. You might also become fatigued from sitting in class after class. When one class immediately follows another, it will be difficult for you to have a last-minute study period immediately before a test because you will be attending another class and are likely to have no more than a fifteen-minute break. Finally, remember that for back-to-back classes, several exams might be held on the same day.

YOUR TURN ▶

Knowing what you know now about your schedule, what will you do differently next term? Will you try to schedule classes close together or spread them apart? Why?

Month(s) October

Monday the _____ 5 _____

7 AM		2	Review for stats Quiz—Wed!
8		3	Do English reading assignment
9		4	↓
10	Stats	5	
11	English 101	6	Gym
NOON		7	
1 PM	Lunch w/Jenn	8	

Tuesday the _____ 6 _____

7 AM		2	
8		3	History (3:30)
9	Gym	4	
10		5	Review for stats Quiz
11	Volunteer @ MSPCA	6	Work 6–11
NOON		7	
1 PM	Biology (1:30)	8	↓

Wednesday the _____ 7 _____

7 AM		2	Do English Reading Assignment
8	Review for stats Quiz	3	
9		4	
10	Stats (Quiz Today!)	5	Meet w/Bio Study Group
11	English 101	6	
NOON		7	
1 PM		8	Volleyball

▲ **FIGURE 2.4**
Example of a weekly schedule viewed monthly.

DON'T OVEREXTEND YOURSELF

Even with the best intentions, some students who use a time-management plan overextend themselves. If there is not enough time to carry your course load and meet your commitments, drop a course before the drop deadline so that you won't have a low grade on your permanent record. If you receive financial aid, keep in mind that you must be registered for a minimum number of credit hours to be considered a full-time student and thereby maintain your current level of financial aid.

If dropping a course is not feasible or if other activities are lower on your list of priorities, which is likely for most college students, assess your other time commitments and let go of one or more. Doing so can be very difficult, especially if you think that you are letting other people down. However, it is far preferable to excuse yourself from an activity than to fail to come through at the last minute because you have committed to more than you can possibly achieve.

REDUCE DISTRACTIONS

Where should you study? Some students find that it's best not to study in places associated with leisure, such as the kitchen table, the living room, or in front of the TV, because these places lend themselves to interruptions and other distractions. Similarly, it might be unwise to study on your bed because you might drift off to sleep. Instead, find quiet places, both on campus and at home, where you can concentrate and develop a study mind-set each time you sit down to do your work.

Try to stick to a routine as you study. If you have larger blocks of time available on the weekend, for example, take advantage of that time to review or catch up on major projects, such as term papers, that can't be completed effectively in fifty-minute blocks. Break down large tasks and take one thing at a time.

Here are some more tips to help you deal with distractions:

- Turn off the computer, TV, CD player, DVD, iPod, or radio unless the background noise or music really helps you concentrate on your studies or drowns out more distracting noises (people laughing or talking in other rooms or hallways, for instance). Consider silencing your cell phone so that you aren't distracted by incoming calls or text messages.
- Stay away from the computer if you're going to be tempted to check e-mail or Facebook.
- Try not to let personal concerns interfere with studying.
- Develop an agreement with your roommate(s) or family about quiet hours. If that's not possible, find a quiet place where you can go to concentrate.

Respecting Others' Time

In college, if you repeatedly arrive late for class or leave before class periods have officially ended, you are breaking the basic rules of politeness, and you are intentionally or unintentionally showing a lack of respect for your instructors and your classmates. In college, punctuality is a virtue.

Be in class early enough to shed your coat, shuffle through your backpack, and have your assignments, notebooks, and writing utensils ready to go. Likewise, be on time for scheduled appointments. Avoid disruptive behaviors such as leaving class to feed a parking meter or answer your cell phone, returning five or ten minutes later. Similarly, text messaging, sending instant messages, doing homework for another class, falling asleep, or talking (even whispering) disrupts the class. Make adequate transportation plans in advance, get enough sleep at night, wake up early enough to be on time for class, and complete assignments prior to class.

Time management is a lifelong skill. Securing a good job after college will likely mean managing your own time and possibly that of other people you supervise. If you decide to go to graduate or professional school, time management will continue to be essential to your success. But not only is time management important for you, it is also a way in which you show respect for others: your friends, family, and college instructors.

Where to go FOR HELP...

ON CAMPUS ▶

Academic Skills Center Along with assistance in studying for exams, reading textbooks, and taking notes, your campus academic skills center has specialists in time management who can offer advice for your specific problems.

Counseling Center If your problems with time management involve emotional issues you are unable to resolve, consider visiting your school's counseling office.

Your Academic Advisor/Counselor If you have a good relationship with this person, he or she might be able to offer advice or to refer you to another person on campus, including those in the offices mentioned above.

A Fellow Student A friend who is a good student and willing to help you with time management can be one of your most valuable resources.

MY INSTITUTION'S RESOURCES ▶

_____
_____
_____
_____
_____

Now that you have read and discussed this chapter, consider how you can apply what you have learned to your academic and personal life. The following prompts will help you reflect on chapter material and its relevance to you both now and in the future.

1. Review the "Overcoming Procrastination" section of this chapter. Think of one upcoming assignment in any of your current classes and describe how you can avoid waiting until the last minute to get it done. Break down the assignment and list each step that you will take to complete the assignment. Give yourself a due date for each step and one for completing the assignment.

2. After reading about effective time-management strategies, consider the ways in which you manage your own time. If you were grading your current set of time-management skills, what grade (A, B, C, or lower) would you give yourself? Why? What is your biggest challenge to becoming a more effective time manager?

One-Minute PAPER...

Chapter 2 gives you a lot of tips for managing your time. It can be frustrating to realize that you have to spend time organizing yourself in order to manage your time effectively. Did any of the time-management tips in this chapter really appeal to you? If so, which ones and why? Did anything in this chapter leave you with more questions than answers? If so, what are your questions?

Building Your PORTFOLIO...

TIME IS OF THE ESSENCE

This chapter includes many great tips for effectively managing your time. Those skills are necessary for reducing the stress of everyday life, but have you thought about managing your time over the long term? What are your long-term goals? Preparing yourself for a particular career is probably high on your list, and it's not too early to begin thinking about what kind of preparation is necessary for the career (or careers) you are considering.

First, to help you determine the careers you're most interesting in pursuing, schedule an appointment with the career center on your campus and ask for information on career assessments to help you identify your preferences and interests. This portfolio assignment will help you realize that it is important to plan ahead and consider what implications your long-term goals have for managing your time right now.

1. In a Word document or Excel spreadsheet create a table like the example on page 32.

2. Choose a career or careers in which you're most interested. In this example, a student needs to plan ahead for activities that will help to prepare for a future as a certified public accountant. It is OK if you have not decided on just one major or career; this is a process that you can repeat as your interests change. An "action step" is something that you need to do within a certain time frame.

3. Talk with someone in the career center, a professor, an upperclass student in your desired major, or a professional in your chosen career to get an idea of what you need to be considering, even now.

4. Fill in the action steps, To-Dos, time line, and notes sections of your own chart, and update the chart as you learn more about the career you are exploring.

5. Save your work in your portfolio on your personal computer or flash drive.

Example Career: Certified Public Accountant (CPA)			
Action Step	**To-Do**	**Time line**	**Notes**
Make sure I'm taking the courses necessary to pursue this career.	Set up an appointment to talk with my academic advisor.	I should do this as soon as possible.	What prerequisites do I need for these courses?
Consider job shadowing.	Check with the career center to learn whether they can help me job shadow with a college alum in this career.	I should do this as soon as possible.	This action step will help me to determine whether this is really a career that I wish to pursue.
Check out campus clubs, organizations, and volunteer work.	Join a club or organization and consider becoming an officer, such as treasurer.	I should do this as soon as possible.	This will give me practical experience that relates to my field.
Determine whether I need a master's degree, certificate, or license.	Explore these options and the benefits of each.	I should begin thinking about this in my junior and senior years.	I need to know how long a degree will take and consider how to finance it.

3

Understanding Emotional Intelligence

In this chapter you will explore

- What emotional intelligence is
- Why emotional intelligence matters in college and in life
- How to assess your emotional intelligence
- Specific skills that are connected to emotional intelligence
- What you can do to improve your emotional competencies

ing. That's not necessarily true, but the popular belief embodies a key aspect of education that is often overlooked. The ability to understand and get along with people is vital for success in school, work, and life. Another element of success is the ability to manage time well and get things done. Why do some individuals handle stressful situations with ease while others fall apart? Although we tend to think of these abilities as inborn personality traits that can't be changed, the fact is that social skills and stress-management skills can be learned and improved.

Particularly in the first year of college, many students who are intellectually capable of succeeding have difficulty establishing positive relationships with others, dealing with pressure, or making wise decisions. Other students exude optimism and happiness and seem to adapt to their new environment without any trouble. The difference lies not in academic talent but in emotional intelligence (EI), or the ability to recognize and manage moods, feelings, and attitudes. A growing body of evidence shows a clear connection between students' EI and whether or not they stay in college.

As you read this chapter, you will develop an understanding of emotional intelligence, and you will learn how to use it to become a more successful student and person. You will begin to look at yourself and others through an EI lens, observe the behaviors that help people do well, get to know yourself better, and take the time to examine why you are feeling the way that you do before you act. Then, as you read each subsequent chapter in this book, try to apply what you have learned about EI and think about how it might relate to the behaviors of successful college students. You can't always control the challenges and frustrations of life, but with practice you *can* control how you respond to them.

What Is Emotional Intelligence?

Emotional intelligence is the ability to identify, use, understand, and manage emotions. Emotions are a big part of who you are; you should not ignore them. The better the emotional read you have on a situation, the more appropriately you can respond to it. Being aware of your own and others' feelings helps you to gather accurate information about the world around you and allows you to respond in appropriate ways.

> **YOUR TURN** ▶
>
> Do you know anybody (including yourself) who is "book smart" but not very good with people? Do you know anyone who has serious problems managing time? What kinds of challenges do these people face? How would improving emotional awareness help?

There are many competing theories about EI, some of them very complex. While experts vary in their definitions and models, all agree that emotions are real, can be changed for the better, and have a profound impact on whether or not a person is successful.

In the simplest terms, emotional intelligence consists of two general abilities:

- **Understanding emotions** involves the capacity to monitor and label feelings accurately (nervous, happy, angry, relieved, and so forth) and to determine why you feel the way you do. It also involves predicting how others might feel in a given situation. Emotions contain information, and the ability to understand and think about that information plays an important role in behavior.

- **Managing emotions** builds on the belief that feelings can be modified, even improved. At times, you need to stay open to your feelings, learn from them, and use them to take appropriate action. Other times, it is better to disengage from an emotion and return to it later. Anger, for example, can blind you and lead you to act in negative or antisocial ways; used positively, however, the same emotion can help you overcome adversity, bias, and injustice.

Identifying and using emotions can help you know which moods are best for different situations and learn how to put yourself in the "right" mood. Developing an awareness of emotions allows you to use your feelings to enhance your thinking. If you are feeling sad, for instance, you might view the world in a certain way, while if you feel happy, you are likely to interpret the same events differently. Once you start paying attention to emotions, you can learn not only how to cope with life's pressures and demands, but also how to harness your knowledge of the way you feel for more effective problem solving, reasoning, decision making, and creative endeavors.[1]

Assessing Your Emotional Intelligence

A number of sophisticated tools can be used to assess emotional intelligence. Some first-year seminars and many campus counseling centers offer the opportunity to complete a professionally administered questionnaire, such as the Emotional Quotient Inventory (EQ-i), which provides a detailed assessment of your emotional skills and a graphic representation of where you stand in comparison with other students. But even without a formal test, you can take a number of steps to get in touch with your own EI. You'll have to dig deep inside yourself and be willing to be honest about how you really think and how you really behave. This can take time, and that's fine. Think of your EI as a work in progress.

---

[1]Adapted with permission from EI Skills Group, "Ability Model of Emotional Intelligence," http://www.emotionaliq.com/. © 2005–2009.

EMOTIONAL INTELLIGENCE QUESTIONNAIRE

Your daily life gives you many opportunities to take a hard look at how you handle emotions. Here are some questions that can help you begin thinking about your own EI.

1. What do you do when you are under stress?
   - ☐ a. I tend to deal with it calmly and rationally.
   - ☐ b. I get upset, but it usually blows over quickly.
   - ☐ c. I get upset but keep it to myself.

2. My friends would say that:
   - ☐ a. I will play, but only after I get my work done.
   - ☐ b. I am ready for fun anytime.
   - ☐ c. I hardly ever go out.

3. When something changes at the last minute:
   - ☐ a. I easily adapt.
   - ☐ b. I get frustrated.
   - ☐ c. It doesn't matter, since I don't really expect things to happen as I plan.

4. My friends would say that:
   - ☐ a. I am sensitive to their concerns.
   - ☐ b. I spend too much time worrying about other people's needs.
   - ☐ c. I don't like to deal with other people's petty problems.

5. When I have a problem to solve, such as too many things due at the end of the week:
   - ☐ a. I write down a list of the tasks I must complete, come up with a plan indicating specifically what I can accomplish and what I can't, and follow my plan.
   - ☐ b. I am very optimistic about getting things done and just dig right in and get to work.
   - ☐ c. I get a little frazzled. Usually I get a number of things done and then push aside the things that I can't do.

Review your responses. A responses indicate that you probably have a good basis for strong emotional intelligence. **B** responses indicate you may have some strengths and some challenges in your EI. **C** responses indicate that your success in life and school could be negatively affected by your EI.

YOUR TURN ▶

Now that you have completed the EI questionnaire, are there any areas that you would like to work on? If so, why do you identify these as areas for improvement? Give specifics. What could you do to improve in these areas?

Identifying Competencies

Emotional intelligence includes many capabilities and skills that influence a person's ability to cope with life's pressures and demands. Reuven Bar-On, a professor at the University of Texas, Austin, and world-renowned EI expert, developed a model that demonstrates how these categories of emotional intelligence directly affect general mood and lead to effective performance (see Figure. 3.1).

Let's take a closer look at the specific skills and competencies that Bar-On has identified as the pieces that make up a person's emotional intelligence.[2]

---

[2]Adapted from R. Bar-On. "The Bar-On Model of Emotional-Social Intelligence (ESI)," *Psicothema*, 2006, 18 (suppl. 13–25): 21. http://www.eiconsortium.org/pdf/baron_model_of_emotional_social_intelligence.pdf.

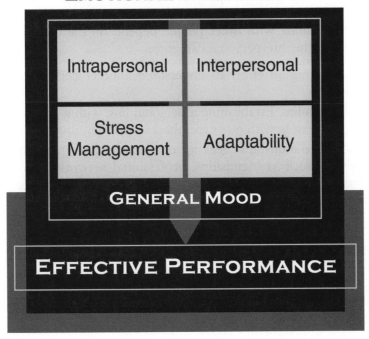

BAR-ON MODEL OF EMOTIONAL INTELLIGENCE

Intrapersonal | Interpersonal

Stress Management | Adaptability

GENERAL MOOD

EFFECTIVE PERFORMANCE

◄ FIGURE 3.1

Bar-On Model of Emotional Intelligence

It's something like a jigsaw puzzle, and when you have put all of the pieces together, you will begin to see yourself and others more clearly.

INTRAPERSONAL SKILLS

The first category, intrapersonal, relates to how well you know and like yourself, as well as how effectively you can do the things you need to do to stay happy. This category is made up of five specific competencies:

- **Emotional self-awareness.** Knowing how and why you feel the way you do.
- **Assertiveness.** Standing up for yourself when you need to without being too aggressive.
- **Independence.** Making important decisions on your own without having to get everyone's opinion.
- **Self-regard.** Liking yourself in spite of your flaws (and we all have them).
- **Self-actualization.** Being satisfied and comfortable with what you have achieved in school, work, and your personal life.

Understanding yourself and why you think and act as you do is the glue that holds all of the EI competencies together. Knowledge of self is strongly connected to respect for others and their way of life. If you don't understand yourself and why you do the things you do, it can be difficult for you to understand others. What's more, if you don't like yourself, you can hardly expect others to like you.

INTERPERSONAL SKILLS

Recent studies have shown that people with extensive support networks are generally happier and tend to enjoy longer, healthier lives. Forging relationships and getting along with other people depend on the competencies that form the basis for the interpersonal category:

- **Empathy.** Making an effort to understand another person's situation or point of view.
- **Social responsibility.** Establishing a personal link with a group or community and cooperating with other members in working toward shared goals.
- **Interpersonal relationships.** Seeking out healthy and mutually beneficial relationships—such as friendships, professional networks, family connections, mentoring, and romantic partnerships—and making a persistent effort to maintain them.

ADAPTABILITY

Things change. Adaptability, the ability to adjust your thinking and behavior when faced with new or unexpected situations, helps you cope and ensures that you'll do well in life, no matter what the challenges. This category includes three key competencies:

- **Reality testing.** Ensuring that your feelings are appropriate by checking them against external, objective criteria.
- **Flexibility.** Adapting and adjusting your emotions, viewpoints, and actions as situations change.
- **Problem solving.** Approaching challenges step by step and not giving up in the face of obstacles.

STRESS MANAGEMENT

In college, at work, and at home, now and in the future, you'll be faced with what can seem like never-ending pressures and demands. Managing the inevitable resulting stress depends on two skills:

- **Stress tolerance.** Recognizing the causes of stress and responding in appropriate ways. Staying strong under pressure.
- **Impulse control.** Thinking carefully about potential consequences before you act and delaying gratification for the sake of achieving long-term goals.

GENERAL MOOD AND EFFECTIVE PERFORMANCE

It might sound sappy, but having a positive attitude really does improve your chances of doing well. Bar-On emphasizes the importance of two emotions in particular:

- **Optimism.** Looking for the "bright side" of any problem or difficulty and being confident that things will work out for the best.

- **Happiness.** Being satisfied with yourself, with others, and with your situation in general.

It makes sense: If you feel good about yourself and manage your emotions, you can expect to get along with others and enjoy a happy, successful life.

┌─ **YOUR TURN** ▶ ───┐

On the basis of what you have learned so far about EI and the competencies that are involved, choose three competencies and describe how being strong in those dimensions will help a student succeed in college.

└───┘

How Emotions Affect Success

Emotions are strongly tied to physical and psychological well-being. For example, some studies have suggested that cancer patients who have strong EI live longer. People who are aware of the needs of others tend to be happier than people who are not. A large study done at the University of Pennsylvania found that the best athletes do well in part because they're extremely optimistic. Despite tremendous obstacles and with the odds stacked against them, emotionally intelligent people nonetheless go on to succeed.

Wired WINDOW

HOW YOU EXPRESS EI ONLINE

We express our EI in many different ways, sometimes without ever being conscious that we are doing it. One space in which students express themselves in subtle and not-so-subtle ways is on social networking sites such as Facebook and MySpace. You may have intentionally posted information in your profile to help others learn about the kind of person you are, your hobbies, your sense of humor, and your personality style. The words that you use and the way in which you try to come across can also tell others about you. Take the groups to which you belong on Facebook, for example. What does being a member of these groups tell others about you? You can learn a lot about people by what they have chosen to share (and what they do not share) on their profile pages. Have you ever read a friend's status update and realized that he or she was having a rough time without your friend's having to say so explicitly? That is an example of one of the subtle ways in which we communicate information about our EI online.

Think Critically

Now that you have examined your groups on Facebook, think critically about your entire profile with a focus on EI. What does your profile (and your online activity such as wall posts) tell you (and others) about how you get along with other people? What other EI dimensions does your profile communicate? Are you assertive? Can you put off having fun until after you've gotten work done? Are you generally happy? Do you handle stress well? Have you found differences in the ways in which you communicate your EI online and your actual EI? If so, how can you fix these discrepancies?

YOUR TURN ▶

Describe yourself as a successful person ten years after college. What kinds of skills will you have? Don't just focus on your degree or a job description, but include the EI competencies that help explain why you have become successful.

A number of studies link strong emotional intelligence skills to college success in particular. Here are a few highlights:

- **Emotionally intelligent students get higher grades.** Researchers looked at students' grade point averages at the end of the first year of college. Students who had tested high for intrapersonal skills, stress tolerance, and adaptability when they entered in the fall did better academically than those who had lower overall EI test scores.

- **Students who can't manage their emotions struggle academically.** Some students have experienced full-blown panic attacks before tests. Others who are depressed can't concentrate on coursework. And far too many turn to risky behaviors (drug and alcohol abuse, eating disorders, and worse) in an effort to cope. Dr. Richard Kadison, Chief of Mental Health Service at Harvard University, notes that "the emotional well-being of students goes hand-in-hand with their academic development. If they're not doing well emotionally, they are not going to reach their academic potential."[3] Even students who manage to succeed academically in spite of emotional difficulties can be at risk if unhealthy behavior patterns follow them after college.

- **Students who can delay gratification tend to do better overall.** Impulse control leads to achievement. In the famous "Marshmallow Study" performed at Stanford University, researchers examined the long-term behaviors of individuals who, as four-year olds, did or did not practice delayed gratification. The children were given one marshmallow and told that if they didn't eat it right away, they could have another. Fourteen years later, the children who ate their marshmallow immediately were more likely to experience significant stress, irritability, and inability to focus on goals. The children who waited scored an average of 210 points higher on the SAT; had better confidence, concentration, and reliability; held better-paying jobs; and reported being more satisfied with life. The following box details the differences between the two groups of students after fourteen years.

- **EI skills can be enhanced in a first-year seminar.** In two separate studies, one conducted in Australia and another conducted in the United States, researchers found that college students enrolled in a first-year seminar who demonstrated good EI skills were more likely to do better in college than students who did not exhibit those behaviors. A follow-up study indicated that the students who had good EI skills also raised their scores on a measure of emotional intelligence.

---

[3]Richard Kadison and Theresa Foy DiGeronimo, *College of the Overwhelmed: The Campus Mental Health Crisis and What to Do About It* (San Francisco: Jossey-Bass, 2004), p. 156.

THE STANFORD MARSHMALLOW STUDY

Impulse Controlled	Impulsive
■ Assertive	■ Indecisive
■ Cope with frustration	■ Overreact to frustration
■ Work better under pressure	■ Overwhelmed by stress
■ Self-reliant, confident	■ Lower self-image
■ Trustworthy	■ Stubborn
■ Dependable	■ Impulsive
■ Delay gratification	■ Don't delay gratification
■ Academically competent	■ Poorer students
■ Respond to reason	■ Prone to jealousy and envy
■ Concentrate	■ Provoke arguments
■ Eager to learn	■ Sharp temper
■ Follow through on plans	■ Give up in face of failure
■ SAT: 610 verbal, 652 math	■ SAT: 524 verbal, 528 math

Source: Y. Shoda, W. Mischel, and P. K. Peake, "Predicting Adolescent Cognitive and Self-Regulatory Competencies from Preschool Delay of Gratification," *Developmental Psychology*, 1990, 26(6), 978–86.

Without strong EI in college, it is possible to do well enough to get by, but you might miss out on the full range and depth of competencies and skills that can help you to succeed in your chosen field and have a fulfilling and meaningful life.

How to Improve Your Emotional Intelligence

Developing your EI is an important step toward getting the full benefit of a college education. Think about it. Do you often give up because something is just too hard or you can't figure it out? Do you take responsibility for what you do, or do you blame others if you fail? Can you really be successful in life if you don't handle change well or if you are not open to diverse groups and their opinions? How can you communicate effectively if you are not assertive or if you are overly aggressive? If you're inflexible, how can you solve problems, get along with coworkers and family members, or learn from other people's points of view?

The good news is you can improve your EI. It might not be easy—old habits are hard to change—but it can definitely be done. Here are some suggestions:

1. **Identify your strengths and weaknesses.** Take a hard look at yourself, and consider how you respond to situations. Most people have trouble assessing their own behaviors realistically, so ask someone you trust and respect for insight. And if you have an opportunity to take a formal emotional intelligence test or to meet with a behavioral counselor, by all means, do.

2. **Set realistic goals.** As you identify areas of emotional intelligence that you would like to improve, be as specific as possible. Instead of deciding to be more assertive, for example, focus on a particular issue that is giving you trouble, such as nagging resentment toward a friend who always orders the most expensive thing on the menu and then expects to split the whole check evenly.

3. **Formulate a plan.** With a particular goal in mind, identify a series of steps you could take to achieve the goal, and define the results that would indicate success. As you contemplate your plan, consider all of the emotional competencies discussed on pages 36–39 of this chapter: You might find that to be more assertive with your friend about the restaurant situation, for instance, you need to figure out why you're frustrated (emotional self-awareness), identify possible causes for your friend's behavior (empathy), and consider what you might be doing to encourage it (reality testing).

4. **Check your progress on a regular basis.** Continually reassess whether or not you have met your goals, and adjust your strategy as needed.

Suppose you know that you don't handle stress well. When things get tough—too many things are due at once, your roommate leaves clothes and leftover food all over the place, and your significant other seems a bit distant—you begin to fall apart. Here is a model you might use for improving the way you handle stress.

> **EI competency:** Stress tolerance
> **Specific goal:** To get control of the things that are causing stress this week
> **Plan:** Identify each stressor, and select a strategy for addressing it.

- List everything that needs to be done this week. Allot time for each item on the list, and stick to a schedule. Reassess the schedule many times during the week.
- Ask yourself whether your roommate is bothering you only because you are stressed. Do you do some of the same things your roommate does? Ask yourself what the next step should be: Talking to your roommate? Looking for another place to study?
- Ask yourself whether your significant other is acting differently for any reason. Is he or she under stress? Are you overreacting because you feel insecure in the relationship? After answering these questions, decide what the next step will be: Talking to your significant other and sharing your feelings with him or her? Reassessing the situation in another week when things calm down?
- Identify what reduces stress for you and still allows you to stay on target to get things done. Is it exercise? Working in small chunks with rewards when you finish something? Playing a musical instrument?

Success Indicator: You are feeling less stressed, and you have accomplished many of the things on your list. You are working out three times a week. Your significant other seems just fine, and your place is still a mess but it's not bothering you. You leave your room and decide to study in the library.

YOUR TURN ▶

Using the preceding example as a model, select an EI competency that you would like to improve, choose a specific goal, and formulate a plan for accomplishing it. What kinds of results do you hope to achieve? How will improving your EI in this area help you become a happier, more confident person?

It's important not to try to improve everything at once. Instead, identify specific EI competencies that you can define, describe, and identify, and then set measurable goals for change. Don't expect success overnight. Remember that it took you a while to develop your specific approach to life, and it will take commitment and practice to change it.

Where to go
FOR HELP...

If you think that you might need some help developing some of these EI skills, especially if you feel that you are not happy or optimistic or you're not handling stress well, do something about it. Although you can look online and get some tips about being an optimistic person, for example, there is nothing like getting some help from a professional. Consider visiting your academic advisor or a wellness or counseling center on campus. Look for any related workshops that are offered on campus or nearby. Remember that the good news about EI is that with persistence it can be improved.

MY INSTITUTION'S RESOURCES ▶

_____

_____

_____

_____

_____

_____

_____

③ Applying What You've LEARNED...

Now that you have read and discussed this chapter, consider how you can apply what you have learned to your academic and personal life. The following prompts will help you reflect on the chapter material and its relevance to you both now and in the future.

1. Managing stress is an important skill in college. Take a look through your course syllabi, and make a list of assignments, exams, and the due dates. Do any of your assignments or exams seem to cluster around the same time in the term? Can you anticipate times when you might be especially likely to get stressed? What can you do in advance to avoid becoming overwhelmed and overstressed?

2. College life offers many opportunities to meet new people and to develop a new support network. But finding friends and mentors you can trust is not always easy. What steps have you taken so far to meet new people and build a network of support in college?

One-Minute PAPER...

Emotional intelligence might be a term that you were not familiar with before reading this chapter. What did you find to be the most interesting information in this chapter? Make a note of any information that was hard to understand or apply to your own life. What kinds of questions do you still have for your instructor?

Building Your PORTFOLIO...

KNOW THYSELF

Understanding your own behavior can sometimes be more difficult than understanding someone else's. Review the questionnaire on page 36 of this chapter. Were you honest in your assessment of yourself?

1. In a Word document, list the questions from page 36 that you answered with a B or a C. For example, did you rate yourself with a B or a C on a question such as "I am okay when things change at the last minute"?

2. Next, note the EI competencies that relate to each question. For the example above, the key competency is adaptability, as evidenced in reality testing, flexibility, and problem solving.

3. For each question that you have listed, describe your strategy for improving your response to certain situations. For example, when things change suddenly, you might say, "I am going to take a few minutes to think about what I need to do next. I will remind myself that I am still in control of my actions."

4. Save your responses in your portfolio on your personal computer or flash drive. Revisit your responses to the questions listed above as you experience similar situations.

Pay special attention to how your emotional intelligence affects your daily life. As you become more aware of your emotions and actions, you will begin to see how you can improve in the areas that are most difficult for you.

4

Discovering How You Learn

In this chapter you will explore

- Many approaches to understanding your learning styles or preferences
- How learning styles and teaching styles often differ
- How to optimize your learning style in any classroom setting
- How to understand and recognize a learning disability

Have you ever thought about how you learn? People

learn differently. This is hardly a novel idea, but if you are to do well in college, it is important that you become aware of your preferred way, or style, of learning. Experts agree that there is no one best way to learn.

Maybe you have trouble paying attention to a long lecture, or maybe listening is the way you learn best. You might love classroom discussion, or you might consider hearing what other students have to say in class a big waste of time.

Perhaps you have not thought about how college instructors, and even particular courses, have their own inherent styles, which can be different from your preferred style of learning. Many instructors rely almost solely on lecturing; others use lots of visual aids, such as PowerPoint outlines, charts, graphs, and pictures. In science courses, you will conduct experiments or go on field trips where you can observe or touch what you are studying. In dance, theater, or physical education courses, learning takes place in both your body and your mind. And in almost all courses, you'll learn by reading both textbooks and other materials. Some instructors are friendly and warm; others seem to want little interaction with students. It's safe to say that in at least some of your college courses, you won't find a close match between the way you learn most effectively and the way you're being taught. This chapter will help you first to understand how you learn best and then to think of ways in which you can create a link between your style of learning and the expectations of each course and instructor.

There are many ways of thinking about and describing **learning styles**. Some of these will make a lot of sense to you; others might initially seem confusing or counterintuitive. Some learning style theories are very simple, and some are complex. You will notice some overlap between the different theories, but using several of them might help you do a more precise job of discovering your learning style. If you are interested in reading more about learning styles, the library and campus learning center will have many resources.

In addition to its focus on learning styles, this chapter will also explore **learning disabilities**, which are very common among college students. You might know someone who has been diagnosed with a learning disability, such as dyslexia or attention deficit disorder. It is also possible that you have a special learning need and are not aware of it. This chapter seeks to increase your self-awareness and your knowledge about such challenges to learning. In reading this chapter, you will learn more about common types of learning disabilities, how to recognize them, and what to do if you or someone you know has a learning disability.

YOUR TURN ▶

Which of your current classes would you describe as your favorite? Do you think that your choice has anything to do with the instructor's teaching style? Why or why not?

The VARK Learning Styles Inventory

The VARK Inventory focuses on how learners prefer to use their senses (hearing, seeing, writing, reading, or experiencing) to learn. The acronym VARK stands for "Visual," "Aural," "Read/Write," and "Kinesthetic." Visual learners prefer to learn information through charts, graphs, symbols, and other visual means. Aural learners prefer to hear information. Read/Write learners prefer to learn information that is displayed as words. Kinesthetic learners prefer to learn through experience and practice, whether simulated or real. To determine your learning style according to the VARK Inventory, respond to the following questionnaire.

THE VARK QUESTIONNAIRE, VERSION 7.0

This questionnaire is designed to tell you something about your preferences for the way you work with information. Choose answers that explain your preference. Check the box next to those items. Please select as many boxes as apply to you. If none of the response options apply to you, leave the item blank.

1. You are helping someone who wants to go to your airport, town center, or railway station. You would:
   - ☐ a. go with her.
   - ☑ b. tell her the directions.
   - ☐ c. write down the directions (without a map).
   - ☐ d. draw, or give her a map.

2. You are not sure whether a word should be spelled "dependent" or "dependant." You would:
   - ☐ a. see the words in your mind and choose by the way they look.
   - ☐ b. think about how each word sounds and choose one.
   - ☑ c. find it in a dictionary.
   - ☐ d. write both words on paper and choose one.

3. You are planning a holiday for a group. You want some feedback from them about the plan. You would:
   - ☑ a. describe some of the highlights.
   - ☐ b. use a map or Web site to show them the places.
   - ☐ c. give them a copy of the printed itinerary.
   - ☐ d. phone, text, or e-mail them.

4. You are going to cook something as a special treat for your family. You would:
   - ☐ a. cook something you know without the need for instructions.
   - ☐ b. ask friends for suggestions.
   - ☐ c. look through the cookbook for ideas from the pictures.
   - ☑ d. use a cookbook where you know there is a good recipe.

5. A group of tourists want to learn about the parks or wildlife reserves in your area. You would:
   - ☑ a. talk, or arrange a talk for them, about parks or wildlife reserves.
   - ☐ b. show them Internet pictures, photographs, or picture books.
   - ☐ c. take them to a park or wildlife reserve and walk with them.
   - ☐ d. give them a book or pamphlets about the parks or wildlife reserves.

6. You are about to purchase a digital camera or mobile phone. Other than price, what would most influence your decision?
   - ☐ a. Trying or testing it.
   - ☐ b. Reading the details about its features.
   - ☑ c. It is a modern design and looks good.
   - ☐ d. The salesperson telling you about its features.

7. Remember a time when you learned how to do something new. Try to avoid choosing a physical skill (e.g., riding a bike). You learned best by:
   - ☐ a. watching a demonstration.
   - ☑ b. listening to somebody explain it and asking questions.
   - ☐ c. diagrams and charts—visual clues.
   - ☐ d. written instructions—e.g., a manual or textbook.

8. You have a problem with your knee. You would prefer that the doctor:
   - ☑ a. gave you a web address or something to read about it.
   - ☐ b. used a plastic model of a knee to show what was wrong.
   - ☐ c. described what was wrong.
   - ☐ d. showed you a diagram of what was wrong.

9. You want to learn a new program, skill, or game on a computer. You would:
   - ☑ a. read the written instructions that came with the program.
   - ☐ b. talk with people who know about the program.
   - ☐ c. use the controls or keyboard.
   - ☐ d. follow the diagrams in the book that came with it.

10. You like Web sites that have:
    - ☑ a. things you can click on, shift, or try.
    - ☐ b. interesting design and visual features.
    - ☐ c. interesting written descriptions, lists, and explanations.
    - ☐ d. audio channels where you can hear music, radio programs, or interviews.

11. Other than price, what would most influence your decision to buy a new nonfiction book?
    - ☑ a. The way it looks is appealing.
    - ☐ b. Quickly reading parts of it.
    - ☐ c. A friend talks about it and recommends it.
    - ☐ d. It has real-life stories, experiences, and examples.

12. You are using a book, CD, or Web site to learn how to take photos with your new digital camera. You would like to have:

- ☑ a. a chance to ask questions and talk about the camera and its features.
- ☐ b. clear written instructions with lists and bullet points about what to do.
- ☐ c. diagrams showing the camera and what each part does.
- ☐ d. many examples of good and poor photos and how to improve them.

13. You prefer a teacher or a presenter who uses:
    - ☐ a. demonstrations, models, or practical sessions.
    - ☑ b. question and answer, talk, group discussion, or guest speakers.
    - ☐ c. handouts, books, or readings.
    - ☐ d. diagrams, charts, or graphs.

14. You have finished a competition or test and would like some feedback. You would like to have feedback:
    - ☑ a. using examples from what you have done.
    - ☐ b. using a written description of your results.
    - ☐ c. from somebody who talks it through with you.
    - ☐ d. using graphs showing what you have achieved.

15. You are going to choose food at a restaurant or café. You would:
    - ☑ a. choose something that you have had there before.
    - ☐ b. listen to the waiter or ask friends to recommend choices.
    - ☐ c. choose from the descriptions in the menu.
    - ☐ d. look at what others are eating or look at pictures of each dish.

16. You have to make an important speech at a conference or special occasion. You would:
    - ☐ a. make diagrams or get graphs to help explain things.
    - ☐ b. write a few key words and practice saying your speech over and over.
    - ☐ c. write out your speech and learn from reading it over several times.
    - ☐ d. gather many examples and stories to make the talk real and practical.

Source: www.vark-learn.com/english/index.asp

SCORING THE VARK

Use the following scoring chart to find the VARK category to which each of your answers belongs. Circle the letters that correspond to your answers. For example, if you answered b and c for question 3, circle V and R in the 3 row.

Question	A Category	B Category	C Category	D Category
3	K	(V)	(R)	A

Count the number of each of the VARK letters you have circled to get your score for each VARK category.

SCORING CHART

Question	A Category	B Category	C Category	D Category
1	K	A	R	V
2	V	A	R	K
3	K	V	R	A
4	K	A	V	R
5	A	V	K	R
6	K	R	V	A
7	K	A	V	R
8	R	K	A	V
9	R	A	K	V
10	K	V	R	A
11	V	R	A	K
12	A	R	V	K
13	K	A	R	V
14	K	R	A	V
15	K	A	R	V
16	V	A	R	K

Total number of **V**s circled = _____

Total number of **A**s circled = _____

Total number of **R**s circled = _____

Total number of **K**s circled = _____

Because you could choose more than one answer for each question, the scoring is not just a simple matter of counting. It is like four stepping stones across some water. Enter your scores **from highest to lowest** on the stones in the figure, with their V, A, R, and K labels.

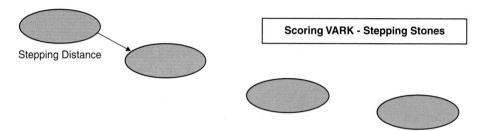

Your stepping distance comes from this table:

The total of my four VARK scores is	My stepping distance is
16–21	1
22–27	2
28–32	3
More than 32	4

Follow these steps to establish your preferences.

1. Your first preference is always your highest score. Check that first stone as one of your preferences.
2. Now subtract your second highest score from your first. If that figure is larger than your stepping distance, you have a single preference. Otherwise, check this stone as another preference and continue with step 3.
3. Subtract your third score from your second one. If that figure is larger than your stepping distance, you have a bimodal preference. If not, check your third stone as a preference and continue with step 4.
4. Last, subtract your fourth score from your third one. If that figure is larger than your stepping distance, you have a trimodal preference. Otherwise, check your fourth stone as a preference, and you have all four modes as your preferences.

Note: If you are bimodal or trimodal or you have checked all four modes as your preferences, you can be described as *multimodal* in your VARK preferences.

YOUR TURN ▶

Did your VARK score surprise you at all? Did you know what type of learner you were before taking the test? If so, when did you discover this? How do you use your modality to your benefit?

USING VARK RESULTS TO STUDY MORE EFFECTIVELY

How can knowing your VARK score help you do better in your college classes? The following table offers suggestions for using learning styles to develop your own study strategies.

Study Strategies by Learning Style

Visual	Aural	Read/Write	Kinesthetic
Underline or highlight your notes.	Talk with others to verify the accuracy of your lecture notes.	Write and rewrite your notes.	Use all your senses in learning: sight, touch, taste, smell, and hearing.
Use symbols, charts, or graphs to display your notes.	Put your notes on tape and listen to them or tape class lectures.	Read your notes silently.	Supplement your notes with real-world examples.
Use different arrangements of words on the page.	Read your notes out loud; ask yourself questions and speak your answers.	Organize diagrams or flow charts into statements.	Move and gesture while you are reading or speaking your notes.
Redraw your pages from memory.		Write imaginary exam questions and respond in writing.	

The Myers-Briggs Type Indicator

One of the best-known and most widely used personality inventories that can also be used to describe learning styles is the Myers-Briggs Type Indicator, or MBTI.[2] While the VARK measures your preferences for using your senses to learn, the MBTI investigates basic personality characteristics and how those relate to human interaction and learning. The MBTI was created by Isabel Briggs Myers and her mother, Katharine Cook Briggs. The inventory identifies and measures psychological type as developed in the personality theory of Carl Gustav Jung, the great twentieth-century psychoanalyst. The MBTI is given to several million people around the world each year. Employers often use this test

[2]Isabel Briggs Myers, *Introduction to Type*, 6th ed. (Palo Alto, CA: CPP, 1998).

to give employees insight into how they perceive the world, go about making decisions, and get along with other people. Many first-year seminar or college success courses also include a focus on the MBTI because it provides a good way to begin a dialogue about human interaction and how personality type affects learning.

All the psychological types described by the MBTI are normal and healthy; there is no good or bad or right or wrong—people are simply different. When you complete the Myers-Briggs survey instrument, your score represents your "psychological type"—the combination of your preferences on four different scales. These scales measure how you take in information and how you then make decisions or come to conclusions about that information. Each preference has a one-letter abbreviation. The four letters together make up your type. Although this book doesn't include the actual survey, you will find a description of the basic MBTI types on page 53. Which one sounds most like you?

Wired WINDOW

USING TECHNOLOGY TO AID LEARNING

If you scored as having an aural, visual, or read/write preference on the VARK Inventory, you can use technology to enhance how you learn course material. Students with an aural preference can use a digital recorder or microcassette recorder to record lectures and then listen to them again later. If you have an iPod, you can purchase a microphone attachment that allows you to use the iPod as a digital audio recorder, and you can organize your recorded lectures using iTunes. Many other MP3 players also have recording capabilities. Before you record any lecture, make sure that you have your professors' permission to do so. In addition to recording lectures, you can find supplemental course material through podcasts and via iTunes. A number of institutions provide free podcasts for many courses on iTunes. You can browse through course offerings in the iTunesU section, or you can search for a term in the iTunes store and limit it to iTunesU results. Try searching the Web to find podcasts and audio files to help you enhance your knowledge of a certain topic. (Hint: Try searching for a specific subject and the word *podcast*. For instance, you might search "Introduction to Philosophy podcast.")

Students with a visual preference can use Web sites such as YouTube to help supplement their learning. Institutions such as Stanford University have their own profiles on YouTube, and they post videos that feature faculty members explaining concepts in their field of study. In the same way you search for audio files on the Web and iTunesU, you can search YouTube to find videos to enhance your knowledge of concepts covered in class. (For your psychology class, for example, you might watch a video based on Stanley Milgram's obedience experiments.)

Thinking Critically

Search for an audio or video file to supplement a concept or lecture from one of your courses. Once you have found the file, evaluate it on the basis of the criteria for evaluating Internet sources found in Chapter 10. Can you identify the creator of the work? Is the person reliable? Does the podcast or video cite the sources that are used? Is the information in this podcast or video more or less reliable than the information contained in your textbook? In what way or ways?

EXTRAVERSION (E) VERSUS INTROVERSION (I): THE INNER OR OUTER WORLD

The E-I preference indicates whether you direct your energy and attention primarily toward the outer world of people, events, and things or the inner world of thoughts, feelings, and reflections.

Extraverts tend to be outgoing, gregarious, and talkative. They often think "with the volume on," saying out loud what is going through their minds. They are energized by people and activity, and they seek this in both work and play. They are people of action; they like to spend more time doing things than thinking about them. At their best, they are good communicators who are quick to act and lead. However, they might seem to talk too much and too loudly, drowning others out or acting before they think. (Note that when the term is being used in the context of psychological type and the MBTI, *extravert* is spelled with an *a* and not an *o*, even though *extrovert* is the more common spelling.)

Introverts prefer to reflect carefully and think things through before taking action. They think a lot, but if you want to know what's on their minds, you might have to ask them. They are refreshed by quiet and privacy. At their best, introverts are good, careful listeners whose thoughts are deep and whose actions are well considered. On the other hand, they might seem too shy and not aware enough of the people and situations around them, or they can think about things so long that they neglect to actually start doing anything.

YOUR TURN ▶

After reading this description, do you consider yourself an extravert or an introvert? Why? Do you ever wish you were like the other? If so, when and why?

SENSING (S) VERSUS INTUITION (N): FACTS OR IDEAS

The S-N preference indicates how you perceive the world and take in information: directly, through your five senses, or indirectly, by using your intuition.

Sensing types are interested above all in the facts, what is known and what they can be sure of. Typically sensing types are practical, factual, realistic, and down-to-earth. They can be very accurate, steady, precise, patient, and effective with routine and details. They are often relatively traditional and conventional. They dislike unnecessary complication, and they prefer to practice skills they already know. At their best, sensing types can be counted on to do things right, taking care of every last detail. However, they can plod along while missing the point of why they are doing what they do, not seeing the forest (the whole picture) for the trees (the details).

Intuitive types are fascinated by possibilities—not so much the facts themselves, but what those facts mean, what concepts might describe those facts, how those might relate to other concepts, and what the implications of the facts would be. Intuitive types are less tied to the here and now and tend to look farther into the future and the past. They need inspiration and meaning for what they do, and they tend to work in bursts of energy and enthusiasm. Often, they are original, creative, and nontraditional. They can have trouble with routine and details, however, and they would rather learn a new skill than keep practicing one they have already mastered. They can exaggerate facts sometimes without realizing it. At their best, intuitive types are bright, innovative people who thrive in academic settings and the world of invention and ideas, although they can also be impractical dreamers whose visions fall short because of inattention to detail.

THINKING (T) VERSUS FEELING (F): LOGIC OR VALUES

The T-F preference indicates how you prefer to make your decisions: through logical, rational analysis or through your subjective values, likes, and dislikes. *Thinking* types are usually logical, rational, analytical, and critical. They pride themselves on reasoning their way to the best possible decisions. They tend to decide things relatively impersonally and objectively, and they are less swayed by feelings and emotions—both their own and other people's. In fact, other people's feelings sometimes puzzle or surprise them. They can deal with interpersonal disharmony and can be firm and assertive when they need to be. In all their dealings, they need and value fairness. At their best, thinking types are firm, fair, logical, and just. On the other hand, they can seem cold, insensitive to other people's feelings, and overly blunt and hurtful in their criticisms.

Feeling types are typically warm, empathic, sympathetic, and interested in the happiness of others as well as themselves. They need and value harmony, and they can become distressed and distracted by argument and conflict. They sometimes have trouble being assertive when it would be appropriate to do so. Above all, they need and value kindness. At their best, feeling types are warm and affirming, and they facilitate cooperation and goodwill among those around them while pursuing the best human values. However, feeling types can be illogical, emotionally demanding, reluctant to tackle unpleasant tasks, and unaffected by objective reason and evidence.

JUDGING (J) VERSUS PERCEIVING (P): ORGANIZATION OR ADAPTABILITY

The J-P preference indicates how you characteristically approach the outside world: by making decisions and judgments or by observing and perceiving instead.

Judging types approach the world in a planned, orderly, organized way; they try to order and control their part of it as much as possible. They make their decisions relatively quickly and easily because they like to make and follow plans. They are usually punctual and tidy, and they appreciate those traits in others. At their best, judging types are natural organizers who get things done and get them done on time. However, judging types might jump to conclusions prematurely, be too judgmental of people, make decisions too hastily without enough information, and have trouble changing their plans even when those plans are not working.

Perceiving types don't try to control their world as much as adapt to it. Theirs is a flexible, wait-and-see approach. They deal comfortably and well with changes, unexpected developments, and emergencies, adjusting their plans and behaviors as needed. They tend to delay decisions so that they can keep their options open and gather more information. They might procrastinate to a serious degree, however, and they can try to juggle too many things at once without finishing any of them. At their best, perceiving types are spontaneous, flexible individuals who roll with the punches and find ways to take the proverbial lemons in life and turn them into lemonade. On the other hand, perceiving types can be messy, disorganized procrastinators.

HOW TO USE YOUR STRONGEST AND WEAKEST PREFERENCES

Because there are two possible choices for each of four different preferences, there are sixteen possible psychological types. No matter what your Myers-Briggs type, all components of personality have value in the learning process. The key to success in college, therefore, is to use all of the attitudes and functions (E, I, S, N, T, F, J, and P) in their most positive sense. As you go about your studies, here is a system we recommend:

1. *Sensing*: Get the facts. Use sensing to find and learn the facts. How do we know facts when we see them? What is the evidence for what is being said?
2. *Intuition*: Get the ideas. Now use intuition to consider what those facts mean. Why are those facts being presented? What concepts and ideas are being supported by those facts? What are the implications? What is the big picture?
3. *Thinking*: Critically analyze. Use thinking to analyze the pros and cons of what is being presented. Are there gaps in the evidence? What more do we need to know? Do the facts really support the conclusions? Are there alternative explanations? How well does what is presented hang together logically? How could our knowledge of it be improved?
4. *Feeling*: Make informed value judgments. Why is this material important? What does it contribute to people's good? Why might it be important to you personally? What is your personal opinion about it?
5. *Introversion*: Think it through. Before you take any action, carefully review everything you have encountered so far.
6. *Judging*: Organize and plan. Don't just dive in! Now is the time to organize and plan your studying so that you will learn and remember everything you need to. Don't just plan in your head either; write your plan down, in detail.
7. *Extraversion*: Take action. Now that you have a plan, act on it. Do whatever it takes. Create note cards, study outlines, study groups, and so on. If you are working on a paper, now is the time to start writing.
8. *Perceiving*: Change your plan as needed. Be flexible enough to change something that isn't working. Expect the unexpected, and deal with the unforeseen. Don't give up the whole effort the minute your original plan stops working. Figure out what's wrong, and come up with another, better plan and start following that.

Multiple Intelligences

Another way of measuring how we learn is the theory of *multiple intelligences*, developed in 1983 by Howard Gardner, a professor of education at Harvard University. Gardner's theory is based on the premise that the traditional notion of human intelligence is very limited. He proposes eight different intelligences to describe how humans learn.

As you might imagine, Gardner's work is controversial because it questions our long-standing definitions of intelligence. Gardner argues that students should be encouraged to develop the abilities they have and that evaluation should measure all forms of intelligence, not just linguistic and logical-mathematical intelligence.

As you think of yourself and your friends, what kinds of intelligences do you have? Do college courses measure all the ways in which you are intelligent? Here is a short inventory that will help you recognize your multiple intelligences.

MULTIPLE INTELLIGENCES INVENTORY

According to Gardner, all human beings have at least eight different types of intelligence. Depending on your background and age, some intelligences are likely to be more developed than others. This activity will help you find out what your intelligences are. Knowing this, you can work to strengthen the other intelligences that you do not use as often. Put a check mark next to the items that apply to you.

Verbal/Linguistic Intelligence

_____ I enjoy telling stories and jokes.

_____ I enjoy word games (for example, Scrabble and puzzles).

_____ I am a good speller (most of the time).

_____ I like talking and writing about my ideas.

_____ If something breaks and won't work, I read the instruction book before I try to fix it.

Logical/Mathematical Intelligence

_____ I really enjoy my math class.

_____ I like to find out how things work.

_____ I enjoy computer and math games.

_____ I love playing chess, checkers, or Monopoly.

_____ If something breaks and won't work, I look at the pieces and try to figure out how it works.

Visual/Spatial Intelligence

_____ I prefer a map to written directions.

_____ I enjoy hobbies such as photography.

_____ I like to doodle on paper whenever I can.

_____ In a magazine, I prefer looking at the pictures rather than reading the text.

_____ If something breaks and won't work, I tend to study the diagram of how it works.

Bodily/Kinesthetic Intelligence

_____ My favorite class is gym because I like sports.

_____ When looking at things, I like touching them.

_____ I use a lot of body movements when talking.

_____ I tend to tap my fingers or play with my pencil during class.

_____ If something breaks and won't work, I tend to play with the pieces to try to fit them together.

Musical/Rhythmic Intelligence

_____ I enjoy listening to CDs and the radio.

_____ I like to sing.

_____ I like to have music playing when doing homework or studying.

_____ I can remember the melodies of many songs.

_____ If something breaks and won't work, I tend to tap my fingers to a beat while I figure it out.

Interpersonal Intelligence

_____ I get along well with others.

_____ I have several very close friends.

_____ I like working with others in groups.

_____ Friends ask my advice because I seem to be a natural leader.

_____ If something breaks and won't work, I try to find someone who can help me.

Intrapersonal Intelligence

_____ I like to work alone without anyone bothering me.

_____ I don't like crowds.

_____ I know my own strengths and weaknesses.

_____ I find that I am strong-willed, independent, and don't follow the crowd.

_____ If something breaks and won't work, I wonder whether it's worth fixing.

Naturalist Intelligence

_____ I am keenly aware of my surroundings and of what goes on around me.

_____ I like to collect things like rocks, sports cards, and stamps.

_____ I like to get away from the city and enjoy nature.

_____ I enjoy learning the names of living things in the environment, such as flowers and trees.

_____ If something breaks down, I look around me and try to see what I can find to fix the problem.

A verbal/linguistic learner likes to read, write, and tell stories and is good at memorizing information. A logical/mathematical learner likes to work with numbers and is good at problem-solving and logical processes. A visual/spatial learner likes to draw and play with machines and is good at puzzles and reading maps and charts. A bodily/kinesthetic learner likes to move around and is good at sports, dance, and acting. A musical/rhythmic learner likes to sing and play an instrument and is good at remembering melodies and noticing pitches and rhythms. An interpersonal learner likes to have many friends and is good at understanding people, leading others, and mediating conflicts. Intrapersonal learners like to work alone, understand themselves well, and are original thinkers. A naturalistic learner likes to be outside and is good at preservation, conservation, and organizing a living area. You can use your intelligences to help you make decisions about a major, choose activities, and investigate career options. Which intelligences best describe you?

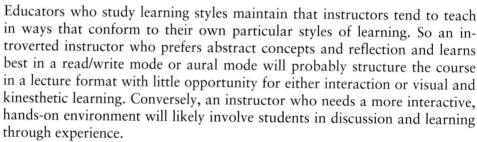

TOTAL SCORE

_____ Verbal/Linguistic
_____ Musical/Rhythmic
_____ Logical/Mathematical
_____ Interpersonal
_____ Visual/Spatial
_____ Intrapersonal
_____ Bodily/Kinesthetic
_____ Naturalist

Add the number of check marks you made in each section. Your score for each intelligence will be a number between 1 and 5. Your high scores of 3 or more will help you to get a sense of your own multiple intelligences.

Source: www.ldrc.ca/projects/miinventory/mitest.html.

YOUR TURN ▶

Do you agree with Howard Gardner that there are eight styles of learning? Why or why not?

When Learning Styles and Teaching Styles Conflict

Educators who study learning styles maintain that instructors tend to teach in ways that conform to their own particular styles of learning. So an introverted instructor who prefers abstract concepts and reflection and learns best in a read/write mode or aural mode will probably structure the course in a lecture format with little opportunity for either interaction or visual and kinesthetic learning. Conversely, an instructor who needs a more interactive, hands-on environment will likely involve students in discussion and learning through experience.

Do you enjoy listening to lectures, or do you find yourself gazing out the window or dozing? When your instructor assigns a group discussion, what is your immediate reaction? Do you dislike talking with other students, or is that the way you learn best? How do you react to lab sessions when you have to conduct an actual experiment? Is this an activity you look forward to or one that you dread? Each of these learning situations appeals to some students more than others, but each is inevitably going to be part of your college experience. Your college professors or university administrators have intentionally designed courses for you to have the opportunity to listen to professors who are experts in their field, interact with other students in structured groups, and learn through doing. Because these are all important components of your college education, it's important for you to make the most of each situation.

When you recognize a mismatch between how you best learn and how you are being taught, it is important that you take control of your learning process. Don't depend on the instructor or the classroom environment to give you everything you need to maximize your learning. Employ your own preferences, talents, and abilities to develop many different ways to study and retain information. Look back through this chapter to remind yourself of the ways in which you can use your own learning styles to be more successful in any class you take.

Learning with a Disability

While everyone has a learning style, a portion of the population has what is characterized as a learning disability. Learning disabilities are usually recognized and diagnosed in grade school, but some students can successfully compensate for a learning problem, perhaps without realizing that's what it is, and reach college without having been properly diagnosed or assisted.

Learning disabilities affect people's ability to interpret what they see and hear or to link information across different parts of the brain. These limitations can show up as specific difficulties with spoken and written language, coordination, self-control, or attention. Such difficulties can impede learning to read, write, or do math. The term *learning disability* covers a broad range of possible causes, symptoms, treatments, and outcomes. Because of this, it is difficult to diagnose a learning disability or pinpoint the causes. The types of learning disabilities that most commonly affect college students are attention disorders and disorders that affect the development of academic skills including reading, writing, and mathematics.

ATTENTION DISORDERS

Attention disorders are common in children, adolescents, and adults. Some students who have attention disorders appear to daydream excessively, and once you get their attention, they can be easily distracted. Individuals with attention deficit disorder (ADD) or attention deficit hyperactivity disorder (ADHD) often have trouble organizing tasks or completing their work. They don't seem to listen to or follow directions, and their work might be messy or appear careless. Although they are not strictly classified as learning disabilities, ADD and ADHD can seriously interfere with academic performance, leading some educators to classify them along with other learning disabilities.

If you have trouble paying attention or getting organized, you won't really know whether you have ADD or ADHD until you are evaluated. Check out resources on campus or in the community. After you have been evaluated, follow the advice you get, which might or might not mean taking medication. If you do receive a prescription for medication, be sure to take it according to the physician's directions. In the meantime, if you're having trouble getting and staying organized, whether or not you have an attention disorder, you can improve your focus through your own behavioral choices. The National Institutes of Mental Health offer the following suggestions (found on their Web site) for adults with attention disorders:

> Adults with ADD or ADHD can learn how to organize their lives by using "props," such as a large calendar posted where it will be seen in the morning, date books, lists, and reminder notes. They can have a special place for keys, bills, and the paperwork of everyday life. Tasks can be organized into sections so that completion of each part can give a sense of accomplishment. Above all, adults who have ADD or ADHD should learn as much as they can about their disorder (http://www.nimh.nih.gov/health/publications/attention -deficit-hyperactivity-disorder/can-adults-have-adhd.shtml).

COGNITIVE LEARNING DISABILITIES

Other learning disabilities are related to cognitive skills. Dyslexia, for example, is a common developmental reading disorder. A person can have problems with any of the tasks involved in reading. However, scientists have found that a significant number of people with dyslexia share an inability to distinguish or separate the sounds in spoken words. For instance, dyslexic individuals sometimes have difficulty assigning the appropriate sounds to letters, either individually or when letters combine to form words. However, there is more to reading than recognizing words. If the brain is unable to form images or relate new ideas to those stored in memory, the reader can't understand or remember the new concepts. So other types of reading disabilities can appear when the focus of reading shifts from word identification to comprehension.

Writing, too, involves several brain areas and functions. The brain networks for vocabulary, grammar, hand movement, and memory must all be in good working order. So a developmental writing disorder might result from problems in any of these areas. Someone who can't distinguish the sequence of sounds in a word will often have problems with spelling. People with writing disabilities, particularly expressive language disorders (the inability to express oneself using accurate language or sentence structure), are often unable to compose complete, grammatical sentences.

A student with a developmental arithmetic disorder will have difficulty recognizing numbers and symbols, memorizing facts such as the multiplication table, aligning numbers, and understanding abstract concepts such as place value and fractions.

Anyone who is diagnosed with a learning disability is in good company. The pop star Jewel; Michael Phelps, the Olympic gold medal swimmer; and actors Keira Knightley, Orlando Bloom, Patrick Dempsey, and Vince Vaughn are just a few of the famous and successful people who have diagnosed learning disabilities. A final important message: A learning disability is a learning difference but is in no way related to intelligence. Having a learning disability is not a sign that you are stupid. In fact, some of the most intelligent individuals in human history have had a learning disability.

The following questions may help you determine whether you or someone you know should seek further screening for a possible learning disability:

- Do you perform poorly on tests even when you feel you have studied and are capable of performing better?
- Do you have trouble spelling words?
- Do you work harder than your classmates at basic reading and writing?
- Do your instructors tell you that your performance in class is inconsistent, such as answering questions correctly in class but incorrectly on a written test?
- Do you have a really short attention span, or do your family members or instructors say that you do things without thinking?

Although responding "yes" to any of these questions does not mean that you have a disability, the resources of your campus learning center or the office for student disability services can help you address any potential problems and devise ways to learn more effectively.

Where to go
FOR HELP...

ON CAMPUS ▶

To learn more about learning styles and learning disabilities, talk to your first-year seminar instructor about campus resources. Most campuses have a learning center or a center for students with disabilities. You might also find that instructors in the areas of education or psychology have a strong interest in the processes of learning. Finally, don't forget your library or the Internet. A great deal of published information is available to describe how we learn.

BOOKS ▶

Learning Outside the Lines Edward M. Hallowell (Foreword), Jonathan Mooney, and David Cole, *Two Ivy League Students with Learning Disabilities and ADHD Give You the Tools for Academic Success and Educational Revolution* (New York: Fireside, 2000).

Kathleen G. Nadeau, *Survival Guide for College Students with ADD or LD* (Washington, DC: Magination Press, 1994).

ADD and the College Student Patricia O. Quinn, MD (ed.), *A Guide for High School and College Students with Attention Deficit Disorder* (Washington, DC: Magination Press, 2001).

ONLINE ▶

LD Pride www.ldpride.net/learningstyles.MI.htm. This site was developed in 1998 by Liz Bogod, an adult with learning disabilities. It provides general information about learning styles and learning disabilities and offers an interactive diagnostic tool to determine your learning style.

Support 4 Learning www.support4learning.org.uk/ education/learning_styles.cfm. This site is supported by HERO (Higher Education and Research Opportunities), which is the official online gateway to U.K. universities, colleges, and research organizations. The site provides learning style inventories and helpful hints about how to use your learning style to do well in college courses.

National Center for Learning Disabilities www.ncld .org. This is the official Web site of the National Center for Learning Disabilities. The site provides a variety of resources on diagnosing and understanding learning disabilities.

Facebook www. facebook.com. There are groups on Facebook that were created by students who have learning disabilities or ADHD. These groups are a great way to connect with other students with learning disabilities at your college or university or at other institutions. If you have been diagnosed with a disability, the members of these groups can offer support and help you seek out appropriate resources in order to be successful in college.

MY INSTITUTION'S RESOURCES ▶

_____

_____

_____

_____

_____

_____

_____

_____

_____

_____

_____

_____

_____

_____

Applying What You've LEARNED...

Now that you have read and discussed this chapter, consider how you can apply what you have learned to your academic and personal life. The following prompts will help you reflect on chapter material and its relevance to you both now and in the future.

1. It is almost certain that you will find yourself in a class where your learning style conflicts with your instructor's preferred style of teaching. After reading this chapter, describe what you can do to take control and make the most of your strongest learning preferences.

2. It is important to understand various learning styles in the context of education, but it is also important to understand how learning preferences affect career choices. Considering your own learning styles, what might be the best careers for you? Why?

One-Minute PAPER...

Recognizing that people have different ways of learning can be a relief. After reading this chapter, do you have a better understanding of your own learning style? What did you find to be the most interesting point in this chapter? What would you like to learn more about?

Building Your PORTFOLIO...

ARE WE ON THE SAME PAGE?

After reading about the Myers-Briggs Type Indicator in this chapter, can you guess what type you are?

1. Create a Word document, and note each type that you think best fits your personality.

> *Example*
>
> **E**xtravert **or I**ntrovert
> I think I am an _____
>
> **S**ensing **or** Intuitio**N**
> I think I am _____
>
> **T**hinking **or F**eeling
> I think I am _____
>
> **J**udging **or P**erceiving
> I think I am _____

2. Note what you think your four MBTI letters would be (for example, ESTP).

3. Using your favorite Internet search engine, search for "suggested careers for MBTI types." You will find several Web sites that suggest specific careers based on specific personality types.

4. Visit one site, and list at least two careers that are recommended for the MBTI type that you identify. Have you thought about these careers before? Do you think they would be a good fit for you? Why or why not?

   (Example: Careers recommended for ESTP: Sales representatives, marketers, police, detectives, paramedics, medical technicians, computer technicians, computer technical support, entrepreneurs. Suggestions found at http://www .geocities.com/lifexplore/mbcareer.htm.)

5. Save your findings in your portfolio on your personal computer or flash drive. Revisit this document as you continue to explore different majors and careers.

5 Thinking Critically: The Basis of a College Education

In this chapter you will explore

- Why critical thinking is essential for success
- The meaning and value of a liberal education
- Why there are no "absolutely right" or "positively wrong" answers to important questions
- How to sharpen your critical-thinking skills
- How logical reasoning can help you make sense of conflicting ideas

Many educators would argue that the most important skill you'll acquire in college is the ability and confidence to think for yourself. Courses in every discipline will encourage you to ask questions, to sort through competing information and ideas, to form well-reasoned opinions, and to defend them. A liberal college education teaches you to investigate all sides of an issue and all possible solutions to a problem before you reach a conclusion or decide on a plan of action. Indeed, the word *liberal* (from the Latin *libero*, meaning "to free") has no political connotation in this context but represents the purpose of a college education: to liberate your mind from biases, superstitions, prejudices, and lack of knowledge so that you'll be in a better position to seek answers to difficult questions.

YOUR TURN ▶

In your own words, define *liberal education*. Why would a "free" mind be an asset for you now and in the future?

If you have just completed high school, you might be experiencing an awakening as you adjust to college. If you're an older returning student, discovering that your instructors trust you to find valid answers could be both surprising and stressful. If a high school teacher asked, "What are the three branches of the U.S. government?" there was only one acceptable answer: "legislative, executive, and judicial." A college instructor, on the other hand, might ask, "Under what circumstances might conflicts arise among the three branches of government, and what does this reveal about the democratic process?" There is no simple—or single—answer, and that's the point of higher education. Questions that suggest complex answers engage you in the process of critical thinking.

Most important questions don't have simple answers, and finding satisfactory answers can be elusive. To reach them, you will have to discover numerous ways to view important issues. You will need to become comfortable with uncertainty. And you must be willing to challenge assumptions and conclusions, even those presented by so-called experts. It is natural to find critical thinking difficult, to feel frustrated by answers that are seldom entirely wrong or right. Yet the complicated questions are usually the ones that are most worthy of study, and working out the answers can be both intellectually exciting and personally rewarding. In this chapter, we will explain how developing and applying your critical-thinking skills can make the search for truth a worthwhile and stimulating adventure.

What Is Critical Thinking and Why Is It Important?

Let's start with what critical thinking is *not*. By "critical," we do not mean "negative" or "harsh." Rather, the term refers to thoughtful consideration of the information, ideas, and arguments that you encounter. Critical thinking is the ability to think for yourself and to reliably and responsibly make the decisions that affect your life.

As Richard Paul and Linda Elder of the National Council for Excellence in Critical Thinking explain it, "critical thinking is that mode of thinking about any subject, content, or problem in which the thinker improves the quality of his or her thinking by skillfully . . . imposing intellectual standards upon [his or her thoughts]."[1] They believe that much of our thinking, left to itself, is biased, distorted, partial, uninformed, or downright prejudiced. Yet the quality of our life and the quality of what we produce, make, or build depend precisely on the quality of our thought.

Paul and Elder also caution that shoddy thinking is costly. How so? You probably know people who simply follow authority. They do not question, are not curious, and do not challenge people or groups who claim special knowledge or insight. These people do not usually think for themselves but rely on others to think for them. They might indulge in wishful, hopeful, and emotional thinking, assuming that what they believe is true simply because they wish it, hope it, or feel it to be true. As you might have noticed, such people tend not to have much control over their circumstances or to possess any real power in business or society.

Critical thinkers, in contrast, investigate problems, ask questions, pose new answers that challenge the status quo, discover new information, question authorities and traditional beliefs, challenge received dogmas and doctrines, make independent judgments, and develop creative solutions. When employers say they want workers who can find reliable information, analyze it, organize it, draw conclusions from it, and present it convincingly to others, they are seeking individuals who are critical thinkers.

YOUR TURN ▶

On the basis of the explanation above, how would you rate yourself as a critical thinker?

Whatever else you do in college, make it a point to develop and sharpen your critical-thinking skills. You won't become an accomplished critical thinker overnight. But with practice, you can learn how to tell whether information is truthful and accurate. You can make better decisions, come up with fresh solutions to difficult problems, and communicate your ideas strategically and persuasively.[2]

Becoming a Critical Thinker

In essence, critical thinking is a search for truth. In college and in life, you'll be confronted by a mass of information and ideas. Much of what you read and hear will seem suspect, and a lot of it will be contradictory. (If you have ever talked back to a television commercial or doubted a politician's campaign promises, you know this already.) How do you decide what to believe?

Paul and Elder remind us that there may be more than one right answer to any given question. The task is to determine which of the "truths" you

---

[1]http://www.criticalthinking.org/print-page.cfm?pageID=766.
[2]Liz Brown, *Critical Thinking* (New York: Weigl Publishers, 2008), p. 4.

read or hear are the most plausible and then draw on them to develop ideas of your own. Difficult problems practically demand that you weigh options and think through consequences before you can reach an informed decision. Critical thinking also involves improving the way you think about a subject, statement, or idea. To do that, you'll need to ask questions, consider several different points of view, and draw your own conclusions.

> **YOUR TURN ▶**
>
> Think of a problem you had to solve in the past. How did you do it? How can you draw on that experience to improve your ability to solve academic problems?

ASK QUESTIONS

The first step of thinking critically is to engage your curiosity. Instead of accepting statements and assertions at face value, question them. When you come across an idea or a "fact" that strikes you as interesting, confusing, or suspicious, ask yourself first what it means. Do you fully understand what is being said, or do you need to pause and think to make sense of the idea? Do you agree with the statement? Why or why not? Can the material be interpreted in more than one way?

Don't stop there. Ask whether you can trust the person or institution making a particular claim, and ask whether they have provided enough evidence to back up an assertion (more on this later). Ask who might be likely to agree or disagree and why. Ask how a new concept relates to what you already know, where you might find more information about the subject, and what you could do with what you learn. Finally, ask yourself about the implications and consequences of accepting something as truth.

Will you have to change your perspective or give up a long-held belief? Will it require you to do something differently? Will it be necessary to investigate the issue further? Do you anticipate having to try to bring other people around to a new way of thinking?

> **YOUR TURN ▶**
>
> Imagine that your state has just approved a license plate design incorporating a cross and the slogan "I Believe." Almost immediately, a number of organizations begin protesting that this is a violation of the First Amendment of the U.S. Constitution. What kinds of questions will you ask to get at the truth?

CONSIDER MULTIPLE POINTS OF VIEW

Once you start asking questions, you'll typically discover a slew of different possible answers competing for your attention. Don't be too quick to latch onto one and move on. To be a critical thinker, you need to be fair and open-minded, even if you don't agree with certain ideas at first. Give them all a fair hearing, because your goal is to find the truth or the best action, not to confirm what you already believe.

Often you will recognize the existence of competing points of view on your own, perhaps because they're held by people you know personally. You might discover them in what you read, watch, or listen to for pleasure. Reading assignments might deliberately expose you to conflicting arguments and theories about a subject, or you might encounter differences of opinion as you do research for a project.

In class discussions also, your instructors might often insist that more than one valid point of view exists: "So, for some types of students, you agree that bilingual education might be best? What types of students might not benefit?" Your instructors will expect you to explain in concrete terms any point you reject: "You think this essay is flawed. Well, what are your reasons?" They might challenge the authority of experts: "Dr. Fleming's theory sounds impressive. But here are some facts he doesn't account for . . ." Your instructors will also sometimes reinforce your personal views and experiences: "So something like this happened to you once, and you felt exactly the same way. Can you tell us why?"

The more ideas you entertain, the more sophisticated your own thinking will become. Ultimately, you will discover not only that is it okay to change your mind, but that a willingness to do so is the mark of a reasonable, educated person.

DRAW CONCLUSIONS

Once you have considered different points of view, it's up to you to reach your own conclusions, to craft a new idea based on what you've learned, or to make a decision about what you'll do with the information you have.

This process isn't necessarily a matter of figuring out the best idea. Depending on the goals of the activity, it might be simply the one that you think is the most fun or the most practical, or it might be a new idea of your own creation. For a business decision, it might involve additional cost-benefit analysis to decide which computer equipment to purchase for your office. In a chemistry lab, it might be a matter of interpreting the results of an experiment. In a creative writing workshop, students might collaborate to select the most workable plot for a classmate's short story. Or a social worker might conduct multiple interviews before recommending a counseling plan for a struggling family.

Drawing conclusions involves looking at the outcome of your inquiry in a more demanding, critical way. If you are looking for solutions to a problem, which ones really seem most promising after you have conducted an exhaustive search for materials? Do some answers conflict with others? Which ones can be achieved? If you have found new evidence, what does that new evidence show? Do your original beliefs hold up? Do they need to be modified? Which notions should be abandoned? Most important, consider what you would need to do or say to persuade someone else that your ideas are valid. Thoughtful conclusions aren't very useful if you can't share them with others.

How Collaboration Fosters Critical Thinking

A 1995 study by Professor Anuradha A. Gokhale at Western Illinois University, published in the *Journal of Technology Education*, found that students who participated in collaborative learning performed significantly better on a test requiring critical thinking than did students who studied individually. The study also found that the two groups did equally well on a test that required only memorization.[3]

Having more than one student involved in the learning process generates a greater number of ideas. People think more clearly when they are talking as well as listening (a very good reason to participate actively in your classes). Creative brainstorming and group discussion encourage original thought. These habits also teach participants to consider alternative points of view carefully and to express and defend their own ideas clearly. As a group negotiates ideas and learns to agree on the most reliable thoughts, it moves closer to a surer solution.

YOUR TURN ▶

If you never have worked with a study group, now is the time to try it and discover how much more learning can take place in a shorter period of time. How do you think you could benefit from joining a study group? What reasons might you give for not joining one?

Collaboration occurs not only face to face, but also over the Internet. Christopher P. Sessums, creator of an award-winning blog, writes:

> Weblogs offer several key features that I believe can support a constructive, collaborative, reflective environment. For one, it's convenient. The medium supports self-expression and "voice." Collaboration and connectivity can be conducted efficiently, especially in terms of participants' time or place. Publishing your thoughts online forces you to concretize your thoughts.

"Collaborative weblogs," Sessums concludes, "promote the idea of learners as creators of knowledge, not merely consumers of information."[4] So do online discussion groups, wikis (which allow users to add, update, and otherwise improve material that others have posted), and, of course, face-to-face collaboration.

Whether in person or through electronic communication, teamwork improves your ability to think critically. As you leave college and enter the

[3]Anuradha Gokhale, "Collaborative Learning Enhances Critical Thinking," *Journal of Technology Education*, 1995, 7.1.

[4]Christopher Sessums, Eduspaces weblog, November 9, 2005. Available at: http://eduspaces .net/csessums/weblog/archive/2005/11.

world of work, you will find that collaboration is essential in almost any career you pursue, not only with people in your work setting, but also with others around the globe.

Thinking Critically about Arguments

What does the word *argument* mean to you? If you're like most people, the first image it conjures up might be an ugly fight you had with a friend, a yelling match you witnessed on the street, or a heated disagreement between family members. True, such unpleasant confrontations are arguments. But the word also refers to a calm, reasoned effort to persuade someone of the value of an idea.

When you think of it this way, you'll quickly recognize that arguments are central to academic study, work, and life in general. Scholarly articles, business memos, and requests for spending money all have something in common: The effective ones make a general claim, provide reasons to support it, and back up those reasons with evidence. That's what argument is.

As we have already seen, it's important to consider multiple points of view, or arguments, in tackling new ideas and complex questions. But arguments are not all equally valid. Good critical thinking involves think-

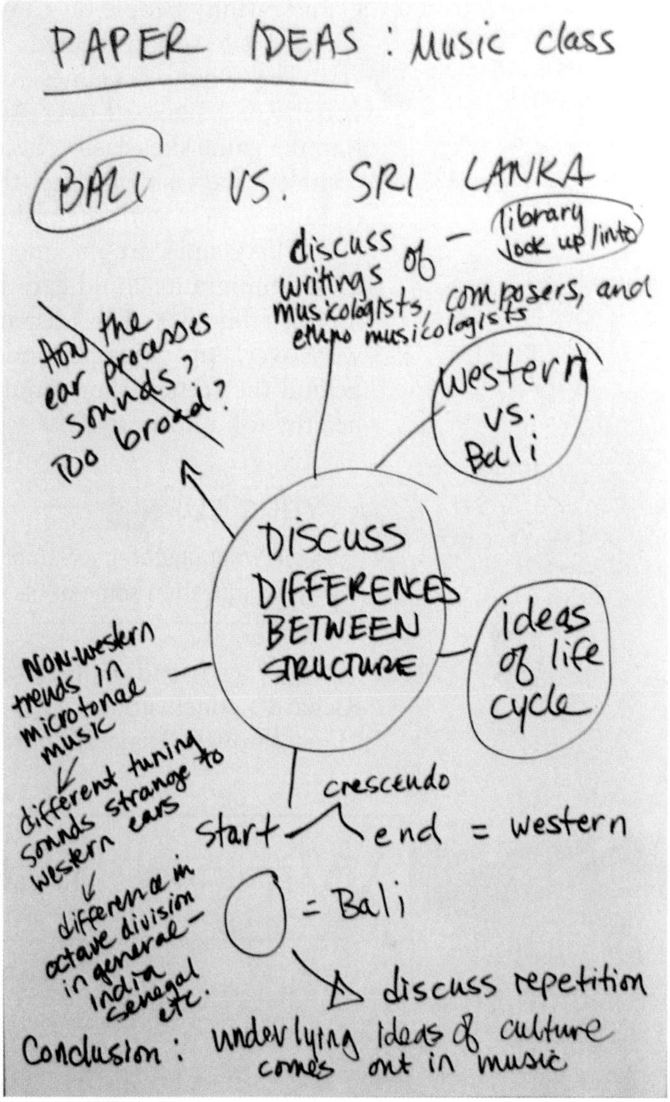

▶ **FIGURE 5.1**   Brainstorming on Paper

ing creatively about the assumptions that might have been left out and scrutinizing the quality of the evidence that is used to support a claim. Whether examining an argument or communicating one, a good critical thinker is careful to ensure that ideas are presented in an understandable, logical way.

CHALLENGE ASSUMPTIONS

All too often, our beliefs are based on gut feelings or on blind acceptance of something we've heard or read. To some extent, that's unavoidable. If we made a habit of questioning absolutely everything, we would have trouble making it through the day. Yet some assumptions should be examined more thoughtfully, especially if they will influence an important decision or serve as the foundation for an argument.

For an example, imagine that the mayor of the city where your school is located has announced that he wants to make a bid to host the Olympic

Games. Many people on campus are excited at the prospect, but your friend Richard is less than thrilled.

"The Olympic Games just about ruined my hometown," Richard tells you. "Road signs all over Atlanta had to be changed so that visitors could find the game sites easily. Because the city couldn't supply enough workers to complete the task on time, the organizers brought thousands of immigrants to town to help with the task, and some of them were illegal aliens.

"The Games are intended to foster national and international pride, but these immigrants could care less about that. They were there to earn money for their families. The Hispanic population nearly doubled once the Games were over. And if people understood how much political corruption went on behind the scenes, they would understand why the Olympic Games are not healthy for a host city."

YOUR TURN ▶

So far, what unstated assumptions do you see in Richard's argument? Explain why you question some of his claims.

Another friend, Sally, overhears your conversation, and she's not buying Richard's conclusions. "How do you know all of that is accurate?" she asks. "I just know it," says Richard.

Wired WINDOW

USING CRITICAL THINKING IN THE BLOGOSPHERE

Weblogs, or blogs, allow anyone, even those with limited Web publishing experience, to post online journals that appear professional. Blogs emerged in 2003, and their popularity has exploded since then. Bloggers are currently posting over 900,000 new entries every day.[5] Because there are so many blogs, they cover just about any topic you can think of—from politics to purchasing, from movies to money, from sex to Silicon Valley. If you want to know bloggers' opinions about anything, you can find them in the blogosphere. Because there are so many blogs, opinions about an issue can range widely among bloggers—some supporting a certain viewpoint, some being against it, and many others being somewhere in between. Keep in mind that the vast majority of bloggers are not experts in their field and that most blogs are not reviewed for accuracy. This allows for a richer examination of all possible viewpoints, but you must hone your critical-thinking skills to evaluate blogs effectively.

Thinking Critically

Blogs present a wonderful opportunity for you to improve your critical-thinking skills. Many bloggers are perfectly comfortable sharing their thinking process with their audience. Can you find a blogger who discusses a common topic yet provides a viewpoint that is not represented in the mainstream? Search for a blog with commentary on a current event that you find interesting. (Hint: Search for the topic keywords plus the word *blog*.) Find two blogs with different viewpoints on the same topic. Then answer the following questions: What is each blogger's viewpoint? Do the people who leave comments generally agree or disagree with the blogger's point of view? Why does the blogger hold that point of view? Is there any evidence on the blog that supports the blogger's view? Do you have an opinion on the topic? Which blogger do you most agree with? Why?

[5]Technorati, 2008. Available at: http://technorati.com/blogging/state-of-the-blogosphere.

Eager to get at the truth of the matter, Sally decides to look into other points of view. She does a quick web search and finds an article about the Atlanta Olympics in the *American Historical Review*, the journal of record for the history profession in the United States. Its author notes that "the Games provided an enormous engine for growth" and comments that the city's "surging population is the most obvious marker of Atlanta's post-Olympic transformation." The article continues: "By the 1996 Games the metro population had reached three million, and today [is] 4,458,253. Winning the Olympic bid marked a turning point that put Atlanta on the world's radar screen."[6]

YOUR TURN ▶

What's the difference between Richard's approach to the truth and Sally's? Which is more sensible? Why?

Although Sally has found good information from a reputable source, you should be uncomfortable with the totally upbeat tone of the article. If you and Sally dig a little further, you might land on the Web site of the Utah Office of Tourism, which includes a report that was prepared when that state was investigating the potential impacts of hosting the 2002 Winter Games in Salt Lake City. According to the report, "Among the key legacies of the Atlanta Olympics was the regeneration of certain downtown districts that had fallen into urban decay." The authors also note that "the Olympic-spurred development in [Atlanta] has provided a much-needed stimulus for revitalization."[7]

Finding a second positive analysis would give you a compelling reason to believe that the Olympic Games are good for a city, but Richard might easily discover a report from the European Tour Operators Association, which concludes that visitors are likely to stay away from host countries during and following the Games, causing a significant long-term decline in revenue for hotels and other businesses that depend on tourism.[8]

Unfortunately, simply learning more about the benefits and costs of hosting the Olympics doesn't yield any concrete answers. Even so, you, Richard, and Sally have uncovered assumptions and have developed a better understanding of the issue. That's an important first step.

YOUR TURN ▶

In your opinion, is hosting the Olympics good or bad for a city? Why? How can you reconcile Richard's views on the subject with Sally's findings? If you think the truth lies in between, how would you go about discovering it?

---

[6]Mary G. Rolinson, visiting lecturer in the Georgia State University History Department, "Atlanta Before and After the Olympics." Copyright © American Historical Association. Available at: http://www.historians.org/perspectives/issues/2006/0611/0611ann6.cfm.

[7]Utah Office of Tourism, *Observations from Past Olympic Host Communities: Executive Summary.* Available at: http://travel.utah.gov/research_and_planning/2002_olympics.

[8]"Olympics Have Negative Effect on Tourism," July 10, 2008. Available at: http://www.travelbite.co.uk.

EXAMINE THE EVIDENCE

The evidence that is offered as support for an argument can vary in quality. While Richard started with no proof other than his convictions ("I just know it"), Sally looked to expert opinion and research studies for answers to her question. Even so, one of her sources sounded overly positive, prompting a need to confirm the author's claims with additional evidence from other sources.

Like Sally, critical thinkers are careful to check that the evidence supporting an argument—whether someone else's or their own—is of the highest possible quality. To do that, simply ask a few questions about the arguments as you consider them:

- What general idea am I being asked to accept?
- Are good and sufficient reasons given to support the overall claim?
- Are those reasons backed up with evidence in the form of facts, statistics, and quotations?
- Does the evidence support the conclusions?
- Is the argument based on logical reasoning, or does it appeal mainly to the emotions?
- Do I recognize any questionable assumptions?
- Can I think of any counterarguments? What facts can I muster as proof?
- What do I know about the person or organization making the argument?

> **YOUR TURN ▶**
>
> What, if anything, is wrong with making decisions purely on the basis of your emotions?

If, after you have evaluated the evidence used in support of a claim, you're still not certain of its quality, it's best to keep looking. Drawing on questionable evidence for an argument has a tendency to backfire. In most cases, a little persistence will help you find something better. (You can find tips on how to find and evaluate sources in Chapter 10, "Developing Library, Research, and Information Literacy Skills.")

BEWARE OF LOGICAL FALLACIES

A critical thinker has an attitude—an attitude of wanting to avoid nonsense, to find the truth, and to discover the best action. It's an attitude that rejects intuiting what is right in favor of requiring reasons. Instead of being defensive or emotional, critical thinkers aim to be logical.

Although logical reasoning is essential to solving any problem, whether simple or complex, you need to go one step further to make sure that an argument hasn't been compromised by faulty reasoning. Here are some of the most common missteps people make in their use of logic:

- **Attacking the person.** It's perfectly acceptable to argue against other people's positions or to attack their arguments. It is not okay, however, to go after their personalities. Any argument that resorts to personal attack ("Why should we believe a cheater?") is unworthy of consideration.

- **Begging.** "Please, officer, don't give me a ticket because if you do, I'll lose my license, and I have five little children to feed and won't be able to feed them if I can't drive my truck." None of the driver's statements offer any evidence, in any legal sense, as to why she shouldn't be given a ticket. Pleading *might* work, if the officer is feeling generous, but an appeal to facts and reason would be more effective: "I fed the meter, but it didn't register the coins. Since the machine is broken, I'm sure you'll agree that I don't deserve a ticket."

- **Appealing to false authority.** Citing authorities, such as experts in a field or the opinions of qualified researchers, can offer valuable support for an argument. But a claim based on the authority of someone whose expertise is questionable relies on the appearance of authority rather than real evidence. We see this all the time in advertising: Sports stars who are not doctors, dieticians, or nutritionists urge us to eat a certain brand of food, or famous actors and singers who are not dermatologists extol the medical benefits of a pricey remedy for acne.

- **Jumping on a bandwagon.** Sometimes we are more likely to believe something if a lot of other people believe it. Even the most widely accepted truths, however, can turn out to be wrong. There was a time when nearly everyone believed that the world was flat—until someone came up with evidence to the contrary.

- **Assuming that something is true because it hasn't been proven false.** Go to a bookstore, and you'll find dozens of books detailing close encounters with flying saucers and extraterrestrial beings. These books describe the person who had the close encounter as beyond reproach in integrity and sanity. Because critics could not disprove the claims of the witnesses, the events are said to have really occurred. Even in science, few things are ever proved completely false, but evidence can be discredited.

- **Falling victim to false cause.** Frequently, we make the assumption that just because one event followed another, the first event must have caused the second. This reasoning is the basis for many superstitions. The ancient Chinese once believed that they could make the sun reappear after an eclipse by striking a large gong, because they knew that the sun reappeared after a large gong had been struck on one such occasion. Most effects, however, are usually the result of a complex web of causes. Don't be satisfied with easy before-and-after claims; they are rarely correct.
- **Making hasty generalizations.** If someone selected one green marble from a barrel containing a hundred marbles, you wouldn't assume that the next marble would be green. After all, there are still ninety-nine marbles in the barrel, and you know nothing about the colors of those marbles. However, given fifty draws from the barrel, each of which produced a green marble after the barrel had been shaken thoroughly, you would be more willing to conclude that the next marble drawn would also be green. Reaching a conclusion based on the opinion of one source is like figuring that all the marbles in the barrel are green after pulling out only one.

YOUR TURN ▶

Have you ever used any of these fallacies to justify a decision? Why was it wrong to do so? Can you think of other errors of logic that might push you farther from the truth?

Fallacies like these can slip into even the most careful reasoning. One false claim can derail an entire argument, so be on the lookout for weak logic in what you read and write. Never forget that accurate reasoning is a key factor for success in college and in life.

Critical Thinking in College and Everyday Life

As you practice the skills of critical thinking in college, they start to become a natural part of your life. Eventually, you will be able to think your way through many everyday situations, such as these:

- You try to reach a classmate on the phone to ask a question about tomorrow's quiz. When you can't reach her, you become so anxious that you can't study or sleep.
- On the day an important paper is due, a heavy snowstorm rolls in. You brave the cold to get to class. When you arrive, no one—including the teacher—is there. You take a seat and wait.

Now let's transform you into a critical thinker and examine the possible outcomes:

- When you can't reach a classmate on the phone to ask a question about tomorrow's quiz, you review the material once more, then call one or more other classmates. Then you consider their views and those of your textbook and class. Instead of deciding on one point of view for each important topic, you decide to keep in mind all of those that make sense, leaving your final decision until you have the quiz in your hand.

■ Before heading out to class in a big snowstorm, you check the college Web site and discover that classes have been canceled. You stay at home.

YOUR TURN ▶

Suppose you're shopping for a surround-sound system. One good friend urges you to buy the top of the line. Another well-meaning friend steers you to a different brand, claiming it's just as good as the more expensive brand leader. Now all you know is that two of your good friends have offered information that might or might not be true. How do you think critically about which system to choose?

If you hang onto the guidelines in this chapter, we can't promise your classes will be easier, but they will certainly be more interesting. You will now know how to use critical thinking to figure things out instead of depending purely on how you feel or what you've heard. As you listen to a lecture, try to predict where it is heading and why. When other students raise issues, ask yourself whether they have enough information to justify what they have said. And when you raise your hand, remember that asking a sensible question can be more important than trying to find the elusive—and often nonexistent— "right answer."

Imagine a world in which physicians tried a new procedure on a patient before it had been tested, your history course was taught by someone who never studied history, and you put your total faith in a hair restorer just because the advertising said it would grow hair in two weeks.

As a critical thinker, you would know better.

Where to go
FOR HELP...

ON CAMPUS ▶

Logic Courses Check out your philosophy department's introductory course in logic. This might be the single best course designed to teach you critical-thinking skills. Nearly every college offers such a course.

Argument Courses and Critical Thinking Courses These are usually offered in the English department. They will help you develop the ability to formulate logical arguments and avoid such pitfalls as logical fallacies.

Debating Skills Some of the very best critical thinkers developed debating skills during college. Go to either your student activities office or your department of speech/drama, and find out whether your campus has a debate club or team. Debating can be fun, and chances are you will meet some interesting student thinkers that way.

LITERATURE ▶

12 Angry Men **by Reginald Rose** (New York: Penguin Classics, 2006) This is a reprint of the original teleplay, which was written in 1954 and made into a film in 1958. It is also available on DVD. The stirring courtroom drama pits twelve jurors against one another as they argue the outcome of a murder trial in which the defendant is a teenage boy. Where critical thinking is needed to arrive at the truth, all but one juror employ every noncritical argument in the book to arrive at a guilty verdict until the analysis of the one holdout produces remarkable changes in their attitudes.

ONLINE ▶

Check the following Web site for a critical review of *The Encyclopedia of Stupidity:* http://arts.independent.co.uk/books/reviews/article112328.ece.

A Guide to Critical Thinking About What You See on the Web: http://www.ithaca.edu/library/training/think.html.

MY INSTITUTION'S RESOURCES ▶

_____

_____

_____

_____

_____

_____

_____

_____

_____

_____

_____

_____

_____

_____

5 Applying What You've LEARNED...

Now that you have read and discussed this chapter, consider how you can apply what you have learned to your academic and personal life. The following prompts will help you reflect on chapter material and its relevance to you now and in the future.

1. After reading this chapter, think of professions (for example, physicians, engineers, marketing professionals) for whom problem solving and thinking "outside of the box" is necessary. Choose one career, and describe why you think critical thinking is a necessary and valuable skill.

2. In your opinion, is it harder to think critically than to base your arguments on how you feel about a topic? Why or why not? What are the advantages of finding answers based on your feelings? Based on critical thinking? How might you use both approaches in seeking answers?

One-Minute PAPER...

One major shift from being a high school student to being a college student involves the level of critical thinking your college instructors expect of you. After reading this chapter, how would you describe critical thinking to a high school student?

Building Your PORTFOLIO...

MY INFLUENCES

Our past experiences have shaped the way in which we think and perceive the world around us. Sometimes it is easy to interpret things without stopping to think about why we feel the way we do. How have other people shaped the way you see the world today?

1. In your personal portfolio, create a Word document and:

   - Describe at least three people (such as family, friends, celebrities, national leaders) who you feel have most influenced the way you think.

   - Describe how these individuals' values, actions, expectations, and words have shaped the way you think about yourself and the world.

2. Describe a situation that you have dealt with since coming to college that has challenged you to think about an issue in a new and different way.

3. Save your work on your personal computer or flash drive.

6 Being Engaged in Learning: Listening, Taking Notes, and Participating in Class

In this chapter you will explore

- How to use your senses in learning and remembering
- How to prepare before class
- Why you should participate in class by speaking up
- How to listen critically
- How to assess and improve your note-taking skills
- Why it is important to review your notes and textbook materials soon after class
- How being engaged in the classroom improves your learning

In virtually every college class you take, you'll

need to master certain skills to earn high grades, such as listening, taking notes, and being engaged in learning. Engagement in learning means that you take an active role in your classes by listening critically, asking questions, contributing to discussions, and providing answers. These active learning behaviors will enhance your ability to understand abstract ideas, find new possibilities, organize those ideas, and recall the material once the class is over.

Your academic success relies on practicing the habits of active engagement both in and out of class. In the classroom, engagement starts with the basics: listening, taking notes, and participating in class discussions. Many of the questions on college exams will be drawn from class lectures and discussions. Therefore you need to attend each class and be actively involved. In addition to taking notes, you might consider recording the lecture and discussion if you have the instructor's permission. If there are points you don't understand, take the time to meet with the instructor after class or during office hours, or meet with a study group to compare your understanding of course material with that of your classmates.

This chapter reviews several note-taking methods. Choose the one that works best for you. Because writing down everything the instructor says is probably not possible and you might not be sure what is most important, ask questions in class. Reviewing your notes with a tutor, someone from your campus learning center, or a friend from class can also help you clarify the most important points.

Most of all, be sure to speak up. You will be more likely to remember what happens in class if you are an active participant.

YOUR TURN ▶

What kind of notes did you take in high school? Do you think you learned how to take good notes? Is the same method working for you now? Why or why not?

Using Your Senses in the Learning Process

You can enhance your memory by using as many of your senses as possible while learning. How do you believe you learn most effectively?

1. **Aural**: Are you an auditory learner? Do you learn by listening to other people talk?
2. **Visual**: Do you like reading? Do you learn best when you can see the words on the printed page? During a test, can you actually visualize where the information appears in your text?
3. **Interactive**: Does talking about information from the lecture or the text help you remember it?

4. **Tactile:** Do you learn through your sense of touch?

5. **Kinesthetic:** Can you learn better when your body is in motion? Do you learn more effectively by doing something than by listening or reading about it?

6. **Olfactory:** Does your sense of taste or smell contribute to your learning process?

Two or three of these modes probably describe your preferred ways of learning. At the college level, faculty members tend to share information primarily via lecture and the textbook. However, many students like to learn through visual and interactive means. This difference can create a mismatch between learning and teaching styles. It is a problem only if you do not learn how to adapt lecture material and the text to your preferred modes of learning.

BEFORE CLASS TIPS

1. **Do the assigned reading.** Otherwise, you might find the lecturer's comments disjointed, and you might not understand some terms that your instructor will use. Some instructors refer to assigned readings for each class session; others might distribute a **syllabus** (course outline) and assume you are keeping up with the assigned readings. As you read, take good notes. In books that you own, **annotate** (add critical or explanatory margin notes), highlight, or underline the text. In books that you do not own, such as library books, make a photocopy of the pages and then annotate or highlight.

2. **Pay careful attention to your course syllabus.** Syllabi are formal statements of course expectations, requirements, and procedures. Instructors assume that students will understand and follow course requirements with few or no reminders once they have received a syllabus.

3. **Make use of additional materials provided by the instructors.** Many instructors post lecture outlines or notes on a Web site before class. Download and print these materials for easy reference during class.

4. **Warm up for class** by reviewing chapter introductions and summaries, referring to related sections in your text, and scanning your notes from the previous class period. This prepares you to pay attention, understand, and remember.

5. **Get organized.** Decide what type of notebook will work best for you. Many study skills experts suggest using three-ring binders because you can punch holes in syllabi and other course handouts and keep them with class notes. If you take notes on your laptop, keep your files organized in separate folders for each of your classes, and make sure that the file name of each document reflects the date and topic of the class.

Philosophy 101: Introduction to Philosophy
Descartes: Meditations on First Philosophy
Meditation 1

Lecture Notes

Historical Introduction

- b. 1596, LaHaye (now 'Descartes'), France; d. 1650, Stockholm, Sweden.
- Trained in classical literature, history, rhetoric, higher mathematics, and philosophy.
- Unimpressed with traditional, scholastic philosophy; all of it open to doubt; shaky foundations.
- Sought to develop a new model for science and philosophy based on the certainty of mathematical reasoning.

Introduction to the *Meditations*

- Not a philosophical treatise, but an exercise in thinking.
- Written as a thought process, "stream of consciousness".
- Written in first person, allows reader to imagine him/herself as engaging in this thought process.
- Goal: discover a foundation for knowledge.

Meditation 1

- Foundation of knowledge must be certain.
- Why? Anything built upon certainty will also be certain. Anything built upon uncertain foundations will also be uncertain.

Relation between knowledge and belief

- To know something *X*, one must believe *X*.
- Belief is a necessary condition for knowledge.

What kinds of beliefs do we have?

- Observational beliefs (grass is green, I have hands, etc.)
- Predictive beliefs (the sun will rise tomorrow)
- General inductive beliefs (all swans are white)
- General definitional beliefs (all bachelors are unmarried)
- Mathematical beliefs (2 + 3 = 5)

Descartes only focuses on two of these categories: observational beliefs and mathematical beliefs.

- Can we be certain with respect to either of these categories of belief?
- Observational
  - Sources of doubt: senses sometimes deceive; we could be dreaming.
- Mathematical
  - Sources of doubt: omnipotent God, omnipotent evil genius.

Can we be certain about any belief?

- Descartes finds such a belief in Meditation 2.

End of Meditation 1

- While doubt forces us to discard practically all of our beliefs, we naturally fall back into agreement with them.

Preparing for Class

In your first-year classes, you'll be listening to and reading material that might seem hard to understand. Beginning on the first day of class, you will be more likely to remember what you hear and read if you try to link it to something you have already learned or experienced.

Because some lectures are hard to follow and understand, you need to be prepared before class begins. You would not want to be unprepared to give a speech, interview for a job, plead a case in court, or compete in a sport. For each of these situations, you would prepare in some way. For the same reasons, you should begin listening, learning, and remembering before the lecture.

Even if lectures don't allow for active participation, you can do a number of things to become more engaged and to make your listening and note-taking more efficient.

Participating in Class

To really learn, you must listen critically, talk about what you are learning, write about it, relate it to past experiences, and make what you learn part of yourself. Participation is the heart of **active learning**. When we say something in class, we are more likely to remember it than we will when someone else says something. So when a teacher tosses a question your way or you have a question to ask, you're actually making it easier to remember the day's lesson.

LISTENING CRITICALLY AND WITH AN OPEN MIND

Knowing how to listen in class can help you get more out of what you hear, understand better what you have heard, and save time.

Here are some suggestions:

1. **Be ready for the message.** If you have done the assigned reading, you will already know details from the text, so you can focus your notes on key concepts during the lecture. You will also be able to notice information that the text does not cover.

2. **Listen to the main concepts and central ideas, not just to fragmented facts and figures.** Although facts are important, they will be easier to remember and will make more sense when you can place them in a context of concepts, themes, and ideas.

3. **Listen for new ideas.** Even if you are an expert on a topic, you can still learn something new. As a critical thinker, make a note of questions that arise in your mind as you listen, but save the judgments for later.

4. **Repeat mentally.** Words can go in one ear and out the other unless you make an effort to retain them. If you cannot translate the information into your own words, ask the instructor for further clarification.

5. **Decide whether what you have heard is not important, somewhat important, or very important.** If it's very important, make it a major point in your notes by highlighting or underscoring it, or use it as a major topic in your outline.

6. **Keep an open mind.** Every class holds the promise of letting you discover new ideas and uncover different perspectives. Some teachers might intentionally present information that challenges your value system. Instructors want you to think for yourself; they don't necessarily expect you to agree with everything they or your classmates say. However, if you want people to respect your values and ideas, you must show respect for theirs as well.

7. **Ask questions.** Some teachers prefer to save questions for the end or want students to ask questions during separate discussion sections or office hours. To some extent, this preference might depend on the nature and size of the class. If your teacher answers questions as they arise, do not hesitate to ask if you did not hear or understand what was said. If you can't hear another student's question or response, ask that it be repeated.

8. **Sort, organize, and categorize.** When you listen, try to match what you are hearing with what you already know.

SPEAKING UP

Naturally, you will be more likely to participate in a class in which the teacher emphasizes interactive discussion, calls on students by name, shows signs of approval and interest, and avoids criticizing students for an incorrect answer. Often, answers you and others offer that are not quite correct can lead to new perspectives on a topic.

Large classes can be intimidating. If you speak up in a class of 100 and think you have made a fool of yourself, you also believe that 99 other people will know it. That's somewhat unrealistic, since you have probably asked a question that others were too timid to ask. To take full advantage of these opportunities, try using the following techniques:

1. **Take a seat as close to the front as possible.** If students are seated by name and your name begins with Z, request to be moved up front.

2. **Keep your eyes trained on the teacher.** Sitting up front will make this easier to do.

3. **Focus on the lecture.** Do not let yourself be distracted. It might be wise not to sit near friends who can distract you.

4. **Raise your hand when you don't understand something.** The instructor might answer you immediately, ask you to wait until later in the class, or throw your question to the rest of the class. In each case, you benefit in several ways. The instructor will get to know you, other students will get to know you, and you will learn from both the instructor and your classmates.

5. **Speak up in class.** Ask a question or volunteer to answer a question or make a comment. Speaking up becomes easier every time you do it.

6. **Never feel that you're asking a stupid question.** If you don't understand something, you have a right to ask for an explanation.

7. **When the instructor calls on you to answer a question, don't bluff.** If you know the answer, give it. If you're not certain, begin with, "I think . . . , but I'm not sure I have it all correct." If you don't know, just say so.

YOUR TURN ▶

Is it hard or easy for you to raise your hand and ask questions in most of your classes? Why? How can you become more involved?

---

8. **If you have recently read a book or article that is relevant to the class topic, bring it in.** Use it either to ask questions about the topic or to provide information that was not covered in class.

Taking Effective Notes

What are "effective notes"? They are notes that prepare you to do well on quizzes or exams. Becoming an effective note-taker takes time and practice, but this skill will help you improve your learning and your grades.

NOTE-TAKING FORMATS

You can make class time more productive by using your listening skills to take effective lecture notes, but first you have to decide on a system.

Cornell Format. Using the Cornell format, you create a "recall" column on each page of your notebook by drawing a vertical line about two to three inches from the left border (see Figure 6.1). As you take notes during lecture, write only in the wider column on the right; leave the recall column on the left blank. (If this method seems unwieldy, consider using the back of the previous notebook page for your recall column.) The recall column is where you write down the main ideas and important details for tests and examinations as you sift through your notes as soon as feasible after class, preferably within an hour or two. Many students have found the recall column to be a critical part of effective note-taking.

Outline Format. Some students find that an outline is the best way for them to organize their notes. If you use this approach, try to determine the instructor's outline and re-create it in your notes. Add details, definitions, examples, applications, and explanations (see Figures 6.2 and 6.5).

Paragraph Format. You might decide to write summary paragraphs when you are taking notes on what you are reading. This method might not work as well for class notes because it's difficult to summarize a topic until your instructor has covered it completely. By the end of the lecture, you might have forgotten critical information (see Figure 6.5).

Psychology 101, 1/31/11
Theories of Personality

Personality trait: define	Personality trait = "durable disposition to behave in a particular way in a variety of situations"
Big 5: Name + describe them	Big 5 - McCrae + Costa - (1)extroversion, (or positive emotionality)=outgoing, sociable, friendly, upbeat, assertive; (2) neuroticism=anxious, hostile, self-conscious, insecure, vulnerable; (3)openness to experience=curiosity, flexibility, imaginative; (4) agreeableness=sympathetic, trusting, cooperative, modest; (5)conscientiousness=diligent, disciplined, well organized, punctual, dependable
Psychodynamic Theories: Who?	Psychodynamic Theories—focus on unconscious forces Freud-psychoanalysis—3 components of personality—(1)id=primitive, instinctive, operates according to pleasure principle (immediate gratification);
3 components of personality: name and describe	(2)ego=decision-making component, operates according to reality principle (delay gratification until appropriate); (3)superego=moral component, social standards, right + wrong
3 levels of awareness: name and describe	3 levels of awareness—(1) conscious=what one is aware of at a particular moment; (2)preconscious=material just below surface, easily retrieved; (3)unconscious=thoughts, memories, + desires well below surface, but have great influence on behavior

◄ **FIGURE 6.1**

Note-taking in the Cornell Format

List Format. This format can be effective in taking notes on lists of terms and definitions, facts, or sequences, such as the body's pulmonary system. It is easy to use lists in combination with the Cornell format, with key terms on the left and their definitions and explanations on the right (see Figure 6.4).

YOUR TURN ►

Which of these four note-taking methods (Cornell, outline, paragraph, list) is most like the one you use? How well does your current system work for you? Explain your answer. What changes will you make in how you take notes now that you have read this portion of the chapter?

Psychology 101, 1/31/11: Theories of Personality

I. Personality trait = "durable disposition to behave in a particular way in a variety of situations"
II. Big 5-McCrae + Costa
  A. Extroversion, (or positive emotionality)=outgoing, sociable, friendly, upbeat, assertive
  B. Neuroticism=anxious, hostile, self-conscious, insecure, vulnerable
  C. Openness to experience=curiosity, flexibility, imaginative
  D. Agreeableness=sympathetic, trusting, cooperative, modest
  E. Conscientiousness=diligent, disciplined, well organized, punctual, dependable
III. Psychodynamic Theories-focus on unconscious forces—Freud-psychoanalysis
  A. 3 components of personality
    1. Id=primitive, instinctive, operates according to pleasure principle (immediate gratification)
    2. Ego=decision-making component, operates according to reality principle (delay gratification until appropriate)
    3. Superego=moral component, social standards, right + wrong
  B. 3 levels of awareness
    1. Conscious=what one is aware of at a particular moment
    2. Preconscious=material just below surface, easily retrieved
    3. Unconscious=thoughts, memories, + desires well below surface, but have great influence on behavior

FIGURE 6.2 ▶

Note-taking in the Outline Format

NOTE-TAKING TECHNIQUES

Whatever note-taking system you choose, follow these important steps:

1. **Identify the main ideas.** The first principle of effective note-taking is to identify and write down the most important ideas around which the lecture is built. Although supporting details are important as well, focus your note-taking on the main ideas. Such ideas can be buried in details, statistics, anecdotes, or problems.

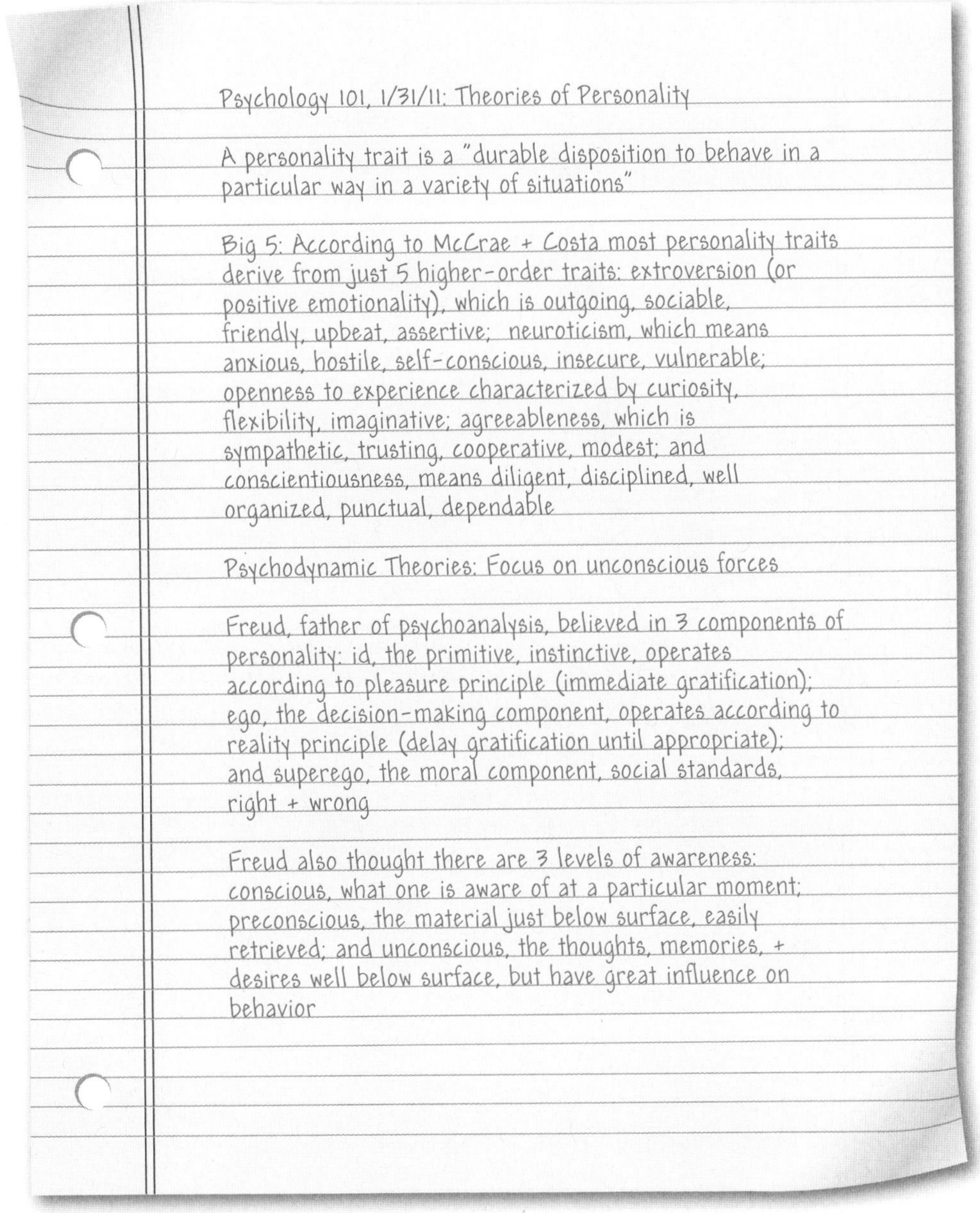

Psychology 101, 1/31/11: Theories of Personality

A personality trait is a "durable disposition to behave in a particular way in a variety of situations"

Big 5: According to McCrae + Costa most personality traits derive from just 5 higher-order traits: extroversion (or positive emotionality), which is outgoing, sociable, friendly, upbeat, assertive; neuroticism, which means anxious, hostile, self-conscious, insecure, vulnerable; openness to experience characterized by curiosity, flexibility, imaginative; agreeableness, which is sympathetic, trusting, cooperative, modest; and conscientiousness, means diligent, disciplined, well organized, punctual, dependable

Psychodynamic Theories: Focus on unconscious forces

Freud, father of psychoanalysis, believed in 3 components of personality: id, the primitive, instinctive, operates according to pleasure principle (immediate gratification); ego, the decision-making component, operates according to reality principle (delay gratification until appropriate); and superego, the moral component, social standards, right + wrong

Freud also thought there are 3 levels of awareness: conscious, what one is aware of at a particular moment; preconscious, the material just below surface, easily retrieved; and unconscious, the thoughts, memories, + desires well below surface, but have great influence on behavior

◀ **FIGURE 6.3**

Note-taking in the Paragraph Format

Some instructors announce the purpose of a lecture or offer an outline, thus providing you with the skeleton of main ideas, followed by the details. Other instructors develop PowerPoint presentations. If they make these materials available on a class Web site before the lecture, you can print them and take notes on the teacher's outline or next to the PowerPoint slides.

If a lecturer says something more than once, chances are it is important. Ask yourself, "What does my instructor want me to know at the end of today's class?"

> Psychology 101, 1/31/11: Theories of Personality
>
> - A personality trait is a "durable disposition to behave in a particular way in a variety of situations"
> - Big 5: According to McCrae + Costa most personality traits derive from just 5 higher-order traits
>   - extroversion, (or positive emotionality)=outgoing, sociable, friendly, upbeat, assertive
>   - neuroticism=anxious, hostile, self-conscious, insecure, vulnerable
>   - openness to experience=curiosity, flexibility, imaginative
>   - agreeableness=sympathetic, trusting, cooperative, modest
>   - conscientiousness=diligent, disciplined, well organized, punctual, dependable
> - Psychodynamic Theories: Focus on unconscious forces
> - Freud, father of psychoanalysis, believed in 3 components of personality
>   - id=primitive, instinctive, operates according to pleasure principle (immediate gratification)
>   - ego=decision-making component, operates according to reality principle (delay gratification until appropriate)
>   - superego=moral component, social standards, right + wrong
> - Freud also thought there are 3 levels of awareness
>   - conscious=what one is aware of at a particular moment
>   - preconscious=material just below surface, easily retrieved
>   - unconscious=thoughts, memories, + desires well below surface, but have great influence on behavior

FIGURE 6.4 ▶

Note-taking in the List Format

2. **Don't try to write down everything.** Some first-year students try to do just that. They stop being thinkers and become stenographers. As you take notes, leave spaces so that you can fill in additional details that you might have missed during class but remember later.

3. **Don't be thrown by a disorganized lecturer.** When a lecture is disorganized, it's your job to try to organize what is said into general and specific frameworks. When the order is not apparent, you will need to indicate in your notes where the gaps lie. After the lecture, consult the reading material or classmates to fill in these gaps, or ask your instructor. Most instructors have regular office hours for student appointments, yet it is amazing how few students use these opportunities for one-on-one instruction.

4. **Keep your notes and supplementary materials for each course in a separate three-ring binder.** Label the binder with the course number and

Personality trait	I. Personality trait = "durable disposition to behave in a particular way in a variety of situations"
	II. Big 5-McCrae + Costa
Big 5: Who? Name + describe them	A. Extroversion (or positive emotionality)=outgoing, sociable, friendly, upbeat, assertive
	B. Neuroticism=anxious, hostile, self-conscious, insecure, vulnerable
	C. Openness to experience=curiosity, flexibility, imaginative
	D. Agreeableness=sympathetic, trusting, cooperative, modest
	E. Conscientiousness=diligent, disciplined, well organized, punctual, dependable
	III. Psychodynamic Theories-focus on unconscious forces--Freud-psychoanalysis
Psychodynamic Theories: Who? 3 components. Name, define, relate each to a principle	A. 3 components of personality
	1. Id=primitive, instinctive, operates according to pleasure principle (immediate gratification)
	2. Ego=decision-making component, operates according to reality principle (delay gratification until appropriate)
	3. Superego=moral component, social standards, right + wrong
	B. 3 levels of awareness
3 levels of awareness: name and describe	1. conscious=what one is aware of at a particular moment
	2. preconscious=material just below surface, easily retrieved
	3. unconscious=thoughts, memories, + desires well below surface, but have great influence on behavior

◄ **FIGURE 6.5**

Cornell Format combined with Outline Format

name. If the binders are too bulky to carry in your backpack, create a separate folder for each class. Before class, label and date the paper you will be using for taking notes. Then, as soon as possible after class, move your notes from the folder to the binder.

5. **Download any notes, outlines, or diagrams, charts, graphs, and other visuals** from the instructor's Web site before class and bring them with you. You can focus on the ideas being presented while adding your own labels and notes to the visual images.

6. **Organize your notes chronologically in your binder.** Then create separate tabbed sections for homework, lab assignments, returned tests, and other materials.

7. **If handouts are distributed in class, label them and place them in your binder** near the notes for that day. Buy a portable three-ring hole-punch that can be kept in your binder. Do not let handouts accumulate in your folders; add any handouts to your binders as you review your notes each day.

Taking Notes in Nonlecture Courses. Always be ready to adapt your note-taking methods to match the situation. Group discussion is becoming a popular way to teach in college because it engages students in active participation. You might also have **Supplemental Instruction** (SI) classes on your campus that provide further opportunity to discuss the information presented in lectures. Assume you are taking notes in a problem-solving group assignment. You would begin your notes by asking yourself, "What is the problem?" and writing down the answer. As the discussion progresses, you would list the solutions that are offered. The important details might include the positive and negative aspects of each view or solution. The important thing to remember is that you need to record the information presented by your classmates as well as by the instructor and to consider all reasonable ideas, even though they might differ from your own.

When a course has separate lecture and discussion sessions, you will need to understand how the discussion sessions relate to and augment the lectures. If different material is covered in lecture or discussion, you might need to ask for guidance in organizing your notes.

How to organize the notes you take in a class discussion depends on the purpose or form of the discussion. It usually makes good sense to begin with the list of issues or topics that the discussion leader announces. Another approach is to list the questions that participants raise for discussion. If the discussion explores reasons for and against a particular argument, divide your notes into columns or sections for pros and cons. When conflicting views are presented in discussion, record different perspectives and the rationales behind them.

Taking Notes in Science and Mathematics Courses. Many mathematics and science courses build on each other from term to term and from year to year. For example, when taking organic chemistry, you might need to refer to notes taken in earlier chemistry courses. This review step can be particularly important when time has passed since your last related course, such as after a summer break. On page 91 are some tips to keep in mind specifically when taking notes in quantitative and scientific classes.

Using Technology to Take Notes. While some students use laptops for note-taking, others prefer taking notes by hand so they can easily circle important items or copy complex equations or diagrams while these are being presented. If you handwrite your notes, entering them on a computer after class for review purposes might be helpful, especially if you are a kinesthetic learner. After class you can also cut and paste diagrams and other visual representations into your notes and print a copy that might be easier to read than notes you wrote by hand.

TIPS FOR NOTE-TAKING IN QUANTITATIVE AND SCIENCE CLASSES

- Write down any equations, formulas, diagrams, charts, graphs, and definitions that the instructor puts on the board or screen.

- Quote the instructor's words as precisely as possible. Technical terms often have exact meanings and cannot be paraphrased.

- Use standard symbols, abbreviations, and scientific notation.

- Write down all worked problems and examples step by step. They often provide the template for exam questions. Actively engage in solving the problem yourself as it is being solved at the front of the class. Be sure that you can follow the logic and understand the sequence of steps. If you have questions you cannot ask during lecture, write them down in your notes so that you can ask them in discussion, in the lab, or during the instructor's office hours.

- Consider taking your notes in pencil or erasable pen. You will probably need to use an eraser or make changes in your notes when copying long equations while also trying to pay attention to the instructor or when you copy problems that other students are solving at the board. You want to keep your notes as neat as possible. Later, you can use colored ink to add other details.

- Listen carefully to other students' questions and the instructor's answers. Take notes on the discussion and during question-and-answer periods.

- Use asterisks, exclamation points, question marks, or symbols of your own to highlight important points in your notes or questions that you need to come back to when you review.

- Refer to the textbook after class; the text might contain more accurate diagrams and other visual representations than you can draw while taking notes in class. If they are not provided in handouts or on the instructor's Web site, you might even want to scan or photocopy diagrams from the text and include them with your notes in your binder.

- Keep your binders for math and science courses until you graduate (or even longer if there is any chance that you will attend graduate school at some point in the future). They will serve as beneficial review materials for later classes in math and science and for preparing for standardized tests such as the Graduate Record Exam (GRE) and the Medical College Admission Test (MCAT).

Some students, especially aural learners, find it is advantageous to record lectures. But if you record, resist the temptation to become passive in class instead of actively listening. Students with specific types of disabilities might be urged to record lectures or use the services of note-takers who type on a laptop while the student views the notes on a separate screen.

Reviewing Your Notes

Most forgetting takes place within the first twenty-four hours of encountering the information. In two weeks, you will have forgotten up to 70 percent of it! Forgetting can be a serious problem when you are expected to learn and remember many different facts, figures, concepts, and relationships for a number of classes. Once you understand how to improve your ability to remember, you will retain information more easily and completely. Retaining information will help your overall understanding as well as your ability to recall important details during exams.

Don't let the forgetting curve take its toll on you. As soon after class as possible, review your notes and fill in the details you still remember but missed writing down. One way to remember is to recite important data to yourself every few minutes. If you are an aural learner, you might want to repeat your notes out loud. Another idea is to tie one idea to another idea, concept, or name so that thinking of one will prompt recall of the other.

For interactive learners, the best way to learn something might be to teach it to someone else. You will understand something better and remember it longer if you try to explain it. (Asking and answering questions in class can also provide you with the feedback you need to make certain your understanding is accurate.) Now you're ready to embed the major points from your notes in your memory. Use the three important steps on page 93 for remembering key points for your exams.

Wired WINDOW

TECHNOLOGY TO HELP YOU TAKE NOTES

You will discover many options for using technology to enhance your note-taking skills and your engagement with learning. Some students prefer to bring their laptops to class and either type their notes or use the tablet feature to handwrite their notes into digital files. We think it's important to strike a balance between taking notes on your computer and paying attention to class discussion. Most students can't type as quickly as they can write and will need to be very selective about the information they choose to enter on a computer. You might face a greater challenge extracting the most important points of the lecture or discussion while it is happening. Evernote (evernote.com), a free service, allows you to use your cell phone to take pictures of documents, including PowerPoint presentations, whiteboard notes, and overheads, and have these converted to digital documents automatically. If you choose to use such a service, make sure you have obtained permission from your professors to reproduce their notes. Evernote has a useful Web interface and offers a free

desktop application that allows you to search for text within your notes. Using the Web interface or the application, you can organize your notes in "notebooks" (it is helpful to keep a notebook for each of your courses). With Evernote, you don't have to worry about making sure that you copy every detail from your professor's notes, and you can stay focused on the topic being discussed.

Think Critically

What note-taking method do you prefer (notebook, laptop, Evernote, recorder)? Why is this method effective for you? What are some adjustments that you can make to your preferred method to enhance your note-taking success? One example, if you use your laptop to take notes, might be to find a better way to organize your files on your computer so they are easier to locate. What are some other examples? If you have never used a service such as Evernote, think about whether this kind of service would be helpful to you. In what ways would it help? In what ways might it detract from your learning?

KEYS TO REMEMBERING

1. **Write down the main ideas.** For five or ten minutes, quickly review your notes and select key words or phrases that will act as labels or tags for main ideas and key information in your notes.

2. **Recite your ideas out loud.** Recite a brief version of what you understand from the class. If you don't have a few minutes after class when you can concentrate on reviewing your notes, find some other time during that same day to review what you have written. You might also want to ask your instructor to glance at your notes to determine whether you have identified the major ideas.

3. **Review your notes from the previous class just before the next class session.** As you sit in class the next time it meets, waiting for the lecture to begin, use the time to quickly review your notes from the previous class session. This review will put you in tune with the lecture that is about to begin and prompt you to ask questions about material from the previous lecture that might not have been clear to you.

What if you have three classes in a row and no time for studying between them? Recall and recite as soon after class as possible. Review the most recent class first. Never delay recall and recitation longer than one day; if you do, it will take you longer to review, select main ideas, and recite. With practice, you can complete the review of your main ideas from your notes quickly.

COMPARING NOTES

You might be able to improve your notes by comparing notes with another student or in a study group, Supplemental Instruction session, or a learning community. Knowing that your notes will be seen by someone else will prompt you to make your notes well organized, clear, and accurate. Compare your notes: Are they as clear and concise as those of other students? Do you agree on the most important points? Share with each other how you take and organize your notes. You might get new ideas for using abbreviations. Take turns testing each other on what you have learned. Testing each other will help you predict exam questions and determine whether you can answer them. Comparing notes is not the same as copying somebody else's notes. You simply cannot learn as well from someone else's notes, no matter how good they are, if you have not attended class.

If your campus has a note-taking service, check with your instructor about making use of this for-pay service, but keep in mind that such notes are intended to supplement the ones you take, not to substitute for them. Unless you are a tactile learner, copying or typing your notes might not help you learn the material. A more profitable approach might be to summarize your notes in your own words.

Finally, have a backup plan in case you need to be absent because of illness or a family emergency. Exchange phone numbers and e-mail addresses with other students so that you can contact one of them to learn what you missed and get a copy of their notes. Also contact your instructor to explain your absence and set up an appointment during office hours to make sure you understand the work you missed.

CLASS NOTES AND HOMEWORK

Good class notes can help you complete homework assignments. Follow these steps:

1. **Take ten minutes to review your notes.** Skim the notes, and put a question mark next to anything you do not understand at first reading. Draw stars next to topics that warrant special emphasis. Try to place the material in context: What has been going on in the course for the past few weeks? How does today's class fit in?

2. **Do a warm-up for your homework.** Before doing the assignment, look through your notes again. Use a separate sheet of paper to rework examples, problems, or exercises. If there is related assigned material in the textbook, review it. Go back to the examples. Cover the solution, and attempt to answer each question or complete each problem. Look at the author's work only after you have made a serious effort to remember it. Keep in mind that it can help to go back through your course notes, reorganize them, highlight the essential items, and thus create new notes that could be better than the originals.

3. **Do any assigned problems, and answer any assigned questions.** When you start doing your homework, read each question or problem and ask: What am I supposed to find or find out? What is essential and what is extraneous? Read each problem several times, and state it in your own words. Work the problem without referring to your notes or the text, as though you were taking a test.

4. **Persevere.** Don't give up too soon. When you encounter a problem or question that you cannot readily handle, move on only after a reasonable effort. After you have completed the entire assignment, come back to any items that stumped you. You might need to mull over a particularly difficult problem for several days. Let your unconscious mind have a chance. Inspiration might come when you are waiting at a stoplight or just before you fall asleep.

5. **Complete your work.** When you finish an assignment, talk to yourself about what you learned from it. Think about how the problems and questions were different from one another, which strategies were successful, and what form the answers took. Be sure to review any material you have not mastered. Seek assistance from the instructor, a classmate, a study group, the campus learning center, or a tutor.

> **YOUR TURN ▶**
>
> What is your reaction to these suggestions about taking notes and studying for class? Which ideas will you implement in your note-taking strategies? Why? Do you think they have the potential to help you earn better grades? If so, in what way?

Becoming Engaged in Learning

No matter how good your listening and note-taking techniques are, you will not get the most out of college unless you become an engaged learner.

Engaged students devote the time and the energy necessary to develop a real love of learning, both in and out of class.

Although you might acquire knowledge by listening to a lecture, you might not be motivated to think about what that knowledge means to you. When you are actively engaged in learning, you will learn not only the material in your notes and textbooks, but also how to:

- Work with others
- Improve your critical thinking, listening, writing, and speaking skills
- Function independently and teach yourself
- Manage your time
- Gain sensitivity to cultural differences

Engagement in learning requires that you be a full and active participant in the learning process. Your instructors will set the stage and provide valuable information, but it's up to you to do the rest. Your college experience will be most rewarding if you take advantage of the resources your college offers, including the library, cultural events, the faculty, and other students. This approach to learning has the potential to make you well rounded in all aspects of life. The hexagon in Figure 6.6 depicts seven aspects of development, with intellectual development at its center. All of these aspects of development support each other, and each affects the way that specific issues (such as those in the shaded area) are handled.

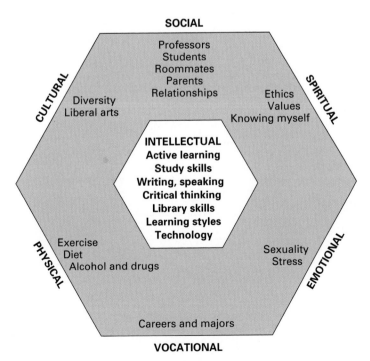

SOCIAL
Professors
Students
Roommates
Parents
Relationships

CULTURAL
Diversity
Liberal arts

SPIRITUAL
Ethics
Values
Knowing myself

INTELLECTUAL
Active learning
Study skills
Writing, speaking
Critical thinking
Library skills
Learning styles
Technology

PHYSICAL
Exercise
Diet
Alcohol and drugs

EMOTIONAL
Sexuality
Stress

Careers and majors

VOCATIONAL

◀ **FIGURE 6.6**

Aspects of Student Development

OTHER TIPS FOR ENGAGEMENT

- Before choosing a class, ask friends which instructors encourage active learning.
- Go beyond the required reading. Investigate other information sources in the library or on the Internet.
- If you disagree with what your instructor says, politely offer your opinion. Most instructors will listen. They might still disagree with you, but they might also think more of you for showing you can think independently.
- Interact with professors, staff members, and other students. One easy way is through e-mail. Some professors offer first-year students the opportunity to collaborate in research projects and service activities. You will also find many opportunities to become involved in campus organizations. Getting involved in out-of-class opportunities will help you develop relationships with others on campus.
- Use Facebook to connect with other students and with campus activities and groups. Join in discussions that are happening in those groups.

Where to go FOR HELP...

ON CAMPUS ▶

Learning Assistance Center Almost every campus has one of these, and this chapter's topic is one of their specialties. More and more, the best students—and good students who want to be better students—use learning centers as much as students who are having academic difficulties. Services at learning centers are offered by both full-time professionals and highly skilled student tutors.

Fellow College Students Often, the best help we can get comes from those who are closest to us: fellow students. Keep an eye out in your classes, residence hall, co-curricular groups, and other places for the most serious, purposeful, and directed students. Those are the ones to seek out. Find a tutor. Join a study group. Students who do these things are most likely to stay in college and be successful. It does not diminish you in any way to seek assistance from your peers.

ONLINE ▶

Toastmasters International offers public speaking tips at http://www.toastmasters.org.

See guidelines for speaking in class at http://www.school-for-champions.com/grades/speaking.htm.

MY INSTITUTION'S RESOURCES ▶

6

Applying What You've LEARNED...

Now that you have read and discussed this chapter, consider how you can apply what you have learned to your academic and personal life. The following prompts will help you reflect on chapter material and its relevance to you both now and in the future.

1. Review the "Using Your Senses in the Learning Process" section of this chapter. Which modes of learning seem to work best for you? If you are not an aural learner, how can you use your preferred ways of learning to master the information that is presented in lecture-style courses? Brainstorm ways to convert lecture material into a format that is a better match for how you best use your five senses in the learning process.

2. Making an intentional effort to learn is not easy. As you try the suggestions in this chapter, consider ways in which you can encourage yourself to keep up the hard work. For example, if you have a big project, try breaking it up into several smaller pieces. As you complete each piece, reward yourself by spending time with friends or taking time to do something you enjoy.

One-Minute PAPER...

This chapter explores multiple strategies for being an effective listener and being engaged in class. What new strategies did you learn that you had never thought about or used before? What questions about effective note-taking do you still have?

Building Your PORTFOLIO...

MAKING MEANING

Chapter 6 includes several examples of note-taking strategies, but did you catch the emphasis on what you should do with your notes after class? Sometimes it is helpful to associate a concept with an interest you have. And preparing to teach someone else how to do something or explaining a complex idea to others can help you understand the information more fully.

Test this idea for yourself.

1. Choose a set of current class notes (it doesn't matter which class they are from), and specifically look for connections between the subject matter and your personal interests and goals (future career, social issue, sports, hobbies, etc.).
2. Next, develop a five-minute presentation using PowerPoint that both outlines your class notes and shows the connection to your interests. Develop the presentation as though you were going to teach a group of students about the concept. Use a combination of graphics, photos, music, and video clips to help your imaginary audience connect with the material in a new and interesting way.
3. Save the PowerPoint in your portfolio on your personal computer or flash drive. Use your PowerPoint presentation as one way to study for your next exam in that course.

You probably won't be creating PowerPoint presentations for all of your class notes, but making a habit of connecting class content to your life is an easy way to help yourself remember information. When it is time to prepare for a test, try pulling your notes into a presentation that you would feel comfortable presenting to your classmates.

7 Reading to Learn: Learning to Remember

In this chapter you will explore

- How to prepare to read
- How to preview reading material
- How to mark your textbooks
- How to review your reading
- How study groups can help you prepare
- How to improve your ability to memorize
- Why a good memory can be an asset but is not all you need if you are to do well in college

Why is reading college textbooks more challenging than reading for pleasure?

College textbooks are loaded with concepts, terms, and complex information that you are expected to learn on your own in a short period of time. Although many students think that the only reason for studying is to do well on exams, a far more important reason is to learn and understand information. If you study to increase your understanding, you are more likely to remember and apply what you learn not only to tests, but also to future courses and to life beyond college. The active reading, understanding, and remembering strategies in this chapter can help you get the most from your college education.

A Plan for Active Reading

When you read actively, you use strategies that help you stay focused. Pleasure reading doesn't require you to annotate, highlight, or take notes. But as you read college textbooks, you'll use all these strategies and more. This plan will increase your focus and concentration, promote greater understanding of what you read, and prepare you to study for tests and exams. The four steps in active reading are

1. Previewing
2. Marking
3. Reading with Concentration
4. Reviewing

> **YOUR TURN ▶**
>
> Which of these four steps do you always, sometimes, or never do? Do any of them seem unnecessary? If so, why? After you read this chapter, go back and see whether you have changed your mind.

PREVIEWING

The purpose of previewing is to get the big picture, that is, to understand how what you are about to read connects with what you already know and to the material the instructor covers in class. Begin by reading the title of the chapter. Ask yourself: What do I already know about this subject? Next, quickly read through the introductory paragraphs. Then read the summary at the beginning or end of the chapter if there is one. Finally, take a few minutes to skim the chapter, looking at the headings and subheadings. Note any study exercises at the end of the chapter.

Keep in mind that different types of textbooks can require more or less time to read. For example, depending on your interests and previous knowledge, you might be able to read a psychology text more quickly than a logic text that presents a whole new symbol system.

Mapping. **Mapping** the chapter as you preview it provides a visual guide for how different chapter ideas fit together. Because many students identify themselves as visual learners, visual mapping is an excellent learning tool for test preparation as well as reading (see Chapter 4, Discovering How You Learn). To map a chapter, use either a wheel structure or a branching structure as you preview the chapter. In the wheel structure, place the central idea of the chapter in the circle. The central idea should be in the introduction to the chapter and might be apparent in the chapter title. Place secondary ideas on the spokes emanating from the circle, and place offshoots of those ideas on the lines attached to the spokes. In the branching map, the main idea goes at the top, followed by supporting ideas on the second tier and so forth. Fill in the title first. Then, as you skim the chapter, use the headings and subheadings to fill in the key ideas.

Alternatives to Mapping. Perhaps you prefer a more linear visual image. If so, consider making an outline of the headings and subheadings in the chapter. You can fill in the outline after you read. Alternatively, make a list. A list can be particularly effective when you are dealing with a text that introduces many new terms and their definitions. Set up the list with the terms in the left column, and fill in definitions, descriptions, and examples on the right after you read.

If you are an interactive learner, make lists or create a flash card for each heading and subheading. Then fill in the back of each card after reading each section in the text. Use the lists or flash cards to review with a partner, or recite the material to yourself.

Previewing, combined with mapping, outlining, or flash cards, might require more time up front, but it will save you time later because you will have created an excellent review tool for quizzes and tests. You will be using your visual learning skills as you create advanced organizers to help you associate details of the chapter with the larger ideas. As you preview the text material, look for connections between the text and the related lecture material. Ask yourself: Why am I reading this? What do I want to know?

MARKING YOUR TEXTBOOK

After completing your preview, you are ready to read the text actively. With your skeleton map or outline, you should be able to read more quickly and with greater comprehension. To avoid marking too much or marking the wrong information, first read without using your pencil or highlighter.

Think a moment about your goals for making marks in your own texts. Some students report that **marking** is an active reading strategy that helps them to focus and concentrate on the material as they read. To meet these goals, some students like to underline, some prefer to highlight, and others use margin notes or annotations. Figure 7.1 provides an example of each method. No matter what method you prefer, remember these two important guidelines:

1. **Read before you mark.** Finish reading a section before you decide which are the most important ideas and concepts. Mark only those

WHAT IS STRESS? **481**

CULTURE AND HUMAN BEHAVIOR 12.1

The Stress of Adapting to a New Culture

(margin note) differences affecting cultural stress

Refugees and immigrants are often unprepared for the dramatically different values, language, food, customs, and climate that await them in their new land. Coping with a new culture can be extremely stress-producing (Johnson & others, 1995). The process of changing one's values and customs as a result of contact with another culture is referred to as *acculturation*. Thus the term **acculturative stress** describes the stress that results from the pressure of adapting to a new culture (Berry, 1994, 2003).

(margin note) acceptance of new culture reduces stress also speaking new language, education, & social support

Many factors can influence the degree of acculturative stress that a person experiences. For example, when the new society is one that accepts ethnic and cultural diversity, acculturative stress is reduced (Shuval, 1993). The ease of transition is also enhanced when the person has some familiarity with the new language and customs, advanced education, and social support from friends, family members, and cultural associations (Finch & Vega, 2003).

(margin note) how attitudes affect stress

Cross-cultural psychologist John Berry has found that a person's *attitudes* are important in determining how much acculturative stress is experienced. When people encounter a new cultural environment, they are faced with two fundamental questions: (1) Should I seek positive relations with the dominant society? (2) Is my original cultural identity of value to me, and should I try to maintain it?

(margin note) 4 patterns of acculturation

The answers to these questions result in one of four possible patterns of acculturation: integration, assimilation, separation, or marginalization (see the diagram). Each pattern represents a different way of cop-

Question 1:
Should I seek positive relations with the dominant society?

Question 2:
Is my original cultural identity of value to me, and should I try to maintain it?

		Yes	No
	Yes	Integration	Separation
	No	Assimilation	Marginalization

Patterns of Adapting to a New Culture According to cross-cultural psychologist John Berry (1994, 2003), there are four basic patterns of adapting to a new culture. Which pattern is followed depends on how the person responds to the two key questions shown.

ing with the stress of adapting to a new culture (Berry, 1994, 2003).

1* *Integrated* individuals continue to value their original cultural customs but also seek to become part of the dominant society. Ideally, the integrated individual feels *comfortable* in both her culture of origin and the culture of the dominant society, moving easily from one to the other (LaFromboise, Coleman, & Gerton, 1993). The successfully integrated individual's level of acculturative stress will be low (Ward & Rana-Deuba, 1999).

2* *Assimilated* individuals give up their old cultural identity and try to become part of the new society. They may adopt the new clothing, religion, and social values of the new environment and *abandon* their old customs and language.

Assimilation usually involves a moderate level of stress, partly because it involves a psychological loss—one's previous cultural identity. People who follow this pattern also

(margin note) possible rejection by both cultures

face the possibility of being rejected either by members of the majority culture or by members of their original culture (LaFromboise & others, 1993). The process of learning new behaviors and suppressing old behaviors can also be moderately stressful.

(margin note) *separation may be self-imposed or discriminating

3* Individuals who follow the pattern of *separation* maintain their cultural identity and avoid contact with the new culture. They may refuse to learn the new language, live in a neighborhood that is primarily populated by others of the same ethnic background, and socialize only with members of their own ethnic group.

(margin note) higher stress with separation

In some instances, such withdrawal from the larger society is self-imposed. However, separation can also be the result of discrimination by the dominant society, as when people of a particular ethnic group are discouraged from fully participating in the dominant society. Not surprisingly, the level of acculturative stress associated with separation is likely to be very high.

4* Finally, the *marginalized* person lacks cultural and psychological contact with *both* his traditional cultural group and the culture of his new society. By taking the path of marginalization, he has lost the important features of his traditional culture but has not replaced them with a new cultural identity.

(margin note) *marginalized = higher level of stress

Marginalized individuals are likely to experience the greatest degree of acculturative stress, feeling as if they don't really belong anywhere. Essentially, they are stuck in an unresolved conflict between the traditional culture and the new social environment. They are also likely to experience feelings of alienation and a loss of identity (Berry & Kim, 1988).

Acculturative Stress As this Sikh family crossing a busy street in Chicago has discovered, adapting to a new culture can be a stressful process. What factors can make the transition less stressful? How can the acculturation process be eased?

▲ FIGURE 7.1

Using a combination of highlighting, arrows, and marginal notes, the reader has boiled down the content of this page for easy review. Without reading the text, note the highlighted words and phrases and the marginal notes, and see how much information you can gather from them. Then read the text itself. Does the markup serve as a study aid? Does it cover the essential points? Would you have marked this page any differently? Why or why not?

particular ideas, using your preferred methods (highlighting, underlining, circling key terms, annotating).

2. **Think before you mark.** When you read a text for the first time, everything can seem important. Only after you have completed a section and have reflected on it will you be ready to identify the key ideas. Ask yourself: What are the most important ideas? What will I see on the test?

Sometimes highlighting or underlining can provide you with a false sense of security. You might have determined what is most important, but you have not necessarily tested yourself on your understanding of the material. When you force yourself to put something in your own words while taking notes, you are not only predicting exam questions but also assessing whether you can answer them. Although these active reading strategies take more time initially, they can save you time in the long run.

READING WITH CONCENTRATION

Many factors can affect your ability to concentrate and understand texts—the time of day, your energy level, your interest in the material, and your study location.

Consider these suggestions:

- Find a study location, such as the campus library, that is removed from traffic and distracting noises. Turn off your cell phone's ringer, and store the phone someplace where you can't easily feel it vibrating. If you are reading an electronic document on your computer, download the information that you need and disconnect from the network.
- Read in blocks of time, with short breaks in between. Some students can read for fifty minutes; others find that a fifty-minute reading period is too long. By reading for small blocks of time throughout the day instead of cramming in all your reading at the end of the day, you should be able to process material more easily.
- Set goals for your study period, such as "I will read twenty pages of my psychology text in the next fifty minutes." Reward yourself with a ten-minute break after each fifty-minute study period.
- If you have trouble concentrating or staying awake, take a quick walk around the library or down the hall. Stretch or take some deep breaths, and think positively about your study goals. Then resume studying.
- Jot study questions in the margins, take notes, or recite key ideas. Reread confusing parts of the text, and make a note to ask your instructor for clarification.
- Focus on the important portions of the text. Pay attention to the first and last sentences of paragraphs and to words in italics or bold print.
- Use the glossary in the text or a dictionary to define unfamiliar terms.

YOUR TURN ▶

Do you have trouble concentrating while you read your textbooks? What strategies do you use to make sure that your mind doesn't wander?

REVIEWING

Many students expect to read through their text material once and be able to remember the ideas four, six, or even twelve weeks later at test time. More realistically, you will need to include regular reviews in your study process. Here is where your notes, study questions, annotations, flash cards, visual maps, or outlines will be most useful. Your study goal should be to review the material from each chapter every week.

Consider ways to use your many senses to review. Recite aloud. Tick off each item in a list on each of your fingertips. Post diagrams, maps, or outlines around your living space so that you will see them often and will likely be able to visualize them while taking the test.

Strategies for Reading Textbooks

As you begin reading, be sure to learn more about the textbook and its author by reading the front matter in the book. Textbooks often have a preface written to the instructor and a separate preface for the students. The foreword is often an endorsement of the book written by someone other than the author, which can add to your understanding of the book and its purpose. Front matter might also include biographical information about the authors that will give you important details about their background.

> **YOUR TURN ▶**
>
> Look at the front material in this book. What does it tell you about the authors and their purpose in writing this book? How do the authors' biographies influence the way you think about what's written in this book?

Some textbooks include questions at the end of each chapter that you can use as a study guide or as a quick check on your understanding of the chapter's main points. Take time to read and respond to these questions.

Although many textbooks seem detailed, they won't necessarily provide all the things you want to know about a topic—the things that can make your reading more interesting. If you find yourself fascinated by a particular topic, go to the **primary sources**—the original research or document. You'll find those referenced in many textbooks, either at the end of the chapters or in the back of the book.

Remember that most texts are not designed to treat topics in depth. Your textbook reading will be much more interesting if you dig a bit further in related sources. Because some textbooks are sold with test banks, your instructors might draw their examinations directly from the text, or they might use the textbook only to supplement the lectures. Ask your instructors what the tests will cover and the types of questions that will be used. In addition, you might try to find a student who has taken a course with your instructor so that you can get a better idea of how that instructor designs tests. Some instructors expect that you will learn the kinds of details that you can get only through the textbook. Other instructors are much more concerned that you be able to understand broad concepts that come from lectures in addition to texts and other readings.

YOUR TURN ▶

What is your favorite text in one of your current courses? Why? Which is your least favorite text? Why?

SUPPLEMENTARY MATERIAL

Whether or not your instructor requires you to read material in addition to the textbook, your understanding will be enriched if you go to some of the primary and supplementary sources that are referenced in each chapter of your text. These sources can take the form of journal articles, research papers, dissertations (the major research papers that students write to earn a doctoral degree), or original essays, and they can be found in your library and on the Internet.

If you are reading a journal article that describes a theory or research study, one technique for easier understanding is to read from the end to the beginning. Read the article's conclusion and discussion sections. Then go back to see how the author performed the experiment or formulated the ideas. If you aren't concerned about the specific method used to collect the data, you can skip over the "methodology" section. In almost all scholarly journals, articles are introduced by an abstract, a paragraph-length summary of the methods and major findings. Reading the **abstract** is a quick way to get the gist of a research article before you dive in.

YOUR TURN ▶

Are you ever tempted not to buy a textbook for one of your courses? Why? What can you do as an alternative? How important do you think textbooks are in your courses? In what other ways can you access the information you want and need to learn?

Monitoring Your Reading

As you read, ask yourself: Do I understand this? If not, stop and reread the material. Look up words that are not clear. Try to clarify the main points and how they relate to one another.

Another way to check comprehension is to try to recite the material aloud, either to yourself or your study partner. Using a study group to monitor your comprehension gives you immediate feedback and is highly motivating.

> **YOUR TURN ▶**
>
> How do you monitor your own reading comprehension? On the basis of the material in this chapter, what are some strategies you could use to ensure that you understand what you are reading?

IF ENGLISH IS NOT YOUR FIRST LANGUAGE

The English language is one of the most difficult languages to learn. Words are often spelled differently from the way they sound, and the language is full of idioms—phrases that are peculiar and cannot be understood from the individual meanings of the words. If you are learning English and are having trouble reading your texts, don't give up. Reading slowly and reading more than once can help you improve your comprehension. Make sure that you have two good dictionaries—one in English and one that links English with your primary language—and look up every word that you don't know. Be

Wired WINDOW

AMAZON KINDLE AND THE FUTURE OF ELECTRONIC READING

Amazon.com developed the Kindle, hoping to popularize electronic reading among mainstream audiences. The Kindle is a book-sized gadget that has a screen, expandable memory, and wireless capability. Electronic readers are not new; however, Amazon.com made some improvements to make the device more useful and marketable. Kindle allows you to download content and even to sample chapters before you agree to purchase the entire book. A growing number of textbooks are available through Kindle, and colleges and universities are starting to experiment with adopting Kindle in their libraries and for use in the curriculum. You might already have read some of your course material digitally. If you have taken an online course, a course that has an online component, or a course shell such as Blackboard, then odds are good that you've read a document online posted by your professor. Some of the active reading strategies you might use for a print book (such as annotating) might not be easy or possible when you are reading something in a digital format.

Think Critically

Pretend that you have been assigned all of your books in a digital format this semester. How would you go about using some of the strategies you've read about in this chapter? How would you take notes on the reading? If you took notes on paper, would you keep them on paper or convert them to a digital format by typing them into a word processing document? How would you highlight the material that you read? How would it feel to be using this kind of technology for reading? Would it be an improvement over traditional books and readings? Why or why not? How do you retain the material that you currently read online (such as news, blog postings, or your friends' status updates)?

sure to practice thinking, writing, and speaking in English, and take advantage of your college's helping services. Your campus might have ESL (English as a Second Language) tutoring and workshops. Ask your advisor or your first-year seminar instructor to help you locate those services.

Listening, note-taking, and reading are the essentials for success in each of your classes. You can perform these tasks without a plan, or you can practice some of the ideas presented in this chapter. If your notes are already working, great. If not, now you know what to do.

Studying to Understand and Remember

While memory is a necessary tool for learning, what's most important is that you study to develop a deep understanding of course information. When you truly comprehend what you are learning, you will be able to exercise your critical thinking abilities.

The human mind has discovered ingenious ways to understand and remember information. Here are some methods that might be useful to you:

1. **Pay attention to what you're hearing or reading.** If you're sitting in class thinking about everything except what the professor is saying or if you're reading and you find that your mind is wandering, you're wasting your time.

YOUR TURN ▶

When you're in class, how would you rate your level of concentration on what the instructor is saying? Is it good, fair, or poor? In which classes do you concentrate best? In which is your concentration worst? Why do you think it's easier to concentrate in some classes than in others?

---

2. **"Overlearn" the material.** After you know and think you understand the material you're studying, go over it again to make sure that you'll retain it for a long time. Recite aloud what you're trying to remember.

3. **Check the Internet.** If you're having trouble remembering what you have learned, Google a key word, and try to find interesting details that will engage you in learning more, not less, about the subject.

TIPS FOR EFFECTIVE STUDYING

Whether you are completing class assignments or preparing for a test, these strategies will help you study more effectively:

1. **Make studying a part of your daily routine**. Don't allow days to go by when you don't crack a book or keep up with course assignments.

2. **Manage your study time wisely**. Create a schedule that will allow you to prepare for exams and complete course assignments on time. Be aware of "crunch times" when you might have several exams or papers due at once. And create some flexibility in your schedule to allow for unexpected distractions.

3. **Collaborate with others**. One of the most effective ways to study is in a group with other students. In your first year of college, gather a group of students who study together. Study groups can meet throughout the term, or they can review for midterms or final exams.

4. **Make your learning style work for you as you study**. Look back at your VARK score from Chapter 4. If you are a visual learner, create diagrams, lists, flash cards, or other visual aids that will enhance memory. If you are an aural learner, be sure to attend discussions and tutorials. Use a digital recorder or tape recorder in class, and replay the lecture when it's study time. Aural learners often find that talking out loud is more effective than reciting in their heads. This might mean that you'll occasionally need to study alone so you won't bother others when you're talking to yourself. If you are a read/write learner, take notes on your notes as you reread them. Turn diagrams and charts into words. If you are a kinesthetic learner, move around the room while you study. Gesture with your arms and hands. Try to convert your notes into real-life examples.

5. **Be alert for external distractions**. Choose a place to study where you can concentrate. That might be in your residence hall or your room at home, or you might have to go somewhere else. The campus library is often the best place to go for uninterrupted study.

6. **Get enough sleep**. Don't cut back on your sleep to cram in additional study hours. Remember that most tests will require you to be able to think clearly about the concepts that you have studied. Especially during final exam weeks, it is important to be well rested so that you can stay alert for extended periods of time.

7. **Follow a regular exercise program**. Walking, jogging, swimming, or other aerobic activities might help you think more clearly and can provide positive and needed study breaks. Exercise releases endorphins in the brain, so it can help improve your mood. Furthermore, research has shown that exercise can potentially increase your brain power by generating new neurons in the hippocampus, an area of the brain that controls learning and memory.[1]

8. **Get a tutor**. Tutoring is not just for students who are failing. Often, the best students seek tutorial assistance to ensure that they understand course material. Most tutors are students, and most campus tutoring services offer their services for free. Ask your academic advisor, counselor, or campus learning center about the availability of tutoring or other kinds of academic support.

[1]http://serendip.brynmawr.edu/bb/neuro/neuro05/web2/mmcgovern.html.

4. **Be sure you have the big picture.** You can talk with someone who has already taken the course, or you can take a brief look at all the reading assignments. Having the big picture will help you understand and remember details.

5. **Look for connections between your life and what's going on in your courses.** For example, if you're taking a music theory course and studying chord patterns, listen for those patterns in contemporary music.

6. **Get organized.** If your desk or your computer is organized, you'll spend less time trying to remember a file name or where you put a particular document.

YOUR TURN ▶

Look around your room and at your computer desktop. Is your living environment neat and organized? How about your "electronic environment"? Does a lack of organization ever cause you to waste time? What strategies could you use to become better organized?

---

7. **Reduce stressors in your life.** Healthy, stress-reducing behaviors, such as meditation, exercise, and sleep, are especially important for college students. Many campuses have counseling or health centers that can provide resources to help you deal with stress.

How Memory Works

Kenneth Higbee describes two different processes involved in memory (see Table 7.1). The first is **short-term memory,** defined as how many items you are able to perceive at one time. Higbee found that information stored in short-term memory is forgotten in less than thirty seconds (and sometimes much faster) unless you take action to either keep that information in short-term memory or move it to long-term memory.

The second memory process is **long-term memory.** Long-term memory can be described in three ways. *Procedural memory* is knowing how to do something, such as solving a mathematical problem or playing a musical instrument. *Semantic memory* involves facts and meanings without regard to where and when you learned those things. *Episodic memory* deals with particular events, their time, and place.[2]

You are using your procedural memory when you get on a bicycle you haven't ridden in years, when you can recall the first piece you learned to play on the piano, when you effortlessly type a letter or class report, and when you drive a car. Your semantic memory is used continuously to recall word meanings or important dates, such as your mother's birthday. Episodic memory allows you to remember events in your life—a vacation, your first day in school, the moment you opened your college acceptance letter.

CONNECTING MEMORY TO DEEP LEARNING

Is a good memory all you need to do well in college? Most memory strategies tend to focus on helping you remember names, dates, numbers, vocabulary, graphic materials, formulas—the bits and pieces of knowledge. However, if you know the date the Civil War began and the fort where the first shots were fired but you don't really know why the Civil War was fought, you're missing the point of a college education. College is about **deep learning,** understanding the "why" and "how" behind the details. So don't forget that while recall of specific facts is certainly necessary, it isn't sufficient. To do well in college courses, you will need to understand major themes and ideas, and you will also need to hone your ability to think critically about what you're learning.

Improving Your Memory

There are many ways to go about remembering. Have you ever had to memorize a speech or lines from a play? How you approach committing the lines to memory might depend on your learning style. If you're an aural learner, you

TABLE 7.1 ▶ Long-Term and Short-Term Memory

Short-Term Memory	Long-Term Memory
Stores information for about thirty seconds	Procedural: remembering how to do something
Can contain from five to nine chunks of information at one time	Semantic: remembering facts and meanings
Information either forgotten or moved to long-term memory	Episodic: remembering the time and place of events

[2]W. F. Brewer and J. R. Pani, "The Structure of Human Memory," in G. H. Bower (Ed.), *The Psychology of Learning and Motivation: Advances in Research and Theory*, vol. 17 (New York: Academic Press, 1983), pp. 1–38.

might choose to record your lines as well as lines of other characters and listen to them on tape. If you're a visual learner, you might remember best by visualizing where your lines appear on the page in the script. If you learn best by reading, you might simply read the script over and over. If you're a kinesthetic learner, you might need to walk or move across an imaginary stage as you read the script.

YOUR TURN ▶

How can you apply your learning style to remembering material for an exam? List some strategies that you already use or might want to try in the future.

Although knowing specific words will help, remembering concepts and ideas can be much more important. To embed such ideas in your mind, ask yourself these questions as you review your notes and books:

1. What is the essence of the idea?
2. Why does the idea make sense? What is the logic behind it?
3. How does this idea connect to other ideas in the material?
4. What are some possible arguments against the idea?

USING REVIEW SHEETS, MIND MAPS, AND OTHER TOOLS

To prepare for an exam that will cover large amounts of material, you need to condense the volume of notes and text pages into manageable study units. Review your materials with these questions in mind: Is this one of the key ideas in the chapter or unit? Will I see this material on the test? You might prefer to highlight, underline, or annotate the most important ideas or create outlines, lists, or visual maps.

Use your notes to develop review sheets. Make lists of key terms and ideas (from the recall column if you've used the Cornell method) that you need to remember. Also, don't underestimate the value of using your lecture notes to test yourself or others on information presented in class.

A **mind map** is essentially a review sheet with a visual element. Its word and visual patterns provide you with highly charged clues to jog your memory. Because they are visual, mind maps help many students recall information more easily.

Figure 7.2 shows what a mind map might look like for a chapter on listening and learning in the classroom. Try to reconstruct the ideas in the chapter by following the connections in the map. Then make a visual mind map for this chapter, and see how much more you can remember after studying it a number of times.

In addition to review sheets and mind maps, you might want to create flash cards. One of the advantages of flash cards is that you can keep them in a pocket of your backpack or jacket and pull them out to study anywhere,

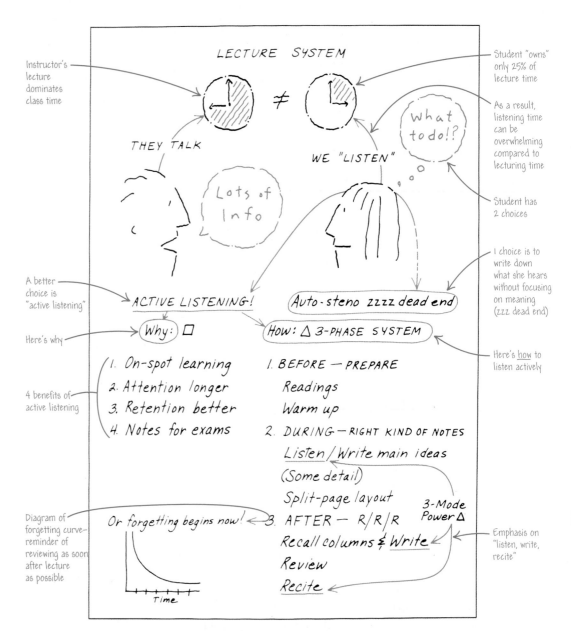

FIGURE 7.2 ▶

Sample Mind Map on Listening and Learning in the Classroom

even when you might not think that you have enough time to take out your notebook to study. Also, you always know where you left off. Flash cards can help you make good use of time that might otherwise be wasted, such as time spent on the bus or waiting for a friend.

Where to go
FOR HELP . . .

ON CAMPUS ▶

Learning Assistance Center Most campuses have learning centers that specialize in reading assistance. Both the best students and struggling students use learning centers, where full-time professionals and skilled student tutors offer services.

Fellow Students Your best help can come from a fellow student. Look for the best students—those who appear to be the most serious and conscientious. Hire a tutor if you can, or join a study group. You are much more likely to be successful.

BOOKS ▶

Buzan, Tony. *Use Your Perfect Memory*, 3rd rev. ed. New York: Penguin Books, 1991.

Higbee, Kenneth L., Ph.D. *Your Memory: How It Works and How to Improve It*, 2nd rev. ed. New York: Marlowe, 2001.

Lorayne, Harry. *Super Memory, Super Student: How to Raise Your Grades in 30 Days*. Boston: Little, Brown, 1990.

ONLINE ▶

Review of the Research on Memory and College Student Learning: http://www.ferris.edu/htmls/academics/center/Teaching_and_Learning_Tips/Memory/indexMemory.htm. This Web site is designed for instructors, though it also includes lots of interesting information for students.

Middle Tennessee State University: http://www.mtsu.edu/~studskl/Txtbook.html. The "Study Skills Help" Web page has a link to "Reading Your Textbooks."

Niagara University's Office for Academic Support: http://www.niagara.edu/oas/learning_center/study_reading_strategies/21_Tips_For_Better_Textbook_Reading.htm. Read these "21 Tips for Better Textbook Reading."

Memorization Techniques: http://www.accd.edu/sac/history/keller/ACCDitg/SSMT.htm. This excellent Web site is maintained by the Alamo Community College District.

MY INSTITUTION'S RESOURCES ▶

_____

_____

_____

_____

_____

_____

_____

_____

_____

_____

_____

_____

_____

_____

7 Applying What You've LEARNED...

Now that you have read and discussed this chapter, consider how you can apply what you have learned to your academic life and your personal life. The following prompts will help you reflect on the chapter material and its relevance to you both now and in the future.

1. Choose a reading assignment for one of your upcoming classes. After previewing the material, begin reading until you reach a major heading or until you have read at least a page or two. Now stop and write down what you remember from the material. Go back and review what you read. Were you able to remember all of the main ideas?

2. The way in which students study in high school is often very different from the way they need to study in college. It can be difficult to adapt to new ways of doing things. Describe the way in which you studied in high school. Describe how you can improve on those habits to do well in college.

One-Minute PAPER...

Doing well on exams is important, but being able to study, comprehend, and remember what you learn has bigger implications for your life. After reading this chapter, do you find yourself thinking about these concepts in a different way? If so, how? What kinds of questions would you ask your instructor about this chapter?

Building Your PORTFOLIO...

THE BIG PICTURE

This chapter introduces a reading strategy called **mapping** as a visual tool for getting the "big picture" of what you are preparing to read. Mapping a textbook chapter can help you quickly recognize how different concepts and terms fit together and make connections to what you already know about the subject. A number of ways of mapping, including wheel maps and branching maps, are described in this chapter. You might also use other types of maps, such as *matrixes* to compare and contrast ideas or show cause and effect, a *spider web* to connect themes, or *sketches* to illustrate images, relationships, or descriptions.

1. Look through your course syllabi, and identify a reading assignment that you need to complete in the next week.

2. Begin by previewing the first chapter of the reading assignment.

3. Practice mapping the chapter by creating your own map using the drawing toolbar in Microsoft Word.

4. Save your map in your portfolio on your personal computer or flash drive.

Example

1. Place the central idea of the chapter in the center of the wheel.

2. Place supporting ideas on the spokes of the wheel.

3. Place important details on the lines attached to the spokes.

Tip: A good place to start is with chapter headings and subheadings. Then move on to terms in bold and graphics such as charts, tables, and diagrams. Textbooks often have study questions at the end of the chapter, which can give you clues about what the author considers the most important concepts.

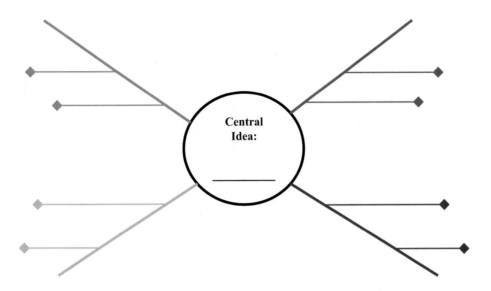

Central Idea:
_____

Reading a textbook efficiently and effectively requires that you develop reading strategies that will help you to make the most of your study time. Mapping can help you organize and retain what you have read, making it a good reading and study tool. Writing, reciting, and organizing the main points, supporting ideas, and key details of the chapter will help you recall the information on test day.

8 Improving Your Performance on Exams and Tests

In this chapter you will explore

- Ways to prepare yourself for exams physically, emotionally, and academically
- How study groups can help you prepare for exams
- How to devise a study plan for an exam
- How to reduce test anxiety
- What to do during the exam
- How to take different types of tests
- How cheating hurts you, your friends, and your college or university

You can prepare for exams in many ways, and certain

methods are more effective than others, depending on the subject matter, your preferred learning style, and the type of test you'll be taking. Sometimes you'll need to be able to recall names, dates, and other specific bits of information, especially if you are taking a multiple-choice or short-answer exam. Many instructors, especially in humanities and social science courses such as literature, history, and political science, will expect you to go beyond names and dates and have a good conceptual understanding of the subject matter. They often prefer essay exams that require you to use higher-level critical thinking skills, such as *analysis, synthesis*, and *evaluation*. They expect you to be able to provide the reasons, arguments, and assumptions on which a given position is based and the evidence that you believe confirms or discounts it. They want you to be able to support your opinions so they can see how you think. They are not looking for answers that merely prove you can memorize the material presented in lecture and the text. Even in math and science courses, your instructors want you not only to remember the correct theory, formula, or equation but also to understand and apply what you have learned.

Knowing your preferred learning style will also help you decide the best ways for you to study, no matter what kind of test or exam you are facing. Remember your VARK score, and review the material in Chapter 4 that helps you link your learning style to strategies for exam preparation.

Getting Prepared for Tests and Exams

Believe it or not, you actually begin preparing for a test on the first day of the term. All of your lecture notes, assigned readings, and homework are part of that preparation. As the test day nears, you should know how much additional time you will need for review, what material the test will cover, and what format the test will take. It is very important to double-check the exam dates on your syllabi, as in Figure 8.1, and to incorporate these dates into your overall plans for time management, for example, in your daily and weekly to-do lists.

Here are some specific suggestions to help you prepare well for any exam:

1. **Ask your instructor.** Find out the purpose, types of questions, conditions (how much time you will have to complete the exam), and content to be covered on the exam. Talk with your instructor to clarify any misunderstandings you might have about your reading or lecture notes. Some instructors might let you see copies of old exams so you can see the types of questions they use. Never miss the last class before an exam, because your instructor might summarize valuable information.

2. **Manage your preparation time wisely.** Create a schedule that will give you time to review effectively for the exam without waiting until the

History 111, US History to 1865
Fall 2010

Examinations
Note: In this course, most of your exams will be on Fridays, except for the Wednesday before Thanksgiving and the final. This is to give you a full week to study for the exam and permit me to grade them over the weekend and return the exams to you on Monday. I believe in using a variety of types of measurements. In addition to those scheduled below, I reserve the right to give you unannounced quizzes on daily reading assignments. Also, current events are fair game on any exam! Midterm and final exams will be cumulative (on all material since beginning of the course). Other exams cover all classroom material and all readings covered since the prior exam. The schedule is as follows:

Friday, 9/3: Objective type

Friday, 9/17: Essay type

Friday, 10/15: Midterm: essay and objective

Friday, 10/29: Objective

Friday, 11/12: Open-book type

Wednesday, 11/24: Essay

Tuesday, 12/14: Final exam: essay and objective

night before. Make sure your schedule has some flexibility to allow for unexpected distractions. If you are able to spread your study sessions over several days, your mind will continue to process the information between study sessions, which will help you during the test. Also, let your friends and family know when you have important exams coming up and how that will affect your time with them.

3. **Focus your study.** Figure out what you can effectively review that is likely to be on the exam. Collaborate with other students to share information, and try to attend all test or exam review sessions offered by your instructor.

PREPARE PHYSICALLY

Maintain your regular sleep routine. To do well on exams, you will need to be alert so that you can think clearly. And you are more likely to be alert when you are well rested. Last-minute, late-night cramming that robs you of sufficient sleep isn't an effective study strategy.

Follow your regular exercise program. Another way to prepare physically for exams is by walking, jogging, or engaging in other kinds of physical activity. Exercise is a positive way to relieve stress and to give yourself a needed break from long hours of studying.

Eat right. Eat a light breakfast before a morning exam, and avoid greasy or acidic foods that might upset your stomach. Limit the amount of caffeinated beverages you drink on exam day, because caffeine can make you jittery. Choose fruits, vegetables, and other foods that are high in energy-rich complex carbohydrates. Avoid eating sweets before an exam. The immediate energy boost they create can be quickly followed by a loss of energy and alertness. Ask the instructor whether you may bring a bottle of water with you to the exam.

PREPARE EMOTIONALLY

Know your material. If you have given yourself adequate time to review, you will enter the classroom confident that you are in control. Study by testing yourself or quizzing others in a study group or learning community so that you will be sure you really know the material.

Practice relaxing. Some students experience upset stomachs, sweaty palms, racing hearts, or other unpleasant physical symptoms of test anxiety. Consult your counseling center about relaxation techniques. Some campus learning centers also provide workshops on reducing test anxiety. If you experience this problem, read the section on test anxiety later in this chapter.

Use positive self-talk. Instead of telling yourself, "I never do well on math tests" or "I'll never be able to learn all the information for my history essay exam," make positive statements such as "I have attended all the lectures, done my homework, and passed the quizzes. Now I'm ready to pass the test!"

YOUR TURN ▶

Are there times when you engage in negative predictions about your academic performance? What do you think causes you to be so hard on yourself? Do you think that changing your predictions could change your performance? Why or why not? How can you reverse your thinking and compliment yourself on your work?

Taking Tests and Exams

Throughout your college career you will take tests in many different formats, in many subject areas, and with many different types of questions. The following box offers test-taking tips that apply to any test situation.

TIPS FOR SUCCESSFUL TEST TAKING

1. **Write your name on the test** (unless you are directed not to) and on the answer sheet.

2. **Analyze, ask, and stay calm**. Before you start the test, take a long, deep breath and slowly exhale. Carefully read all the directions before beginning the test so that you understand what to do. Ask the instructor or exam monitor for clarification if you don't understand something. Be confident. Don't panic. Answer one question at a time.

3. **Make the best use of your time**. Quickly survey the entire test and decide how much time you will spend on each section. Be aware of the point values of different sections of the test. If some questions are worth more points than others, they deserve more of your time.

4. **Jot down idea-starters before the test**. Before you even look at the test questions, turn the test paper over and take a moment to write down the formulas, definitions, and major ideas that you have been studying. (Check with your instructor ahead of time to be sure that he or she is okay with your jotting down idea-starters before the test.) This technique will help you go into the test with a feeling of confidence and knowledge, and it will provide quick access to the information while you are taking the test.

5. **Answer the easy questions first**. Expect that you'll be puzzled by some questions. Make a note to come back to them later. If different sections consist of different types of questions (such as multiple-choice, short-answer, and essay questions), complete the types of question you are most comfortable with first. Be sure to leave enough time for any essays.

6. **If you feel yourself starting to panic or go blank, stop whatever you are doing**. Take a long, deep breath and slowly exhale. Remind yourself you will be OK and that you do know the material and can do well on this test. Then take another deep breath. If necessary, go to another section of the test and come back later to the item that triggered your anxiety.

7. **If you finish early, don't leave**. Stay and check your work for errors. Reread the directions one last time. If you are using a Scantron answer sheet, make sure that all bubbles are filled in accurately and completely.

ESSAY QUESTIONS

Many college instructors have a strong preference for essay exams for a simple reason: Essay exams promote higher-order critical thinking, whereas other types of exams tend to be exercises in memorization. Generally, advanced courses are more likely to include essay exams. To be successful on essay exams, follow these guidelines:

1. **Budget your exam time.** Quickly survey the entire exam, and note the questions that are the easiest for you, along with their point values. Take a moment to weigh their values, estimate the approximate time you should allot to each question, and write the time beside each item number. Be sure you know whether you must answer all the questions or choose among questions. Remember, writing profusely on easy questions that have low value can be a costly error because it takes up precious time you might need for more important questions. Wear a watch so you can monitor your time, and include time at the end for a quick review.

2. **Develop a very brief outline of your answer before you begin to write.** Start working on the questions that are easiest for you, and jot down a few ideas before you begin to write. First, make sure that your outline responds to all parts of the question. Then use your first paragraph to introduce the main points and subsequent paragraphs to describe each point in more depth. If you begin to lose your concentration, you will be glad to have the outline to help you regain your focus. If you find that you are running out of time and cannot complete an essay, provide an outline of key ideas at the very least. Instructors usually assign points on the basis of your coverage of the main topics from the material. Thus you will usually earn more points by responding briefly to all parts of the question than by addressing just one aspect of the question in detail. An outline will often earn you partial credit even if you leave the essay unfinished.

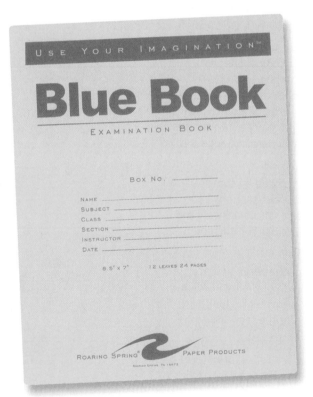

3. **Write concise, organized answers.** Many well-prepared students write good answers to questions that were not asked because they did not read a question carefully or didn't respond to all parts of the question. Other students hastily write down everything they know on a topic. Instructors will give lower grades for answers that are vague and tend to ramble on or for articulate answers that don't address the actual question.

4. **Know the key task words in essay questions.** Being familiar with the **key task word** in an essay question will help you answer it more specifically. The key task words in Table 8.1 (p. 124) appear frequently on essay tests. Take time to learn them so that you can answer essay questions as accurately and precisely as possible.

MULTIPLE-CHOICE QUESTIONS

Preparing for multiple-choice tests requires you to review actively all of the material that has been covered in the course. Reciting from flash cards, summary sheets, mind maps, or the recall column in your lecture notes is a good way to review these large amounts of material.

Take advantage of the many cues that multiple-choice questions contain. Careful reading of each item might uncover the correct answer. Always question choices that use absolute words such as *always*, *never*, and *only*. These choices are often (but not always) incorrect. Also, read carefully for words such as *not*, *except*, and *but*, which are introduced before the choices. Often, the answer that is the most inclusive is correct. Generally, options that do not agree grammatically with the first part of the item are incorrect. For instance, what answers could you rule out in the example in Figure 8.2?

Some students are easily confused by multiple-choice answers that sound alike. The best way to respond to a multiple-choice question is to read the first part of the item and then predict your own answer before reading the options. Choose the letter that corresponds to the option that best matches your prediction.

If you are totally confused by a question, place a check mark in the margin, leave it, and come back later, but always double-check that you are filling in the answer for the right question. Sometimes another question will provide a clue for a question you are unsure about. If you have absolutely no idea, look for an answer that at least contains some shred of information. If there is no penalty for guessing, fill in an answer for every question, even if it is just a guess. If there is a penalty for guessing, don't just choose an answer at random; leaving the answer blank might be a wiser choice.

FILL-IN-THE-BLANK QUESTIONS

In many ways preparing for fill-in-the-blank questions is similar to getting ready for multiple-choice items, but fill-in-the-blank questions can be harder because you do not have a choice of possible answers right in front of you. Not all fill-in-the-blank questions are constructed the same. Some teachers will provide a series of blanks to give you a clue about the number of words in the answer, but if just one long blank is provided, you can't assume that the answer is just one word. If possible, ask the teacher whether the answer is supposed to be a single word per blank or can be a longer phrase.

TRUE/FALSE QUESTIONS

Remember that for a statement to be true, every detail of the sentence must be true. Questions containing words such as *always*, *never*, and *only* tend to be false, whereas less definite terms such as *often* and *frequently* suggest the statement might be true. Read through the entire exam to see whether information in one question will help you answer another. Do not begin to second-guess what you know or doubt your answers just because a sequence of questions appears to be all true or all false.

YOUR TURN ▶

Do you think that essay exams are more appropriate in upper-level courses and multiple-choice exams are more appropriate in first-year courses? Why or why not?

TABLE 8.1 ▶ Key Task Words

Analyze	Divide something into its parts in order to understand it better; show how the parts work together to produce the overall pattern.
Compare	Look at the characteristics or qualities of several things, and identify their similarities or differences. Don't just describe the traits; define how the things are alike and how they are different.
Contrast	Identify the differences between things.
Criticize/ Critique	Analyze and judge something. Criticism can be positive, negative, or both. A criticism should generally contain your own judgments (supported by evidence) and those of authorities who can support your point.
Define	Give the meaning of a word or expression. Giving an example sometimes helps to clarify a definition, but an example by itself is not a definition.
Describe	Give a general verbal sketch of something in narrative or other form.
Discuss	Examine or analyze something in a broad and detailed way. Discussion often includes identifying the important questions related to an issue and attempting to answer these questions. A good discussion explores all relevant evidence and information.
Evaluate	Discuss the strengths and weaknesses of something. Evaluation is similar to criticism, but the word *evaluate* stresses the idea of how well something meets a certain standard or fulfills some specific purpose.
Explain	Clarify something. Explanations generally focus on why or how something has come about.
Interpret	Explain the meaning of something. In science you might explain what an experiment shows and what conclusions can be drawn from it. In a literature course you might explain—or interpret—what a poem means beyond the literal meaning of the words.
Justify	Argue in support of some decision or conclusion by showing sufficient evidence or reasons in its favor. Try to support your argument with both logical and concrete examples.
Narrate	Relate a series of events in the order in which they occurred. Generally, you will also be asked to explain something about the events you are narrating.
Outline	Present a series of main points in an appropriate order. Some instructors want an outline with Roman numerals for main points followed by letters for supporting details. If you are in doubt, ask the instructor whether he or she wants a formal outline.
Prove	Give a convincing logical argument and evidence in support of some statement.
Review	Summarize and comment on the main parts of a problem or a series of statements. A review question usually also asks you to evaluate or criticize.
Summarize	Give information in brief form, omitting examples and details. A summary is short but covers all important points.
Trace	Narrate a course of events. Whenever possible, you should show connections from one event to the next.

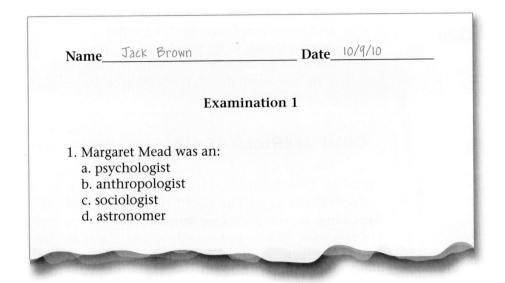

Name Jack Brown   **Date** 10/9/10

Examination 1

1. Margaret Mead was an:
   a. psychologist
   b. anthropologist
   c. sociologist
   d. astronomer

◄ **FIGURE 8.2**
Multiple-choice question

MATCHING QUESTIONS

The matching question is the hardest type of question to answer by guessing. In one column you will find the terms, and in the other you will find their descriptions. Before answering any question, review all of the terms and descriptions. Then match the terms you are sure of. As you do so, cross out both the term and its description, and use the process of elimination to assist you in answering the remaining items. To prepare for matching questions, try using flash cards and lists that you create from the recall column in your notes.

Types of Tests

While you are in college, you will encounter many types of tests. Some tend to be used in particular disciplines; others can be used in any class you might take.

PROBLEM-SOLVING TESTS

In the physical and biological sciences, mathematics, engineering, statistics, and symbolic logic, some tests will require you to solve problems showing all steps. Even if you know a shortcut, it is important to document how you got from step A to step B. On other tests, all that will matter will be whether you have the correct solution to the problem, but doing all the steps will still help ensure that you get the right answer. For these tests, you must also be very careful that you have made no errors in your scientific notation. A misplaced sign, parenthesis, bracket, or exponent can make all the difference.

MACHINE-SCORED TESTS

It is important that you carefully follow the directions for machine-scored tests. In addition to your name, be sure to provide all the necessary information on the answer sheet, such as the instructor's name, the number for the class

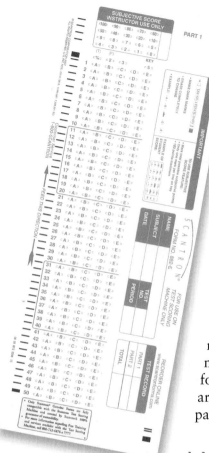

section, or your student ID number. Each time you fill in an answer, make sure that the number on the answer sheet corresponds to the number of the item on the test. If you have questions that you want to come back to (if you are allowed to do so), mark them on the test rather than on the answer sheet.

COMPUTERIZED TESTS

Your comfort with taking computerized tests might depend on how computer-literate you are in general for objective tests as well as your keyboarding skills for essay exams. If your instructor provides the opportunity for practice tests, be sure to take advantage of this chance to get a better sense of how the tests will be structured. There can be significant variations depending on the kind of test, the academic subject, and whether the test was constructed by the teacher or by a textbook company or by another source.

For computerized tests in math and other subjects that require you to solve each problem, record an answer and then move to the next problem. Be sure to check each answer before you submit it. Also, know in advance what materials you are allowed to have on hand, including a calculator and scratch paper for working the problems.

LABORATORY TESTS

In many science courses and in some other academic disciplines, you will be required to take lab tests during which you rotate from one lab station to the next and solve problems, identify parts of models or specimens, explain chemical reactions, and complete other tasks similar to those that you have been performing in lab. At some colleges and universities, lab tests are now administered at computer terminals via simulations. To prepare for lab tests, always attend lab, take good notes, including diagrams and other visual representations as necessary, and be sure to study your lab notebook carefully before the test. If possible, create your own diagrams or models, and then see whether you can label them without looking at your book.

OPEN-BOOK AND OPEN-NOTE TESTS

If you never had open-book or open-note tests in high school, you might be tempted to study less thoroughly, thinking that you will have access to all the information you need during the test. This is a common misjudgment on the part of first-year students. Open-book and open-note tests are usually harder than other exams, not easier.

Most students don't really have time to spend looking things up during an open-book exam. The best way to prepare is to begin the same way you would study for a test in which you cannot refer to your notes or text. But as you do so, develop a list of topics and the page numbers where they are covered in your text. You might want to use the same strategy in organizing your lecture notes. But whatever you do, study as completely as you would for any other test, and do not be fooled into thinking that you don't need to know the material thoroughly.

During the test, monitor your time carefully. Don't waste time unnecessarily looking up information in your text or notes to double-check yourself if you are reasonably confident of your answers. Instead, wait until you have finished the test, and then, if you have extra time, go back and look up answers and make any necessary changes. But if you have really studied, you probably will not find this necessary.

TAKE-HOME TESTS

Like open-book and open-note tests, take-home tests are usually more difficult than in-class tests. Many take-home tests are essay tests, though some instructors will give take-home objective tests. Be sure to allow plenty of time to complete a take-home test. Read the directions and questions as soon

TAKING ONLINE EXAMS

Even if you are typically enrolled in traditional face-to-face courses, you will undoubtedly take an increasing number of your exams online through course management systems (such as Blackboard).

Some of the tips for successful test taking also apply to online exams. Ensure that you will be in a quiet area that is free of distractions while you take the exam. Learn about constraints (e.g., time limit, due date) before the exam by asking your instructor or logging in early to see if the constraints are posted online. If you haven't already done so, take a practice test so that you are familiar with the testing interface. If there is no time limit, take a break after you complete the exam and then go back and recheck your answers. If there is a time limit and the course management system does not show a timer, use a stopwatch or countdown timer to track your progress. (A good rule of thumb is to have the countdown timer sound once with enough time left for you to review the entire exam and then again with five minutes left.) Since you won't have a paper exam, you'll be unable to make notes on the exam itself. Be prepared to have a notepad with you to jot down notes.

You also won't be able to move easily back and forth between the pages of the exam to review your answers or skip questions for later. Therefore when reviewing your answers or going back to previous questions, make sure that you have saved every page of the exam. If you save your exam and have not yet submitted it for grading, you can use your browser's back button to review questions and answers on previous pages.

Thinking Critically

Consider the major differences between taking a paper-and-pencil exam in the classroom and taking it online. What are some ways in which you can apply test-taking strategies to an online environment? What challenges might you encounter when taking exams online? For instance, other open applications and Web sites might distract you. To reduce distractions, close applications and Web sites that you don't need before starting the exam. How can you deliberately set up your desktop workspace and the surrounding area so that you'll do your best on online exams?

as you receive the test to help you gauge how much time you will need. If the test is all essays, consider how much time you might allocate to writing several papers of the same length. Remember that your teacher will expect your essay answers to look more like assigned out-of-class papers than like the essays you would write during an in-class test.

Overcoming Test Anxiety

Test anxiety takes many different forms. Part of combating test anxiety is understanding its sources and identifying its symptoms. Whatever the source, be assured that test anxiety is common.

Test anxiety has many sources. It can be the result of the pressure that students put on themselves to succeed. Without any pressure, students would not be motivated to study; some stress connected with taking exams is natural and can enhance performance. However, when students put too much pressure on themselves or set unrealistic goals, the result is stress that is no longer motivating, only debilitating.

The expectations of parents, a spouse, friends, and other people who are close to you can also induce test anxiety. Sometimes, for example, students who are the first in their families to attend college bear the weight of generations before them who have not had this opportunity. The pressure can be overwhelming!

Finally, some test anxiety is caused by lack of preparation—by not keeping up with assigned reading, homework, and other academic commitments leading up to the test. Procrastination can begin a downward spiral because after you do poorly on the first test in a course, there is even more pressure to do well on subsequent tests to pull up your course grade. This situation becomes even more dire if the units of the course build on one another, as in math and foreign languages, or if the final exam is cumulative. While you are having to master the new material after the test, you are still trying to catch up on the old material as well.

Some test anxiety comes from a negative prior experience. Transcending the memory of negative past experiences can be a challenge. But remember that the past is not the present. Perhaps there are good reasons why you performed poorly in the past. You might not have prepared for the test, you might not have read the questions carefully, or you might not have studied with other students or sought prior assistance from your professor or a tutor. If you carefully follow the strategies in this chapter, you are very likely to do well on all your tests. Remember that a little anxiety is okay. But if you find that anxiety is getting in the way of your performance on tests and exams, be sure to seek help from your campus counseling center.

┌───┐
YOUR TURN ▶

Do you experience any type of test anxiety? If so, what causes you to be anxious? If not, what strategies do you use to stay calm?
└───┘

TYPES OF TEST ANXIETY

Students who experience test anxiety under some circumstances don't necessarily feel it in all testing situations. For example, you might do fine on classroom tests but feel anxious during standardized examinations such as the SAT and ACT. One reason standardized tests are so anxiety provoking is the notion that they determine your future. Believing that the stakes are so high can create unbearable pressure. One way of dealing with this type of test anxiety is to ask yourself: What is the worst that can happen? Remember that no matter what the result, it is not the end of the world. How you do on standardized tests might limit some of your options, but going into these tests with a negative attitude will certainly not improve your chances. Attending preparation workshops and taking practice exams not only can better prepare you for standardized tests, but also can assist you in overcoming your anxiety. And remember that many standardized tests can be taken again at a later time, giving you the opportunity to prepare better and pull up your score.

Some students are anxious only about some types of classroom tests. Practice always helps in overcoming test anxiety; if you fear essay exams, try predicting exam questions and writing sample essays as a means of reducing your anxiety.

Some students have difficulty taking tests at a computer terminal. Some of this anxiety might be related to lack of computer experience. On the other hand, not all computerized tests are user-friendly. You might be allowed to see only one item at a time. Often, you do not have the option of going back and checking over all your answers before submitting them. In preparation for computerized tests, ask the instructor questions about how the test will be structured. Also, make sure you take any opportunities to take practice tests at a learning center or lab.

Test anxiety can often be subject-specific. For example, some students have math test anxiety. It is important to distinguish between anxiety that arises from the subject matter itself and more generalized test anxiety. Perhaps subject-specific test anxiety relates to old beliefs about yourself, such as "I'm no good at math" or "I can't write well." Now is the time to try some positive self-talk and realize that by preparing well, you can be successful even in your hardest courses. If the problem persists, talk to someone in your campus counseling center to develop strategies to overcome irrational fears that can prevent you from doing your best.

SYMPTOMS OF TEST ANXIETY

Test anxiety can manifest itself in many ways. Some students feel it on the very first day of class. Other students begin showing symptoms of test anxiety when it's time to start studying for a test. Others do not get nervous until the night before the test or the morning of an exam day. And some students experience symptoms only while they are actually taking a test.

Symptoms of test anxiety can include butterflies in the stomach, queasiness or nausea, severe headaches, a faster heartbeat, hyperventilating, shaking, sweating, or muscle cramps. During the exam itself, students who are overcome with test anxiety can experience the sensation of "going blank," that is, being unable to remember what they actually know. At this point, students can undermine both their emotional and academic preparation for the test and convince themselves that they cannot succeed.

Test anxiety can impede the success of any college student, no matter how intelligent, motivated, and prepared. That is why it is critical to seek help from your college or university's counseling service or another professional if you think that you have significant test anxiety. If you are not sure where to go for help, ask your advisor, but seek help promptly! If your symptoms are so severe that you become physically ill (with migraine headaches, hyperventilating, or vomiting), you should also consult your physician or campus health service.

STRATEGIES FOR COMBATING TEST ANXIETY

In addition to studying, eating right, and getting plenty of sleep, use these simple strategies to overcome the physical and emotional impact of test anxiety.

First, any time that you begin to feel nervous or upset, take a long, deep breath and slowly exhale to restore your breathing to a normal level. A deep breath is the quickest and easiest relaxation device, and no one even needs to know that you are doing it.

Before you go into the test room, especially before a multiple-hour final exam or before sitting through several exams on the same day, it can help to stretch your muscles just as you would when preparing to exercise. Stretch your calf and hamstring muscles, and roll your ankles. Stretch your arms, and roll your shoulders. Tilt your head to the right, front, and left to stretch your neck muscles.

When you sit down to take the test, pay attention to the way you are sitting. Sit with your shoulders back and relaxed, rather than shrugged forward, and put your feet flat on the floor. Smooth out your facial muscles rather than wrinkling your forehead or frowning. Resist the temptation to clutch your pencil or pen tightly in your fist; take a break and stretch your fingers now and then.

Anxiety-reducing techniques that might be available through your campus counseling center include systematic desensitization, progressive muscle relaxation, and visualization. One of the most popular techniques is creating your own peaceful scene and mentally taking yourself there when you need to relax. Try to use all five senses to recreate your peaceful scene in your mind: What would you see, hear, feel, taste, or smell?

These strategies can assist you in relaxing physically, but meanwhile, you must also pay attention to the mental messages that you are sending yourself. Focus on the positive! If you are telling yourself that you are not smart enough, that you did not study the right material, or that you are going to fail, you need to turn those messages around with a technique called **cognitive restructuring**. We all talk to ourselves, so make sure that your messages are encouraging rather than stress provoking. When you are studying, practice sending yourself positive messages: I really know this stuff. I am going to ace this test!

Similarly, do not allow others, including classmates, your spouse, parents, or friends, to undermine your confidence. If you belong to a study group, discuss the need to stay positive. Sometimes, getting to the test room early will expose you to other students who are asking questions or making comments that are only going to make you nervous. Get to the building early, but wait until just a few minutes before the exam begins to approach the classroom itself. If at any point during a test you begin to feel like you cannot think clearly, or you have trouble remembering or you come to a question you cannot answer, stop for a brief moment, and take another long, deep breath and slowly exhale. Then remind yourself of the positive self-messages you have been practicing.

GETTING THE TEST BACK

Students react differently when they receive their test grades and papers. For some students the thought of seeing the actual graded test produces high levels of anxiety. But unless you look at the instructor's comments and your answers (the correct and incorrect ones), you will have no way to evaluate your own knowledge and test-taking strengths. You might also find that the instructor made an error in the grade that might have cost you a point or two. Be sure to let the instructor know if you find an error.

It is important that you review your graded test. You might find that your mistakes were caused by failing to follow directions, being careless with words or numbers, or overanalyzing a multiple-choice question. If you have any questions about your grade, be sure to talk to the instructor. You might be able to negotiate a few points in your favor, but in any case, you will let your instructor know that you are concerned and want to learn how to do better on graded tests and examinations.

> **YOUR TURN ▶**
>
> What actions do you take when you look at graded tests? Take a look at an exam you got back in one of your classes. What can you learn from it? Would you challenge an instructor if you thought he or she had made a mistake in your grade? Why or why not?

Academic Honesty and Misconduct

Imagine what our world would be like if researchers reported fraudulent results that were then used to develop new machines or medical treatments or to build bridges, airplanes, or subway systems. Integrity is a cornerstone of higher education, and activities that compromise that integrity damage everyone—your country, your community, your college or university, your classmates, and yourself.

CHEATING

Institutions vary widely in how they define broad terms such as "lying" or "cheating." One university defines cheating as "intentionally using or attempting to use unauthorized materials, information, notes, study aids, or other devices. . . [including] unauthorized communication of information during an academic exercise." This definition would apply to looking over a classmate's shoulder for an answer, using a calculator when it is not authorized, obtaining or discussing an exam (or individual questions from an exam) without permission, copying someone else's lab notes, purchasing term papers over the Internet, watching the video instead of reading the book, and duplicating computer files.

PLAGIARISM

Plagiarism, or taking another person's ideas or work and presenting it as your own, is especially intolerable in academic culture. Just as taking someone else's property constitutes physical theft, taking credit for someone else's ideas constitutes intellectual theft.

On most tests, you don't have to credit specific sources. (But some instructors do require that you credit sources you refer to in tests. When in doubt, ask!) In written reports and papers, however, you must give credit any time you use (a) another person's actual words, (b) another person's ideas or theories—even if you don't quote them directly, or (c) any other information that is not considered common knowledge.

Many schools prohibit certain activities in addition to lying, cheating, unauthorized assistance, and plagiarism. Some examples of prohibited behaviors are intentionally inventing information or results, earning credit more than once for the same piece of academic work without permission, giving your work or exam answers to another student to copy during the actual exam or before that exam is given to another section, and bribing in exchange for any kind of academic advantage. Most schools also outlaw helping or attempting to help another student commit a dishonest act.

CONSEQUENCES OF CHEATING AND PLAGIARISM

Although you might see some students who seem to be getting away with cheating or plagiarizing, the consequences of such behaviors can be severe and life-changing. Recent cases of cheating on examinations and plagiarizing major papers have caused some college students to be suspended or expelled and even to have their college degrees revoked. Writers and journalists whose plagiarism has been discovered, such as Jayson Blair, formerly of the *New York Times*, and Stephen Glass, formerly of the *New Republic*, have lost their jobs and their journalistic careers. Even college presidents have occasionally been found guilty of "borrowing" the words of others and using them as their own in speeches and written documents. Such discoveries result not only in embarrassment and shame, but also in lawsuits and criminal actions.

Because plagiarism can be a problem on college campuses, faculty members are now using electronic systems such as www.turnitin.com to identify passages in student papers that have been plagiarized. Many instructors routinely check their students' papers to make sure that the writing is original. So even though the temptation to cheat or plagiarize might be strong, the chance of possibly getting a better grade isn't worth misrepresenting yourself or your knowledge and suffering the potential consequences.

REDUCING THE LIKELIHOOD OF ACADEMIC DISHONESTY

To avoid becoming intentionally or unintentionally involved in academic misconduct, consider the reasons why it could happen:

- **Ignorance.** In a survey at the University of South Carolina, 20 percent of students incorrectly thought that buying a term paper wasn't cheating. Forty percent thought using a test file (a collection of actual tests from previous terms) was fair behavior. Sixty percent thought it was acceptable to get answers from someone who had taken the exam earlier in the same or in a prior term. What do you think?

- **Cultural and campus differences.** In other countries and on some U.S. campuses, students are encouraged to review past exams as practice exercises. Some student government associations maintain test files for use by students. Some campuses permit sharing answers and information for homework and other assignments with friends. Make sure you know the policy on your specific campus.

- **Different policies among instructors.** Because there is no universal code that dictates such behaviors, ask your instructors for clarification. When a student is caught violating the academic code of a particular school or instructor, pleading ignorance of the rules is a weak defense.

- **A belief that grades are all that matter.** This belief might reflect our society's competitive atmosphere. It also might be the result of pressure from parents, peers, or teachers. In truth, grades are nothing if one has cheated to earn them. Even if your grades help you get a job, it is what you have actually learned that will help you keep the job and be promoted. If you haven't learned what you need to know, you won't be ready to work in your chosen field.

- **Lack of preparation or inability to manage time and activities.** If you are tempted to cheat because you are unprepared, ask an instructor to extend a deadline so that a project can be done well.

The following box outlines some steps you can take to reduce the likelihood of problems:

GUIDELINES FOR ACADEMIC HONESTY

1. **Know the rules.** Learn the academic code for your college by going to its Web site. Also learn about any department guidelines on cheating or plagiarism. Study course syllabi. If a teacher does not clarify standards and expectations, ask exactly what they are.

2. **Set clear boundaries.** Refuse when others ask you to help them cheat. Refusing might be hard to do, but you must say no. In test settings, keep your answers covered and your eyes down, and put all extraneous materials away, including cell phones. Now that cell phones enable text messaging, instructors are rightfully suspicious when they see students looking at their cell phones during an exam.

3. **Improve time management.** Be well prepared for all quizzes, exams, projects, and papers. Achieving good preparation might mean unlearning habits such as procrastination (see Chapter 2, "Managing Your Time").

4. **Seek help.** Find out where you can obtain assistance with study skills, time management, and test taking. If your methods are in good shape but the content of the course is too difficult, consult your instructor, join a study group, or visit your campus learning center or tutorial service.

5. **Withdraw from the course.** Your institution has a policy about dropping courses and a deadline to drop without penalty. You might decide to drop only the course that's giving you trouble. Some students choose to withdraw from all classes and take time off before returning to school if they find themselves in over their heads or if a long illness, a family crisis, or some other unexpected occurrence has caused them to fall behind. Before withdrawing, you should ask about campus policies as well as ramifications in terms of federal financial aid and other scholarship programs. See your advisor or counselor.

6. **Reexamine goals.** Stick to your own realistic goals instead of giving in to pressure from family members or friends to achieve impossibly high standards. You might also feel pressure to enter a particular career or profession that is of little or no interest to you. If that happens, sit down with counseling or career services professionals or your academic advisor and explore alternatives.

Where to go FOR HELP . . .

ON CAMPUS ▶

Learning Assistance Center Almost every campus has one of these, and studying for tests is one of its specialties. The best students, good students who want to be the best students, and students with academic difficulties use learning centers and tutoring services. These services are offered by both full-time professionals and highly skilled student tutors and usually are free.

Counseling Services College and university counseling centers offer a wide array of services, often including workshops and individual or group counseling for test anxiety. Sometimes these services are also offered by the campus health center.

Fellow College Students Often the best help we can get is the closest to us. Keep an eye out in your classes, residence hall, and extracurricular activities for the best students, those who appear to be the most serious, purposeful, and directed. Find a tutor. Join a study group. Students who do these things are much more likely to be successful.

ONLINE ▶

The Academic Center for Excellence, University of Illinois at Chicago: http://www.uic.edu/depts/counselctr/ace/examprep.htm.

This Web site provides a list of tips to help you prepare for exams.

Learning Centre of the University of New South Wales in Sydney, Australia: http://www.lc.unsw.edu.au/onlib/exam.html.

Includes the popular SQ3R method.

MY INSTITUTION'S RESOURCES ▶

_____

_____

_____

_____

_____

_____

_____

_____

_____

_____

_____

_____

_____

Applying What You've LEARNED...

Now that you have read and discussed this chapter, consider how you can apply what you have learned to your academic and personal life. The following prompts will help you reflect on the chapter material and its relevance to you both now and in the future.

1. Identify your next upcoming test or exam. What class is it for? When is it scheduled (morning, afternoon, or evening)? What type of test will it be (problem solving, computerized, etc.)? List the specific strategies described in this chapter that will help you prepare for and take this test.

2. Is there one particular course that you find more difficult than others? You probably deal with some form of anxiety when it comes to taking a test in that class. To help you deal with that anxiety, adopt a positive self-message or "mantra"—something to help you stay focused. Think of a phrase or sentence to say to yourself when you begin to doubt your ability to succeed. It could be one of your favorite quotes, lyrics from a song, or even something as simple as "I know I can do this!"

One-Minute PAPER...

As you were reading the tips for improving your performance on exams and tests, were you surprised to see different tips for different subjects, such as math and science, and for different kinds of tests, such as multiple-choice and essay? What did you find to be the most useful information in this chapter? What material was unclear to you?

Building Your PORTFOLIO...

A HIGH PRICE TO PAY

Academic integrity is a supreme value on college and university campuses. Faculty members, staff, and students are held to a strict code of academic integrity, and the consequences of breaking that code can be severe and life-changing. Create a Word document to record your responses to the following activity.

1. Imagine that your college or university has hired you to conduct a month-long academic integrity awareness campaign so that students will learn about and take seriously your campus's guidelines for academic integrity. To prepare for your "new job":

   a. Visit your institution's Web site and use the search feature to find the academic integrity code or policy. Take the time to read through the code, violations, and sanctions.

   b. Visit the judicial affairs office on your campus to learn more about the way your institution deals with violations of academic integrity policies.

   c. Research online resources from other campuses, such as information from the Center for Academic Integrity, hosted by Clemson University (http://www.academicintegrity.org/). This link describes the university's Fundamental Values Project.

    d. Check out several other college and university academic integrity policies and/or honor codes. How do they compare to your institution's code or policy?

2. Outline your month-long awareness campaign. Here are a few ideas to get you started:

    • Plan a new theme every week. Don't forget Internet-related violations.

    • Develop eye-catching posters to display around campus. (Check out the posters designed by students at Elizabethtown College in Pennsylvania, found at http://www.rubberpaw.com/integrity/)

    • Consider guest speakers, debates, skits, or other presentations.

    • Come up with catchy slogans or phrases.

    • Send students a postcard highlighting your institution's policies or honor code.

    • Consider the most effective ways to communicate your message to different groups on campus.

Academic Integrity Awareness Campaign	Events Plan
Week 1	
Week 2	
Week 3	
Week 4	

3. Consider what you have learned through your research. You might want to share your campaign ideas with other students in your class and even select the best ideas for presentation to your campus student affairs office or judicial board.

4. Save your work in your portfolio on your personal computer or flash drive.

9 Writing and Speaking Effectively

In this chapter you will explore

- How writing is a process that leads to a product
- Ways to review and revise your writing
- The importance of recognizing the difference between formal and informal writing
- Six steps to success in preparing a speech
- How best to use your voice and body language
- How to sound organized when speaking on the spot

Writing and speaking are the two basic forms of communication.

The ability to write well and speak well makes a tremendous difference in how the rest of the world perceives you and how well you will be able to communicate throughout your life. But you will find that you often need to communicate differently depending on who is reading or listening to your words. Each time you speak or write, you are addressing an audience. The audience might be one person—a friend, family member, professor, or a potential employer—or your audience might be a group, such as your classmates in college. Some audiences might be unknown to you. For instance, if you're writing a book or an article for publication, a blog entry, or something on your Facebook or MySpace page, you never know who might read your words. To communicate effectively, it's important to think about your audience, what they will understand and expect, and how they will react to what you are saying or writing. It's generally OK to use informal language with your friends, family, and other college students, for example, but your instructors and potential employers will expect more formal writing and speaking.

Experts suggest that there's no single, universally accepted standard for how to speak or write American English. Even so, school systems, professional communicators, and businesses all have standards, and, not surprisingly, the rules do not vary dramatically from place to place. If they did, we would have a hard time understanding one another. Our purpose in this chapter is not to teach you grammar and punctuation (we'll save that for your English classes), but to get you to think of writing and speaking as processes (how you get there) as well as products (the final paper or script) and to help you overcome those writer's and speaker's blocks we all encounter from time to time.

You might wonder: Why can't more people express themselves effectively? The answers vary, but all come back to the same theme: Most people do not think of writing and speaking as processes to be mastered step by step. Instead, they view writing and speaking as products; you knock them out and you're done. Nothing could be further from the truth.

Whatever career you choose, you will be expected to think, create, communicate, manage, and lead. A 2002 survey by the Plain English Network found that 96 percent of the nation's 1,000 largest employers say that employees must have good communication skills to get ahead. This statistic means you will have to be able to write and speak well. You will have to write reports about your work and the performance of others, e-mails to describe problems and propose solutions, and position papers to explain and justify to your superiors why the organization must make certain changes.

As you lead and manage others, you also will need strong speaking skills in order to explain, report, motivate, direct, encourage, and inspire. You might have to give presentations in meetings to your superiors and their subordinates and then follow up with a written report or e-mail. So as you prepare yourself for a career, you need to start thinking of yourself as a person who is both a good thinker and an outstanding communicator.

WRITING

William Zinsser, author of several books on writing, claims, "The act of writing gives the teacher a window into the mind of the student."[1] In other words, your writing provides tangible evidence of how well you think and how well you understand concepts related to the courses you are taking. Your writing might also reveal a good sense of humor, a compassion for the less fortunate, a respect for family, and many other things. Zinsser reminds us that writing is not merely something that writers do; it is a basic skill for getting through life. He claims that far too many Americans cannot perform useful work because they never learned to express themselves.

Using Freewriting to Discover What You Want to Say

Writing expert Peter Elbow asserts that it's impossible to write effectively if you simultaneously try to organize, check grammar and spelling, and offer intelligent thoughts to your readers.[2] He argues that it can't all be done at once, mainly because you use the right—or creative—side of your brain to create thoughts, whereas you use the left—or logical—side for grammar, spelling, organization, and so forth.

Elbow argues that we can free up our writing and bring more energy and voice into it by writing more like the way we speak and trying to avoid the heavy overlay of editing in our initial efforts to write. This preliminary step in the writing process is called "freewriting." By freewriting, Elbow simply means writing that is temporarily unencumbered by mechanical processes, such as punctuation, grammar, spelling, and context. Freewriting is also a way to break the habit of trying to write and edit at the same time.

The freewriting process can be difficult at first because it goes against the grain of how we are accustomed to writing. We normally edit as we write, pausing to collect our thoughts, to recollect the correct spelling of a word, to cross out a sentence that does not belong, to reject a paragraph that doesn't fit with the argument that we are making, or to mentally outline a structure of the argument that we are trying to make. Once you get the hang of it, though, freewriting can become second nature.

YOUR TURN ▶

Have you tried freewriting before? To see what freewriting feels like, write, "My writing speaks for me." Write for at least ten minutes, nonstop, about that statement. Don't think about organization, grammar, punctuation, or spelling, and don't stop writing until the time is up. Discuss with your classmates your reactions to writing this way and what each of you wrote.

---

[1]William Zinsser, *On Writing Well* (New York: Harper Resource 25th Anniversary Edition, 2001).
[2]Peter Elbow, *Writing without Teachers* (New York: Oxford University Press, 1973).

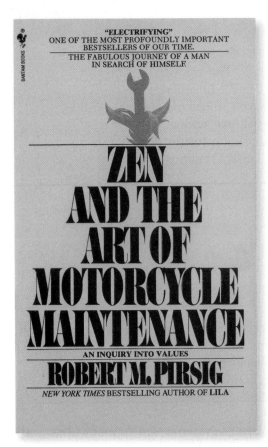

NARROWING YOUR TOPIC

In *Zen and the Art of Motorcycle Maintenance*,[3] Robert Pirsig tells a story about a first-year English class he had taught. Each week he assigned students a 500-word essay to write. One week, a student failed to submit her paper about the town where the college was located, explaining that she had "thought and thought, but couldn't think of anything to write about." Pirsig gave her an additional weekend to complete the assignment. As he said this, an idea flashed through his mind. "I want you to write a 500-word paper just about Main Street, not the whole town," he said. She gasped and stared at him angrily. How was she to narrow her thinking to just one street when she couldn't think of a thing to write about the entire town? On Monday she arrived in tears. "I'll never learn to write," she said. Pirsig's answer: "Write a paper about one building on Main Street. The opera house. And start with the first brick on the lower left side. I want it next class."

The student's eyes opened wide. She walked into the next class with a 5,000-word paper on the opera house. In writing this paper, she had been freewriting but hadn't realized it. "I don't know what happened," she exclaimed. "I sat across the street and wrote about the first brick, then the second, and all of a sudden I couldn't stop." What had Pirsig done for this person? He had helped her find a focus and a place to begin. Getting started is what blocks most students from approaching writing properly. Faced with an ultimatum, the student probably began to see the beauty of the opera house for the first time and had gone on to describe it, to find out more about it in the library, to ask others about it, and to comment on its setting among the other buildings on the block.

Very few writers—even professionally published ones—say what they want to say on their first try. But through practice, an understanding of the writing process, and dedication, most people can improve their writing skills. And being a good writer can translate into good job opportunities and good money.

EXPLORATORY WRITING

Another way to think about writing is to distinguish between exploratory writing and explanatory writing. Those terms practically define themselves, but here are some clearer definitions: **Exploratory writing**, like freewriting, helps you discover what you want to say; **explanatory writing** then allows you to transmit those ideas to others. Explanatory writing is "published," meaning you have chosen to allow others to read it (your teacher, your friends, other students, or the public at large), but it is important that most or all of your exploratory writing be private, to be read only by you as a series of steps toward your published work. Keeping your early drafts under wraps frees

---

[3]Robert Pirsig, *Zen and the Art of Motorcycle Maintenance* (New York: Bantam Books, 1984).

you to say what you mean and mean what you say. Later, you will come back and make adjustments, and each revision will strengthen your message.

Some writers say they gather their best thoughts through exploratory writing: by researching their topic, writing down ideas from their research, and adding their questions and reactions to what they have gathered. As they write, their minds begin to make connections between ideas. At this stage, they don't attempt to organize, to find exactly the right words, or to think about structure. But when they move from exploratory writing to explanatory writing, their preparation will help them form crystal clear sentences, spell correctly, and have their thoughts organized so that their material flows naturally from one point to the next.

The Writing Process

One of the more popular ways of thinking about the writing process includes the following steps:

1. **Prewriting or rehearsing (freewriting).** This step includes preparing to write by filling your mind with information from other sources. It is generally considered the first stage of exploratory writing.

2. **Writing or drafting.** In this step, you build on your exploratory writing to create a rough explanatory draft.

3. **Rewriting or revision.** In this step, you polish your work until it clearly explains what you want to communicate and is ready for your audience. Many students turn in poorly written papers because they skip the first and last steps and make do with the middle one. Perhaps they don't have time because they have overloaded their schedule or they put off things until the night before the paper is due. Whatever the reason, the result is often a poorly written assignment, since the best writing is usually done over an extended period of time, not as a last-minute task. Most professional writers and speakers would never start preparing an assignment only a day or hours before it has to be delivered. For one thing, the mere anxiety such a situation creates would be more than enough to shut down any manner of intelligent thinking. Worrying about your grammar and spelling as you write what might be your only draft can lead to a low grade or a rejection from a career inquiry.

YOUR TURN ▶

Describe your writing process. What steps do you go through when you write a major paper?

PREWRITING: THE IDEA STAGE

Many writing experts, such as Donald Murray,[4] believe that of all the steps, **prewriting** (or freewriting) should take the longest. During freewriting you might question things that seem illogical. You might recall what you've heard other people say. What you read, hear, and question should lead you to write more, to ask yourself whether your views are more reliable than those of others, whether the topic might be too broad or too narrow, and so forth.

What constitutes an appropriate topic or thesis? When is it neither too broad nor too narrow? Test your topic by writing, "The purpose of this paper is to convince my readers that . . ." (but don't use that stilted line in your eventual paper). Pay attention to the assignment. Know the limits of your knowledge, the limitations on your time, and your ability to do the necessary research.

WRITING: THE BEGINNING OF ORGANIZATION

Once you have completed your research and feel you have exhausted the information sources and ideas, it's time to move to the writing, or drafting, stage. It might be a good idea to begin with a **thesis statement** and an outline so that you can put things where they logically belong. A thesis statement is a short statement that clearly defines the purpose of the paper (see Figure 9.1).

Once you have a workable outline and thesis, you can begin paying attention to the flow of ideas from one sentence to the next and from one paragraph to the next, including subheadings where needed. If you have chosen the thesis carefully, it will help you check to see that each sentence relates to your main idea. When you have completed this stage, you will have the first draft of your paper in hand.

> Thesis: Napoleon's dual personality can be explained by examining incidents throughout his life.
> 1. Explain why I am using the term "dual personality" to describe Napoleon.
> 2. Briefly comment on his early life and his relationship with his mother.
> 3. Describe Napoleon's rise to fame from soldier to emperor. Stress the contradictions in his personality and attitudes.
> 4. Describe the contradictions in his relationship with Josephine.
> 5. Summarize my thoughts about Napoleon's personality.
> 6. Possibly conclude by referring to opening question: "Did Napoleon actually have a dual personality?"

FIGURE 9.1 ▶

Thesis Statement

[4]Donald Murray, *Learning by Teaching: Selected Articles on Writing and Teaching* (Portsmouth, NH: Boynton/Cook, 1982).

REWRITING: THE POLISHING STAGE

Are you finished? Not by a long shot. Next comes the stage at which you take a good piece of writing and do your best to make it great. The essence of good writing is rewriting. You read. You correct. You add smoother transitions. You slash through wordy sentences and paragraphs, removing anything that is repetitious or adds nothing of value to your paper. You substitute stronger words for weaker ones. You double-check spelling and grammar. It also might help to share your paper with one or more of your classmates to get their feedback. Having your draft considered carefully by more than one reader is typically called "peer review." Once you have talked with your reviewers about their suggested changes, you can either accept or reject them. At this point, you are ready to finalize your writing and "publish" (turn in) your paper.

ALLOCATING TIME

When writer Donald Murray was asked how long a writer should spend on each of the three stages, he suggested the following:

Prewriting: 85 percent (including research and rumination)

Writing: 1 percent (the first draft)

Rewriting: 14 percent (revising until the essay or paper is suitable for "publication")

Wired WINDOW

WIKIPEDIA: A GOOD SOURCE?

Wikipedia is an online encyclopedia that contains content generated by its users. You might have used Wikipedia to do research for term papers in high school. Unlike the content in traditional encyclopedias, what is found on Wikipedia is never systematically reviewed by topic experts. So who can add or edit content on Wikipedia? The answer is anyone. Sometimes, this creates chaos on Wikipedia pages when users spend a lot of time quarreling over facts. In theory, these discussions can lead to better content on the more popular Wikipedia pages; however, on less popular pages, information can be grossly inaccurate. Knowing this, you should not be surprised that many of your professors will not allow the use of Wikipedia as a source for your research papers.

The discussion of whether or how Wikipedia can be used as a legitimate source continues in the academic world. Many faculty members at one extreme of the debate argue that Wikipedia is nothing more than an opinion-based Web site, while those on the other end argue that the "crowdsourcing" that occurs because of Wikipedia is the ultimate form of peer review. The main point of the argument is that Wikipedia arrives at knowl-edge by bypassing the established process of scientific inquiry, which includes conducting research that meets certain criteria and publishing research in periodicals reviewed by experts in the field. So before you begin your research papers, check with your professors to see whether they will allow you to use Wikipedia as a reference. If they do, use it sparingly, focusing on its ability to provide a quick source of potential information that you can verify (or discount) using other sources that are more acceptable to your instructors.

Thinking Critically

What's your opinion of Wikipedia? Do you think that faculty members should consider Wikipedia the "ultimate form of peer review," or should they treat it as useless? Search for a popular Wikipedia entry that you can corroborate with an external source (such as a textbook or a research article). Are there differences of opinion between the external source and the Wikipedia article? If so, how would you judge what information is correct? How would you suggest improving Wikipedia to make it more acceptable to the academic world?

When readers offer meaningful feedback, you might want to begin the process again, returning to prewriting, then writing, then rewriting (Figure 9.2).

If Murray's figures surprise you, here's a true story about a writer who was assigned to create a brochure. He had other jobs to do and kept avoiding that one. But the other work he was doing had a direct bearing on the brochure he was asked to write. So as he was putting this assignment off, he was also "researching" material for it.

After nearly three months, he finally decided it was time to move forward on the brochure. He sat at his computer and dashed the words off in just under thirty minutes. The more he wrote, the faster the ideas popped into his head. He actually was afraid to stop until he had finished. He read his words, made revisions, sent the result around the office for peer review, incorporated some suggestions, and the brochure was published.

He had spent a long time prewriting (working with related information without trying to write the brochure). He went through the writing stage quickly because his mind was primed for the task. As a result, he had time to polish his work before the first draft.

You can use a similar process. Begin writing the day you get the assignment, even if it's only for ten or fifteen minutes. That way, you won't be confronting a blank screen or piece of paper later. Write something on the assignment every day; the more you write, the better you'll write. Dig for ideas. *Reject nothing* at first, and then revise later. Read good writing; it will help you find your own writing style. Above all, know that becoming a better thinker and writer takes hard work, but practice can make it near perfect.

Choosing the Best Way to Communicate with Your Audience

Before you came to college, you probably spent much more time writing informally than writing formally. Think about all the time you've spent writing e-mails, Facebook and blog comments, text messages, and instant messages

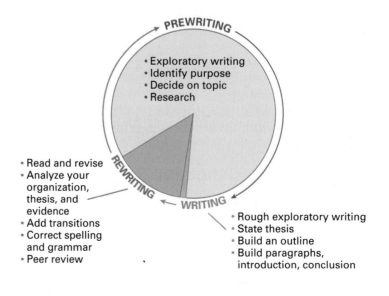

FIGURE 9.2 ▶

The Writing Process

(IMs). Now think about all the time you've spent writing papers for school or work. Typically, writing for wired communications is informal. This can be a detriment to your writing skills. The grammar and structure of e-mail and other types of electronic communication resemble a conversation instead of a formal piece of writing. Additionally, communications via IM and text messaging often use spelling and grammar conventions all their own. As a shortcut, people often condense text messages and IMs by using abbreviations such as "brb," "lol," "y?," and "ttyl." They are abbreviated for good reason—imagine how long it would take to thumb this sentence into a text message. The downside of text messages and IM shortcuts is that they have gradually crept into our writing habits and caused many of us to become careless in our formal writing. It is important to be aware of when it's okay to be sloppy and when you have to be meticulous.

Electronic communication does not convey emotions as well as face-to-face or even telephone conversations do. Electronic communication lacks vocal inflection, visible gestures, and a shared environment. Your correspondent might have difficulty telling whether you are serious or kidding, happy or sad, frustrated or euphoric. Sarcasm is particularly dangerous to use in electronic messages. Therefore your electronic compositions will be different from both your paper compositions and your speech.

Being aware of the differences between formal writing and informal writing will help you build appropriate writing skills for college work. How would you write an e-mail to friends telling them about the volunteer work you did this past weekend? How would you write that same e-mail to a potential employer who might hire you for your first job after college? Another way to improve your writing is to consider the reader's point of view. For the next week, before sending any MySpace or Facebook messages, e-mails, or text messages, reread them and consider how the people who will receive them will perceive your tone. What kind of mood will they think you are in? Will they feel that you are happy to have them as a friend? In how many different ways might your message be interpreted?

YOUR TURN ▶

Have you ever sent or received an e-mail or text message that could be interpreted in more than one way? What did you learn from that experience?

Writing for class projects might be a challenge at first. Visit your institution's writing center when you are starting to work on your paper. Professional staff and trained peer consultants who work in writing centers are available to help students express their ideas clearly through writing. Ask your instructor for examples of papers that have received good grades. You might also ask your instructor to help you review your writing after you have worked with the writing center. Most important, you can practice by using a correct writing style when IMing and text messaging. You'll find that your friends won't fault you for it. (Have you ever seen an IM asking you to "pls stop using proper grammar"?) Since you spend more time with online forms of communication, it's a great way to get real-world practice in the art of academic writing.

SPEAKING

The advice about writing also applies to speaking in public. The major difference, of course, is that you not only have to write the speech, you also have to present it to an audience. Because many people believe that fear of public speaking ranks up there with the fear of death, you might be thinking: What if I plan, organize, prepare, and rehearse, but calamity strikes anyway? What if my mind goes completely blank, I drop my note cards, or I say something totally embarrassing? Remember that people in your audience have been in your position and will understand your anxiety. Just accentuate the positive, rely on your wit, and keep speaking. Your recovery is what they are most likely to recognize; your success is what they are most likely to remember. The guidelines in this chapter can help you improve your speaking skills tremendously, including losing your fear of speaking publicly.

Preparing a Speech

Successful speaking involves six fundamental steps:

> Step 1. Clarify your objective.
> Step 2. Analyze your audience.
> Step 3. Collect and organize your information.
> Step 4. Choose your visual aids.
> Step 5. Prepare your notes.
> Step 6. Practice your delivery.

STEP 1. CLARIFY YOUR OBJECTIVE

Begin by identifying what you want to accomplish. Do you want to persuade your listeners that your campus needs additional student parking? Inform your listeners about the student government's accomplishments? What do you want your listeners to know, believe, or do when you are finished?

STEP 2. ANALYZE YOUR AUDIENCE

You need to understand the people you'll be talking to. Ask yourself:

- **What do they already know about my topic?** If you're going to give a presentation on the health risks of fast food, you'll want to find out how much your listeners already know about fast food so you don't risk boring them or wasting their time.
- **What do they want or need to know?** If your presentation will be about fast food and health, how much interest do your classmates have in nutrition? Would they be more interested in some other aspect of college life?
- **Who are my listeners?** What do the members of your audience have in common with you? How are they different from you?

■ **What are their attitudes toward me, my ideas, and my topic?** How are they likely to feel about the ideas you are planning to present? For instance, what are your classmates' attitudes about fast food?

STEP 3. COLLECT AND ORGANIZE YOUR INFORMATION

Now comes the most critical part of the process: building your presentation by selecting and arranging blocks of information. One useful analogy is to think of yourself as guiding your listeners through the maze of ideas they already have to the new knowledge, attitudes, and beliefs you would like them to have. You can apply the suggestions from earlier in this chapter about creating an outline for writing to composing an outline for a speech.

STEP 4. CHOOSE YOUR VISUAL AIDS

Research has shown that when visual aids are added to presentations, listeners can absorb 35 percent more information, and over time they can recall 55 percent more. You might choose to prepare a chart, show a video clip, write on the board, or distribute handouts. You might also use your computer to prepare overhead transparencies or dynamic PowerPoint presentations. As you select and use your visual aids, consider these rules of thumb:

■ Make visuals easy to follow. Use readable lettering, and don't overload your audience by trying to cover too much on one slide.
■ Explain each visual clearly.
■ Allow your listeners enough time to process visuals.
■ Proofread carefully. Misspelled words hurt your credibility as a speaker.
■ Maintain eye contact with your listeners while you discuss the visuals. Don't turn around and address the screen.

A fancy PowerPoint slideshow can't make up for inadequate preparation or poor delivery skills, but using clear, attractive visual aids can help you organize your material and help your listeners understand what they're hearing. The quality of your visual aids and your skill in using them can contribute to making your presentation effective (see Figure 9.3).

STEP 5. PREPARE YOUR NOTES

If you are like most speakers, having an entire written copy of your speech in front of you might tempt you to read much of your presentation. Even if you can resist that temptation, your presentation could sound canned. On the other hand, your memory might fail you, so speaking without any material at all could be risky. A better strategy is to memorize only the introduction and conclusion of your speech so that you can maintain eye contact during the rest of your speech and thus build rapport with your listeners.

The best speaking aid is a minimal outline, carefully prepared, from which you can speak extemporaneously. Rehearse thoroughly in advance, and you'll be better prepared for how and when you want to present your

Step 4. Choose Your Visual Aids

When visual aids are added to presentations, listeners can absorb 35 percent more information, and over time, they can recall 55 percent more. You might choose to prepare a chart, show a video clip, write on the board, or distribute handouts. You might also use your computer to prepare overhead transparencies or dynamic PowerPoint presentations. As you select and use your visual aids, consider these rules of thumb:
Make visuals easy to follow. Use readable lettering, and don't crowd information. Keep the copy on each slide brief.
Explain each visual clearly.
Allow your listeners enough time to process visuals.
Proofread carefully. Misspelled words hurt your credibility as a speaker.
Maintain eye contact with your listeners while you discuss visuals. Don't turn around and address the screen.

(a) Bad example

Step 4.
Choose Your Visual Aids

- Make visuals easy to follow.
- Explain each visual clearly.
- Allow your listeners time to process visuals.
- Proofread carefully.
- Maintain eye contact with your listeners.

FIGURE 9.3 ▶

Examples of Good and Bad Presentation Slides

(b) Good example

points. Because you are speaking from brief notes, your words will be slightly different each time you give your presentation. That's OK; you'll sound prepared but natural. You might want to use some unobtrusive note cards. If so, it's not a bad idea to number them, just in case you accidentally drop the stack; this has happened to the best of speakers! When you become more comfortable with speaking, you might decide to let your visuals serve as notes. A paper copy of the PowerPoint slides can also serve as your basic outline. Eventually, you might find that you no longer need notes.

STEP 6. PRACTICE YOUR DELIVERY

As you rehearse, form a mental image of success rather than one of failure. Practice your presentation aloud several times beforehand to harness that energy-producing anxiety.

Begin a few days before your target date, and continue until you're about to present it. Rehearse aloud. Talking through your speech can help you much more than thinking through your speech. Practice before an audience— your roommate, a friend, your dog, even the mirror. Talking to something or someone helps simulate the distraction that listeners cause. Consider recording or videotaping yourself to help you pinpoint your own mistakes and to reinforce your strengths. If you ask your practice audience to critique you, you'll have some idea of what changes it might be helpful to make.

YOUR TURN ▶

Think about public speakers you have heard either in person or on TV. Which ones were the most effective? Why? What are some of the specific ways in which the best public speakers communicate with an audience?

Using Your Voice and Body Language

Let your hands hang comfortably at your sides, reserving them for natural, spontaneous gestures. Unless you must stay close to a fixed microphone,

plan to move comfortably and casually around the room. Some experts suggest that you change positions between major points to punctuate your presentation, signaling to your audience, "I've finished with that point; let's shift topics."

Following are some other tips for using your voice and body language:

- Make eye contact with as many listeners as you can. This helps you to read their reactions, demonstrate confidence, and establish command.

- A smile helps to warm up your listeners, although you should avoid smiling excessively or inappropriately. Smiling through a presentation on world hunger would send your listeners a mixed message.

- As you practice your speech, pay attention to the pitch of your voice, your rate of speaking, and your volume. Project confidence and enthusiasm by varying your pitch. Speak at a rate that mirrors normal conversation— not too fast and not too slow. Consider varying your volume for the same reasons you vary pitch and rate—to engage your listeners and to empha- size important points.

- Pronunciation and word choice are important. A poorly articulated word (such as *gonna* for *going to*), a mispronounced word (such as *nuculer* for *nuclear*), or a misused word (such as *anecdote* for *anti- dote*) can quickly erode your credibility. Check meanings and pronun- ciations in a dictionary if you're not sure, and use a thesaurus for word variety. Fillers such as *um, uh, like,* and *you know* are distract- ing, too.

- Consider your appearance. Convey a look of competence, preparedness, and success by dressing professionally.

The GUIDE Checklist

Imagine you've been selected as a campus tour guide for next year's pro- spective first-year students and their families who are visiting your campus. Picture yourself in front of the administration building with a group of people assembled around you. You want to get and keep their attention in order to achieve your objective—increasing their interest in your school. Using the GUIDE method shown in Figure 9.4, you would do the following.

G: GET YOUR AUDIENCE'S ATTENTION

You can relate the topic to your listeners: "Let me tell you what to expect during your college years here—at the best school in the state." Or you can state the significance of the topic: "Deciding which college to attend is one of the most important decisions you'll ever make." Or you can arouse their curiosity: "Do you know the three most important factors that students and their families consider when choosing a college?"

You can also tell a joke (but only if it relates to your topic and isn't of- fensive or in questionable taste), startle the audience, tell a story, or ask a rhetorical question (a question that is asked to produce an effect, especially to

THE GUIDE CHECKLIST

G Get your audience's attention

U "You" – don't forget yourself

I Ideas, ideas, ideas!

D Develop an organizational structure

E Exit gracefully and memorably

make an assertion, rather than to elicit a reply). Regardless of which method you select, remember that a well-designed introduction must not only gain the attention of your listeners, but also develop rapport with them, motivate them to continue listening, and preview what you are going to say during the rest of your speech.

U: YOU (U)–DON'T FORGET YOURSELF

In preparing any speech, don't exclude the most important source of your presentation: you. Even in a formal presentation, you will be most successful if you develop a comfortable style that's easy to listen to. Don't play a role. Instead, be yourself at your best, letting your wit and personality shine through.

I: IDEAS, IDEAS, IDEAS!

Create a list of all the possible points you could make. Then write them out as conclusions you want your listeners to accept. For example, imagine that on your campus tour for prospective new students and their parents, you want to make the following points:

Tuition is reasonable.	The campus is attractive.
The faculty is composed of good teachers.	The library has great resources.
The school is committed to student success.	The campus is safe.
College can prepare you to get a good job.	Faculty members conduct prestigious research.
Student life is awesome.	This college is the best choice.

For a typical presentation, most listeners can process no more than five main points. After considering your list for some time, you decide that the following five points are crucial:

- Tuition is reasonable.
- The faculty is composed of good teachers.
- The school is committed to student success.
- The campus is attractive.
- The campus is safe.

Try to generate more ideas than you think you'll need so that you can select the best ones. As with writing, don't judge your ideas at first; rather, think up as many possibilities as you can. Then use critical thinking to decide which are most relevant to your objectives.

As you formulate your main ideas, keep these guidelines in mind:

- **Main points should be parallel if possible.** Each main point should be a full sentence with a construction similar to that of the others. A poor, *nonparallel* structure might look like this:

  1. Student life is awesome. (a full-sentence main point)
  2. Tuition (a one-word main point that doesn't parallel the first point)

  For a *parallel* second point, try instead:

  2. Tuition is low. (a full-sentence main point)

- **Each main point should include a single idea.** Don't crowd main points with multiple messages, as in the following:

  1. Tuition is reasonable, and the campus is safe.
  2. Faculty members are good teachers and researchers.

Ideas rarely stand on their own merit. To ensure that your main ideas work, use a variety of supporting materials. The three most widely used forms of supporting materials are **examples, statistics,** and **testimony.**

- **Examples** include stories and illustrations, hypothetical events, and specific cases. They can be compelling ways to dramatize and clarify main ideas, but make sure they're relevant, representative, and reasonable.

- **Statistics** are widely used as evidence in speeches. Of course, numbers can be manipulated, and unscrupulous speakers sometimes mislead with statistics. If you use statistics, make sure they are clear, concise, accurate, and easy to understand.
- **Testimony** includes quoting outside experts, paraphrasing reliable sources, and emphasizing the quality of individuals who agree with your main points. When you use testimony, make sure that it is accurate, expert, and credible.

Finally, because each person in your audience is unique, you can best add interest, clarity, and credibility to your presentation by varying and combining the types of support you provide.

D: DEVELOP AN ORGANIZATIONAL STRUCTURE

For example, you might decide to use a chronological narrative approach, discussing the history of the college from its early years to the present. Or you might decide on a problem-solution format in which you describe a problem (such as choosing a school), present the pros and cons of several solutions (the strengths and weaknesses of several schools), and finally identify the best solution (your school!).

Begin with your most important ideas. Writing an outline can be the most useful way to begin organizing. List each main point and subpoint separately on a note card. Spread the cards out on a large surface (such as the floor), and arrange, rearrange, add, and delete cards until you find the most effective arrangement. Then simply number the cards, pick them up, and use them to prepare your final outline.

As you organize your presentation, remember that your overall purpose is to guide your listeners. This means you must not neglect transitions between your main points. For example:

"Now that we've looked at the library, let's move on to the gymnasium."

"The first half of my presentation has identified our recreational facilities. Now let's look at the academic hubs on campus."

"So much for the academic buildings on campus. What about the campus social scene?"

In speaking, as in writing, transitions make the difference between keeping your audience with you and losing them at an important juncture.

E: EXIT GRACEFULLY AND MEMORABLY

Plan your ending carefully, realizing that most of the suggestions for introductions also apply to conclusions.

Whatever else you do, go out with style, impact, and dignity. Don't leave your listeners asking, "So that's it?" Subtly signal that the end is in sight (without the overused "So in conclusion . . ."), briefly summarize your major points, and then conclude confidently.

Speaking on the Spot

Most of the speaking you will do in college and afterward will be on the spot. When your instructor asks your opinion of last night's reading, when another member of your study group asks for your position on an issue, or when your best friend asks you to defend your views, you have to give an impromptu speech.

When you must speak on the spot, it helps to use a framework that allows you to sound organized and competent. Suppose your instructor asks, "Do you think the world's governments are working together effectively to ensure a healthy environment?" One of the most popular ways to arrange your thoughts is through the PREP formula.[5] Short for "preparation," this plan requires the following:

P: **Point of view** Provide an overview—a clear, direct statement or generalization: "After listening to yesterday's lecture, yes, I do."

R: **Reasons** Broadly state why you hold this point of view: "I was surprised by the efforts of the United Nations General Assembly to focus on the environment."

E: **Evidence or examples** Present specific facts or data supporting your point of view: "For example, President Obama has committed to the goal of cutting carbon dioxide emissions 17 percent from 2005 levels by 2020."

P: **Point of view, restated** To make sure you are understood clearly, end with a restatement of your position: "So, yes, the world's governments seem to be concerned and working to improve the situation."

YOUR TURN ▶

Write about your experience of speaking in front of a group. Is public speaking something you enjoy or dread? Are you an anxious or a comfortable speaker? What strategies could you suggest to anyone who wants to become more comfortable when speaking in front of a group?

---

[5]Kenneth Wydro, *Think on Your Feet* (Englewood Cliffs, NJ: Prentice-Hall, 1981).

Where to go
FOR HELP . . .

ON CAMPUS ▶

Writing Center Most campuses have one. Frequently, it is found within the English department.

Learning Assistance Center In addition to help on many other topics, these centers offer help on writing.

Departments of Speech, Theater, and Communications These offer both resources and specific courses to help you develop your speaking skills.

Student Activities One of the best ways to learn and practice speaking skills is to become active in student organizations, especially those like the Student Government Association and the Debate Club.

ONLINE ▶

Writing tips: http://www.uiowa.edu/~histwrit/website/grammar%20help.htm. The University of Iowa's History Department offers help on common writing mistakes.

Plain Language Have you ever been confused by government gobbledygook? Here's a guide to writing user-friendly documents for federal employees: http://www.plainlanguage.gov/howto/guidelines/reader-friendly.cfm.

Toastmasters International offers public speaking tips at http://www.toastmasters.org/pdfs/top10.pdf.

MY INSTITUTION'S RESOURCES ▶

_____

_____

_____

_____

_____

_____

_____

_____

_____

_____

_____

_____

_____

_____

_____

_____

_____

_____

Applying What You've LEARNED . . .

Now that you have read and discussed this chapter, consider how you can apply what you've learned to your academic and personal life. The following prompts will help you reflect on chapter material and its relevance to you both now and in the future.

1. Develop a five-slide PowerPoint presentation to introduce yourself to your classmates in a new way. You might include slides that contain points about your high school years, your hobbies, your jobs, your family, and so forth. Use the effective speaking strategies in this chapter to help you outline your presentation. In addition to text, use visuals such as photos, video clips, and art to engage your audience.

2. Before reading this chapter, had you considered the differences between writing an exam response and writing a blog post or responding to someone on Facebook? Think about the online communications you've had in the last week. Can you say for certain that you knew exactly who your audience was? Did you send anything that could be misinterpreted or end up being read by someone outside your intended audience? What advice about online communications would you give to other students?

One-Minute PAPER . . .

This chapter has information that you can use to improve your writing and speaking skills. Which strategies struck you as methods that you could or should put into practice? If your instructor could cover one area in more depth, what would you want it to be?

Building Your PORTFOLIO . . .

IN THE PUBLIC EYE

The media provide ample opportunities for celebrities and public figures to show off their public speaking skills. As you have probably noticed, some celebrities are much better speakers than others. However, being a good public speaker is not important just for those who are "in the public eye." Whether you want to be a movie star or a marine biologist, potential employers tend to put excellent communication skills at the top of their "must have" list.

1. Identify a public figure who, in your opinion, is a good public speaker.

2. In a Word document, explain why it is important for that person to speak well. List the specific qualities (e.g., humor, eye contact) that you think make that person a good public speaker.

3. Next, re-create the following chart. Recalling the last time you gave a presentation in front of a group and using a scale of 1 to 5 (5 being excellent), rate yourself as a public speaker using the guidelines in the chart.

Public Speaking Skills	1 Poor	2 Fair	3 Average	4 Good	5 Excellent
Level of Preparedness (well prepared and confident, last-minute technology check)					
Professional Appearance (appropriate business attire, including proper shoes)					
Effective Vocal Presentation Style (clear and persuasive, paying attention to the pitch of your voice, rate of speech, volume, and correct grammar)					
Appropriate Behavior and Speech (no chewing gum, being careful to avoid fillers such as *um, uh, like*, and *you know*)					
Natural Body Language (good eye contact with the audience, appropriate facial expressions, relaxed posture)					
Note your lowest scores as areas you need to work on as you prepare for your next presentation.					

4. Save your responses in your portfolio on your personal computer or flash drive. The next time you make a presentation, revisit the chart and spend extra time preparing in the areas in which you rated yourself less than "good."

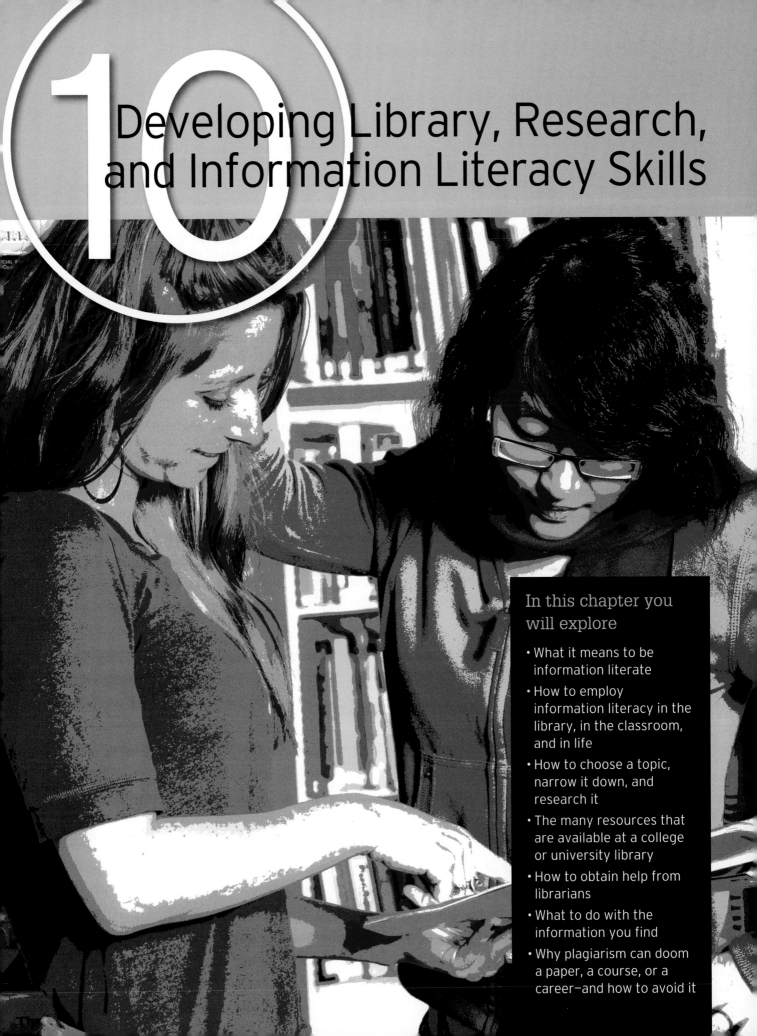

10 Developing Library, Research, and Information Literacy Skills

In this chapter you will explore

- What it means to be information literate
- How to employ information literacy in the library, in the classroom, and in life
- How to choose a topic, narrow it down, and research it
- The many resources that are available at a college or university library
- How to obtain help from librarians
- What to do with the information you find
- Why plagiarism can doom a paper, a course, or a career—and how to avoid it

Which airline or travel service offers the cheapest airfare? Is it

true that certain professors always ask true/false questions? What species of poisonous serpent bit the patient, and which antivenom will work? Which is likely to be more reliable: a Subaru or a Hyundai? What are the relationships between social class and mental illness? At what stress levels will bridge cables snap? How has William Faulkner's fiction influenced contemporary filmmaking? Who steals more from a chain store: customers or employees? What is the best way to shave time from the manufacture and delivery of tractors?

These questions all have something in common. Although some are academic inquiries and others are questions you might ask as part of your job or daily life, they share one important characteristic: The answers to each can be found through research. A doctor would need instant answers for the question about snakebites because a life hangs in the balance. Other situations might not be as critical, but without the ability to find and evaluate information quickly, the world as we know it would eventually fall apart. Research produces discoveries that improve our quality of life.

Developing the skills to locate, analyze, and use information will significantly enhance your ability to keep up with what is going on in the world; to participate in activities that interest you; and to succeed in college, career, and community. The research skills you learn and use as a student will serve you well as a successful professional. That holds true for whatever career path you choose. Whether you're a student of biology, engineering, business, or public relations, your task in college is to manage information for projects and presentations, both oral and written. In a few years, as a lab technician, a project coordinator, a loss prevention specialist, or a campaign manager for a gubernatorial candidate, your task will be the same—to manage and present information for your employers and clients. All colleges and many companies provide libraries for this purpose. But finding and using information involve more than operating a computer or wandering the stacks. To make sense of the vast amount of information at your fingertips in a reasonable amount of time, you'll need to develop a few key research and information literacy skills.

Information Literacy

During the Agricultural Age, most people farmed. Now only a tiny fraction of us work the land, yet edible goods continue to fill our silos and dairy transfer stations and feedlots. During the Industrial Age, we made things. We still do, of course, but automation has made it possible for more goods to be produced by fewer people. Now we live in the Information Age, a name that was created to signify the importance of information in today's economy and our lives.

Most of the global workforce is employed in one way or another in creating, managing, or transferring information. The gross national product (GNP) of the United States is substantially information based. Library science is one of the fastest-growing career opportunities around. Companies such as Google and Yahoo! have earned billions of dollars by simply offering, organizing, and selling information. Put another way, information has value: You can determine its benefits in dollars, and you can compute the cost of not having it.

The challenge is managing it all. There is more information than ever before, and it doubles at rapidly shortening intervals. Because abundance and electronic access combine to produce enormous amounts of retrievable information, people need highly developed **sorting** skills to cope. Information literacy is the premier survival skill for the modern world.

YOUR TURN ▶

Why do you think the chapter states that "Information literacy is the premier survival skill for the modern world"? Do you agree? Why or why not?

What is information literacy? Simply put, it's the ability to find, interpret, and use information to meet your needs. Information literacy has many facets, among them the following:

- **Computer literacy**: Facility with electronic tools, both for conducting inquiries and for presenting to others what you have found and analyzed.
- **Media literacy**: The ability to think critically about material distributed to a wide audience through television, film, advertising, radio, magazines, books, and the Internet.
- **Cultural literacy**: Knowing what has gone on and is going on around you. You have to understand the difference between the Civil War and the Revolutionary War, U2 and YouTube, Eminem and M&Ms, or you will not understand everyday conversation.

Information matters. It helps empower people to make good choices. The choices people make often determine their success in business, their happiness as friends and family members, and their well-being as citizens on this planet.

LEARNING TO BE INFORMATION LITERATE

People marvel at the information explosion, paper inflation, and the Internet. Many confuse mounds of information with knowledge and conclude that they are informed or can easily become informed. But most of us are unprepared for the huge number of available sources and the unsorted, unevaluated mass of information that pours over us at the press of a button. What, then, is the antidote for information overload? To become an informed and successful user of information, keep three basic goals in mind:

1. **Know how to find the information you need.** If you are sick, you need to know whose help to seek. If you lose your scholarship, you need to know where to get financial assistance. If you want to win a lawsuit, you need to know

how to find the outcomes of similar cases. Once you have determined where to look for information, you'll need to ask good questions and to make educated searches of information systems such as the Internet, libraries, and databases. You'll also want to cultivate relationships with information professionals such as librarians, who can help you frame questions, broaden and narrow searches, and retrieve the information you need.

2. **Learn how to interpret the information you find.** It is very important to retrieve information. It is even more important to make sense of that information. What does the information mean? Have you selected a source you can understand? Is the information accurate? Is the source reliable?

3. **Have a purpose.** Even the best information won't do much good if you don't know what to do with it. True, sometimes you'll hunt down a fact simply for your own satisfaction. More often, you'll communicate what you've learned to someone else. You should know not only what form that communication will take—a research paper for a class, a proposal for your boss, a presentation at a hearing—but also what you want to accomplish. Will you use the information to make a decision, develop a new solution to a problem, influence a course of action, prove a point, or something else?

We'll be spending most of this chapter exploring ways to pursue each of these goals.

WHAT'S RESEARCH—AND WHAT'S NOT?

To discover good information that you can use for a given purpose, you'll have to conduct research. You might be working on a college research paper right now—or be anxious about one that's ahead of you. As you contemplate these projects, be sure you understand what research involves.

In the past, you might have completed assignments that asked you to demonstrate how to use a library's electronic book catalog, periodical index, e-mail delivery system, government documents collection, map depository,

and interlibrary loan service. Or you might have been given a subject, such as ethics, and assigned to find a definition or a related book, journal article, or web page. If so, what you accomplished was retrieval. And while retrieving information is an essential element of research, it's not an end in itself.

Nor is research a matter of copying passages or finding a handful of sources and patching together bits and pieces without commentary. In fact, such behavior could easily slip into the category of **plagiarism**, a serious misstep that could result in a failing grade or worse (see p. 177). At the very least, repeating information or ideas without interpreting them puts you at risk of careless use of sources that might be new or old, useful or dangerously in error, reliable or shaky, research based or anecdotal, or objective or biased beyond credibility.

Good research, by contrast, is information literacy in action. Let's take up the ethics topic again. If you were assigned to select and report on an ethics issue, you might pick ethics in politics, accumulate a dozen sources, evaluate them, interpret them, select a few and discard a few, organize the keepers into a coherent arrangement, extract portions that hang together, write a paper or presentation that cites your sources, compose an introduction that explains what you have done, draw some conclusions of your own, and submit the results. That's research. And if you learn to do it well, you'll experience the rush that comes with discovery and the pleasure that accompanies making a statement or taking a stand. The conclusion that you compose on the basis of your research is new information!

EMPLOYING INFORMATION LITERACY SKILLS

By the time you graduate, you should have attained a level of information literacy that will carry you through your professional life. The Association of College and Research Libraries has developed the following best practices for the information-literate student. Learn how to apply them, and you'll do well no matter where your educational and career paths take you.

- **Determine the nature and extent of the information needed.** In general, this information literacy skill involves first defining and articulating what information you need, then identifying a variety of potential sources.
- **Access information effectively and efficiently.** Select the most appropriate research methods, use well-designed search strategies, refine those strategies along the way, and keep organized notes on what you find and where you found it.
- **Evaluate information and its sources critically.** As an information-literate person, you'll be able to apply criteria for judging the usefulness and reliability of both information and its sources. You'll also become skilled at summarizing the main ideas presented by others and comparing new information with what you already know.
- **Incorporate information into your knowledge base and value system.** To incorporate information, you'll determine what information is new, unique, or contradictory and consider whether it has an impact on what's important to you. You'll also validate, understand, or interpret the information through talking with other people. Finally, you'll combine elements of different ideas to construct new concepts of your own making.
- **Use information effectively to accomplish a specific purpose.** You'll apply information to planning and creating a particular product or performance, revising the development process as necessary, and communicating the results to others.
- **Access and use information ethically and legally.** There are economic, legal, and social issues surrounding the retrieval and use of information. You'll need to understand and follow laws, regulations, institutional

policies, and etiquette related to copyright and intellectual property. Most important, you should acknowledge the use of information from sources in everything you write, record, or broadcast.[1]

Choosing, Narrowing, and Researching a Topic

Assignments that require the use of library materials can take many forms and will come in many of your classes. There are numerous ways to search for information to complete an assignment, and we'll consider some of those later in the chapter. Before you start searching, however, you need to have an idea of what you're looking for.

Choosing a topic is often the most difficult part of a research project. Even if an instructor assigns a general topic, you'll need to narrow it down to a particular aspect that interests you enough to make worthwhile the time and energy you'll spend pursuing it. Imagine, for example, that you have been assigned to write a research paper on the topic of political ethics. What steps should you take?

Your first job is to get an overview of your topic. You can begin by looking at general and specific dictionaries and encyclopedias. To learn something about political ethics, for example, you might consult a political dictionary and the *Encyclopedia of American Political History*. Similar broad sources are available for just about any subject area, from marketing to sports psychology to colonial American literature. Check your library's reference area or consult with a librarian for leads.

Once you've acquired some basic information to guide you toward an understanding of the nature of your topic, you have a decision to make: What aspects of the subject will you pursue? Even if you launch the most general of inquiries, you will discover very quickly that your topic is vast and includes many related subtopics. If you look up "political ethics" in the Library of Congress Subject Headings or your library's online catalog, for instance, you will discover some choices:

Civil service, ethics	Judicial ethics
Conflict of interests	Justice
Corporations—corrupt practices	Legislative ethics
Environmental ethics	Political corruption
Ethics, modern	Political ethics
Fairness	Social ethics
Gifts to politicians	

Because the topic is broad, every one of these headings leads to books and articles on political ethics. What you want is a dozen or so focused, highly relevant hits on an aspect of the topic that you can fashion into a coherent, well-organized essay. Begin by assessing what you already know and asking

---

[1]Adapted from *Information Literacy Competency Standards for Higher Education* (2000). http://www.ala.org/ala/acrl/acrlstandards/standards.pdf.

what you would like to learn more about. Perhaps you know a little about the efforts of lobbyists and political action committees to influence legislation, and you're curious about recent efforts to limit what gifts politicians may accept; in that case you might decide on a three-pronged topic—gifts to politicians, political corruption, and lobbyists.

You can follow these steps to focus any topic. By simply consulting a few general sources, you'll find that you can narrow a broad topic to something that interests you and is a manageable size. From reference works and a quick search of a library catalog, periodicals database, or the Internet you will find definitions, introductory materials, some current and historical examples of your topic in action, and related information. You are now ready to launch a purposeful search.

Using the Library

Whenever you have research to do—whether for a class, your job, or your personal life—visit a library. We can't stress this enough. Although the Internet is loaded with billions of pages of information, don't be fooled into thinking it will serve all of your needs. For one thing, you'll have to sort through a lot of junk to find your way to good-quality sources online. More important, if you limit yourself to the Web, you'll miss out on some of the best materials. Although we often think that everything is electronic and can be found through a computer, a great deal of valuable information is still stored in traditional formats and is most easily accessed through a library.

> **YOUR TURN ▶**
>
> Is the library a necessary resource for learning in college? Why or why not?

Every library has books and journals as well a great number of items in electronic databases that aren't available on public Web sites. Most libraries also have several other types of collections such as government documents, microfilm, rare books, manuscripts, dissertations, fine art, photographs, historical documents, maps, and music and films, including archival and documentary productions. Remember that information has been recorded and stored in many forms over the centuries. Libraries maintain materials in whatever form they were first produced and provide access to these materials for free.

TAKING ADVANTAGE OF EVERYTHING YOUR LIBRARY HAS TO OFFER

Books and periodicals are essential, but a college or university library is far more than a document warehouse. For starters, most campus libraries have Web sites that offer lots of help for students. Some provide guidelines on writing research papers, conducting online searches, or navigating the stacks. And all of them provide invaluable services to students and faculty members, including virtual spaces for accessing library holdings and the Web, physical spaces where you can study in quiet or meet with other students, and perhaps even social and entertainment programs.

Of course, no one library can possibly own everything you might need, so groups of libraries share their holdings with each other. If your library does not have a journal or book that looks promising for your project, the interlibrary loan department will be happy to borrow the materials for you. In most cases you can expect to receive the materials in as little as a few days, but it's always a good idea to identify and request what you might need from other libraries as far in advance as possible, in case the material is in high demand.

Are you a commuter or distance education student who cannot easily visit your college library in person? Most libraries provide proxy access to their electronic materials to students off campus. Usually, the library's home page serves as an electronic gateway to its services, which may include the following:

- A searchable catalog of the library's physical holdings
- Electronic databases, some of which let you access the full text of newspaper, magazine, and journal articles from your computer
- Interlibrary loan requests
- Course reserve readings
- Downloadable e-books
- Indexes of Web sites that have been carefully screened for reliability and relevance to particular subject areas
- Online chats with librarians who can help you in real time

To learn more, poke around your library's Web site, or e-mail or phone the reference desk.

Libraries also have a wide variety of physical spaces for students and faculty members to use. From individual study tables to private group rooms to comfortable chairs tucked in quiet corners, you should be able to find a study area that suits you and your needs. You might also discover places to eat, socialize, take in a movie or an art exhibit, check your e-mail and social networking page, search the Web, type your papers, make photocopies, edit videos, give presentations, hold meetings, or take a much-needed nap.

Be sure to use the handouts and guides that are available at the reference desk or online. You will also find tutorials and virtual tours that will help you become familiar with the collections, services, and spaces available at your library.

ASKING A LIBRARIAN

Of all the resources available in a library, the most useful—and often the least used—are the people who staff it. Librarians thrive on helping you. If you're not sure how to start a search, if you're not successful in your first attempts at retrieving information, or if you just need some ideas about what you might try as you pursue a research project, ask a librarian. Librarians are information experts who are trained to assist and guide you to the resources you need. The librarians who work in the reference area or supervise the computer stations might look busy. But they are busy helping people with projects much like yours. You are not interrupting when you ask for assistance, and with rare exceptions, any librarian will be delighted to help you.

You can contact a reference librarian in several ways. E-mail a query, and you are likely to receive a quick reply. Or call the reference desk to ask a question, such as "Do you have a copy of the report *Problems with the Presidential Gifts System*?" You can have a "live chat" online with a library staffer in real time. And of course, you can visit the reference desk in person or make an appointment for a tutorial or consultation. (Hint: You will be most successful if you bring a copy of your assignment and any written instructions you have to your meeting. Tell the librarian what you have tried—if anything.) Remember that there are no silly questions. A good librarian will treat your inquiries with respect.

The information professionals at your library are authorities on how to find information. Most important, they not only know where to find it, but also have the wonderful ability to help you use information to meet your needs, solve problems, provide explanations, open up new possibilities, and ultimately create new knowledge.

Electronic Resources

Online catalogs, periodical databases, and the World Wide Web allow you to quickly and easily locate materials in the vast universe of information. Learning how to use these resources efficiently will save you time and improve your odds of finding the information that best suits your needs.

LIBRARY CATALOGS

The card catalogs that were once common in libraries have been replaced by OPAC (online public access catalogs). These electronic catalogs tell you what books, magazines, newspapers, videos, and other materials are available in a particular library. They might also provide abstracts of the information presented in those materials, tables of contents for individual entries, and related search terms. Typically, they'll provide an identifying number that tells you where in the stacks to locate a particular document. A catalog might also inform you whether an item is already checked out and, if so, when it's due back. The catalog will also allow you to put the material on hold or give you the option of requesting it through interlibrary loan.

You can search the catalogs through terminals at the library or from your home computer or a laptop. The simplest way to search a catalog is by key word (see the guidelines for conducting an effective search on p. 172). You might also search by subject, author, title, date, or a combination of these elements. Be sure to spend a few minutes on the catalog's help or FAQ page, which will guide you through the options and demonstrate ways to customize your search terms. Each system has its own preferences.

PERIODICAL DATABASES

A library catalog helps you search for books and the titles of magazines and journals owned by a particular library. By contrast, periodical databases let you hunt down articles published in hundreds (even thousands) of newspapers, magazines, and scholarly journals. Some databases might provide a full-text copy of the article as part of the record returned from your search; other times you'll have to use the information in the record to find a physical copy in your library or request it through interlibrary loan.

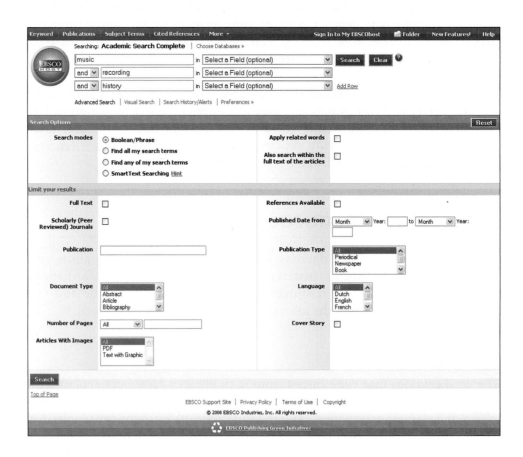

Subscription services such as EBSCO*host*, LexisNexis, and Gale Research compile and maintain electronic periodical databases. These databases are not free to the general public and must be accessed through a library. (Ask at the circulation desk for a barcode number and PIN, which will allow you to access your library's databases from remote terminals.) Most libraries subscribe to multiple databases and subdivide them by broad general categories such as Humanities, Social Sciences, Science and Technology, Business, Health and Medicine, Government Information, or by major. Under "Social Sciences," for example, you might find International Political Science Abstracts (PAIS), America: History and Life, and over twenty other databases. There are also multidisciplinary databases, such as Academic Search Premier, InfoTrac, and Reader's Guide to Periodical Literature, that provide excellent material on most topics you will encounter during your first years of college.

Databases have their own specialties and different strengths, so you'll want to select the best ones for your particular subject or topic. Check your library's subscription list for an overview of what's available, and don't hesitate to ask a librarian to make recommendations about which databases are most relevant to your needs.

Information in a database is usually stored in a single location or on a server that is owned by the subscription service company. Human beings, not computers, do the indexing, so you can be fairly sure the information in a database meets certain criteria for inclusion, such as accuracy, timeliness, and authoritativeness. And because most of the material indexed in a database originally appeared in print, you can be fairly certain that it was reviewed for quality by other scholars or an editorial staff.

THE WORLD WIDE WEB

Searching the Web is a totally different story. The material retrieved by Googling is an aggregation of information, opinion, and sales pitches from the vast universe of servers around the globe. Anybody can put up a Web site, which means you can't be sure of the Web site owner's credibility and reliability. The sources you find on the Web might be written by anyone—a fifth grader, a distinguished professor, a professional society, or a biased advocate.

A recent Google search on the subject "political corruption," for instance, generated over 10 million hits. The first page yielded some interesting results:

A collection of links on politics and political corruption

A Libertarian Party legislative program on political corruption

Two Amazon.com ads

A site that offers "research" on gambling and political corruption

A university site offering research on political corruption in Illinois

These varied results demonstrate that one must be alert when examining Internet sources. Mixed in with credible scholarship on this topic are sales promotions, some arguments against gambling, and useful links to other sources. It isn't always easy to evaluate the quality of Internet sources. Check pages 173–75 in this chapter for some helpful strategies you can use to determine whether a source is credible and authentic.

GUIDELINES FOR EFFECTIVE SEARCHES

Most searches of catalogs and databases are done by using key words. A key word is a single word that would appear in a discussion of the topic you are investigating. Other systems permit searching of phrases. A few databases and web search engines allow a natural language search, in which you can ask a question or type in a sentence that describes what you are looking for. Some databases, such as the *New York Times* Index and ERIC (Education Resources Information Center), have their own approved lists of subject terms that you should consult before searching. Be careful to choose search terms that are relevant to your investigation; this practice will help you retrieve material you can use. A librarian can help you with your search.

To become a successful and savvy user of electronic resources, follow these guidelines:

- **Consult the Help or FAQs link** the first time you use any catalog, database, or search engine to learn specific searching techniques. You will get the best results if you use the tips and strategies suggested by the database provider.

- **Write out your topic or problem as a statement or question.** "Is it right for politicians to take gifts from lobbyists?" Or "The influence of lobbyists or PACs has dramatically changed American political ethics." Doing so will help you identify potentially useful key words.

- **Understand Boolean operators.** Boolean operators are the words *and*, *or*, and *not*. The Bowling Green State University Library Web site describes these terms this way:

    A search for rock AND roll will locate all records containing both the word *rock* and the word *roll*. It will locate items about rock and roll music. It might also locate records that contain both words in a different context, such as "It recommends you roll the rock quickly."

    A search for rock OR roll will locate all records containing either the word *rock* or the word *roll*–not necessarily both. It will retrieve items about bakery rolls, tumbling, rocks, music, gemstones, etc.

    A search for rock NOT roll will locate records containing the word *rock* but NOT the word *roll*. It will retrieve items about rocks, gemstones, diamonds, etc.[2]

- **Write down several terms or synonyms for your topic.** If one search does not yield any useful hits, you have some backup terms on hand. It's also a good idea to search more than one database or engine; different ones might pull up dramatically different sources.

- **Limit your search.** You can often limit a search by date, language, journal name, full text, or word(s) in title. If you still get too many hits, add more search terms.

- **Expand your search.** If you get too few hits, omit a search term. You can also truncate a word by using an asterisk to retrieve broader results. For instance, *lobby** will search for "lobby," "lobbying," "lobbyist," and "lobbyists."

[2]http://www.bgsu.edu/colleges/library/infosrv/lue/boolean.html.

- **Learn the quirks of the databases or search engines you use often.** Some yield better results from Boolean operators (e.g., "politicians AND lobbyists"); others are more attuned to natural language searches (e.g., "ethics in politics" or "gifts to politicians").
- **Check your library's electronic resources page.** Most libraries have links to other commonly used electronic reference tools. These reference tools include online encyclopedias, dictionaries, almanacs, style guides, biographical and statistical resources, and news sources.

YOUR TURN ▶

Talk to a faculty member, a parent, or an older friend who went to college. Ask them how they conducted research before the Internet. Write a short review of the strategies used by former generations to access and use information.

Evaluating Sources

It's easy to assume that huge amounts of available information automatically provide knowledge. Some students might at first be excited about receiving 20,800,000 hits from a Google search on political ethics, but shock takes hold when they realize their discovery is utterly unsorted. They might respond by using only the first several hits, irrespective of quality. A more productive approach is to think critically about the usefulness of potential sources by measuring them against three important criteria: relevance, authority, and bias.

YOUR TURN ▶

How do you find sources for an important paper? Do you go to the first several hits on Google, or do you use a more deliberate process? What strategies can you use to make sure your Internet or library research results in valid information?

RELEVANCE

The first thing to consider in looking at a possible source is how well it fits your needs. That, in turn, will be affected by the nature of your research project and the kind of information you are seeking.

- **Is it introductory?** Introductory information is very basic and elementary. It neither assumes nor requires prior knowledge about the topic. Introductory sources can be useful when you're first learning about a subject. They are less useful when you're drawing conclusions about a particular aspect of the subject.
- **Is it definitional?** Definitional information provides some descriptive details about a subject. It might help you introduce a topic to others or clarify the focus of your investigation.
- **Is it analytical?** Analytical information supplies and interprets data about origins, behaviors, differences, and uses. In most cases it's the kind of information you want.

- **Is it comprehensive?** The more detail, the better. Avoid unsubstantiated opinions, and look instead for sources that consider the topic in depth and offer plenty of evidence to support their conclusions.
- **Is it current?** You should usually give preference to recent sources, although older ones can sometimes be useful (for instance, if your subject is historical or the source is still cited by others in a field).
- **Can you conclude anything from it?** Use the "so what?" test: How important is this information? Why does it matter to my project?

AUTHORITY

Once you have determined that a source is relevant to your project, check that it was created by somebody who has the qualifications to write or speak on the subject. This, too, will depend on your subject and the nature of your inquiry (a fifth grader's opinion might be exactly what you're looking for), but in most cases you'll want expert conclusions based on rigorous evidence.

Make sure you can identify the author and be ready to explain why that author is a reliable source. Good qualifications might include academic degrees, institutional affiliations, an established record of researching and publishing on a topic, or personal experience with a subject. Be wary, on the other hand, of anonymous or commercial sources or those written by someone whose credibility is questionable.

Understand, as well, whether your project calls for scholarly publications, popular magazines, or both. Do you know the difference?

You don't necessarily have to dismiss popular magazines. Many journalists and columnists are extremely well qualified, and their work might well be appropriate for your needs. But as a rule scholarly sources will be more credible.

Scholarly Journals	Popular Magazines
Long articles	Shorter articles
In-depth information on topic	Broad overview of topic
Written by academic experts	Written by journalists or reporters
Graphs, tables, and charts	Photos of people and events
Articles "refereed" or reviewed	Articles not rigidly evaluated
Formally documented	Sources credited informally

BIAS

When you are searching for sources, you should realize that there can be a heavy dose of bias or point of view in some of them. Although nothing is inherently wrong with someone's having a particular point of view, it is dangerous for a reader not to know that the bias is there. A great source for keeping you informed about potential bias is *Magazines for Libraries*,[3] which will tell you about a periodical's editorial and political leanings. *The*

[3]Cheryl LaGuardia, Bill Katz, and Linda S. Katz, *Magazines for Libraries*, 13th ed. (New Providence, NJ: RR Bowker LC, 2004).

Nation, for instance, is generally considered liberal, while *National Review* is conservative.

Some signs of bias indicate that you should avoid using a source. If you detect overly positive or overly harsh language, hints of an agenda, or a stubborn refusal to consider other points of view, think carefully about how well you can trust the information in a document.

YOUR TURN ▶

In your opinion, what newspapers, magazines, or TV networks are biased? Does a biased point of view make you more or less likely to read or watch? Why do you think many people expose themselves only to opinions or viewpoints like their own?

A NOTE ON INTERNET SOURCES

Be especially cautious of material you find online. It is often difficult to tell where something on the Internet came from or who wrote it. The lack of this information can make it very difficult to judge the credibility of the source. And while an editorial board reviews most print matter (books, articles, and so forth) for accuracy and overall quality, it's frequently difficult to confirm that the same is true for information on a Web site—with some exceptions. If you are searching through an online database such as the Human Genome Database or Eldis: The Gateway to Development Information (a poverty database), it is highly likely that documents in these collections have been reviewed. Online versions of print magazines and journals, likewise, have usually been checked out by editors. And information from academic and government Web sites (those whose URLs end in .edu or .gov, respectively) is generally—but not always—trustworthy.

YOUR TURN ▶

One of the most frequently visited sites on the Web is Wikipedia, a collaborative reference work written and maintained by hundreds of volunteers. Most of its articles can be (and have been) edited by anyone with Internet access. What are the pros and cons of using such a site as a source for a research project?

Making Use of What You Find

You have probably heard the saying "Knowledge is power." While knowledge can certainly contribute to power, this is true only if that knowledge is put to use. When you retrieve, sort, interpret, analyze, and synthesize sources from an information center, whether it is the library, a computer database, or the Web, you can produce a product that has power.

But first, you have to decide what form that product will take and what kind of power you want it to hold. Who are you going to tell about your discoveries, and how? What do you hope to accomplish by sharing your conclusions? Remember that a major goal of information literacy is to use information effectively to accomplish a specific purpose. Make it a point to *do* something with the results of your research. Otherwise, why bother?

SYNTHESIZING INFORMATION AND IDEAS

Ultimately, the point of conducting research is that the process contributes to the development of new knowledge. As a researcher, you sought the answer to a question. Now is the time to formulate that answer and share it.

Many students satisfy themselves with a straightforward report that merely summarizes what they found. Sometimes, that's enough. More often, however, you'll want to apply the information to ideas of your own. To do that, first consider all of the information you found and how your sources relate to each other. What do they have in common, and where do they disagree? What conclusions can you draw from those similarities and differences? What new ideas did they spark? How can you use the information you have on hand to support your conclusions? (Refer to Chapter 5 for tips on drawing conclusions from different points of view and using evidence to construct an argument.)

Essentially, what you're doing at this stage of any research project is processing information, an activity known as **synthesis**. By accepting some ideas, rejecting others, combining related concepts, assessing the implications, and pulling it all together, you'll create new information and ideas that other people can use.

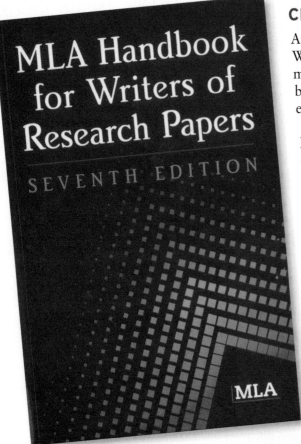

CITING YOUR SOURCES

At some point you'll present your findings. Whether they take the form of an essay, a formal research paper, a script for a presentation or broadcast, a page for a Web site, or something else entirely, you must give credit to your sources.

Citing your sources serves many purposes. For one thing, acknowledging the information and ideas you've borrowed from other writers shows respect for their contributions; it also distinguishes between other writers' ideas and your own. Source citations demonstrate to your audience that you have based your conclusions on thoughtful consideration of good, reliable evidence. Source citations also provide a starting place for anyone who would like more information or is curious about how you reached your conclusions. Most important, citing your sources is the simplest way to avoid plagiarism.

The particular requirements of source citation can get complicated, but it all boils down to two basic rules. As you write, just remember:

- If you use somebody else's exact words, you must give that person credit.
- If you use somebody else's ideas, even if you use your own words to express those ideas, you must give that person credit.

Your instructors will indicate their preferred method for citation: footnotes, references in parentheses included in the text of your paper, or endnotes. If you're not provided with guidelines or if you simply want to be sure that you do it right, consult the most recent edition of a handbook or writing style manual, such as those prepared by the Modern Language Association (*MLA Handbook for Writers of Research Papers*), the American Psychological Association (*Publication Manual of the American Psychological Association*), the University of Chicago Press (*The Chicago Manual of Style*), or the Council of Science Editors (*Scientific Style and Format: The CSE Manual for Authors, Editors, and Publishers*).

ABOUT PLAGIARISM

Several years ago, a serious candidate for the American presidency was forced to withdraw from the race when opponents discovered he had failed to give proper credit to a source he used in one of his speeches. A reporter at a top

Wired WINDOW

PLAGIARISM IN THE DIGITAL AGE

Since the early days of the Internet, professors have seen a rise in plagiarism. In some high schools, the concept of plagiarism is rarely explained, and students might arrive at college with an incomplete understanding of how to cite other people's work. The Internet makes it easier for students to "cut and paste" text and pass that work off as their own—a practice that is considered unethical and, at some institutions, grounds for dismissal. With the advent of new technologies, it is becoming easier to catch students who plagiarize. Some colleges and universities use a Web site called TurnItIn.com, where a student's paper can be uploaded. TurnItIn.com automatically checks the paper against a large database of student papers and against the Web. (It's like doing a Google search on every paper ever written and on the Internet at the same time.) The Web site then provides instructors with an originality report for each student. The professor can then review the originality report to determine whether the student's paper was original. If TurnItIn.com finds a portion of the student's paper that matches something in its database, the portion that matches will be displayed along with the corresponding original work. Remember that most colleges, universities, and professors will not distinguish between deliberately plagiarizing and plagiarizing out of carelessness or because of a lack of understanding about what constitutes plagiarism.

Thinking Critically

Why do higher education institutions take plagiarism so seriously? What are some ways in which you can avoid plagiarizing information that you've found online? Do you think that using a service such as TurnItIn.com is a good idea? Why or why not? How would you feel if you were a faculty member who received a plagiarized paper from a student? How would you handle the situation?

newspaper was fired for deliberately faking his sources, and a famous historian lost her peers' respect (and a portion of her royalties) when another writer noticed that the historian had included passages from her work in a book without citation.

All three writers were accused of plagiarism, but notice that only the reporter plagiarized on purpose. The political candidate and the historian were probably more guilty of poor note-taking than of outright fraud, yet the consequences were just as dire. When information or ideas are put on paper, film, screen, or tape, they become intellectual property. Using those ideas without saying where you got them—even if you do this by mistake—is a form of theft and can cost you a grade, a course, a degree, maybe even a career.

It should go without saying (but we'll say it anyway) that deliberate cheating is a bad idea on many levels. Submitting a paper you purchased from an Internet source or from an individual will cause you to miss out on the discovery and skill development that research assignments are meant to teach. Intentional plagiarism is easily detected and will almost certainly earn you a failing grade, even expulsion.

Although most cases of plagiarism are the result of misunderstanding or carelessness, be aware that "I didn't know" is not a valid excuse. Although your instructors might acknowledge that plagiarism can be an "oops!" thing, they will still expect you to avoid errors, and they will call you on it if you don't. Luckily, plagiarism is relatively easy to avoid. Most important, always cite your sources. Keep careful notes as you conduct your research so that later on you don't inadvertently mistake someone else's words or ideas for your own. Finally, be sure to check out your own campus's definition of what constitutes plagiarism, which you will find in the student handbook or in first-year English course materials. And if you have any questions or doubts about what is and isn't acceptable, ask.

Where to go FOR HELP . . .

ON CAMPUS ▶

Your Instructor Be sure to ask your instructor for help with your information search, especially if you need to narrow your topic.

Library Libraries offer a variety of forms of help, including library orientation sessions, workshops, and, on some campuses, credit-bearing courses to develop your library search and retrieval skills.

Specialized Libraries/Collections At a large university, it is very common to find multiple libraries that are part of separate schools or colleges. For example, if you are a business administration major at such a university, there will probably be a separate business library that you will need to learn to use in addition to the central library. This is true for many majors.

Technology Support Centers Many campuses have units staffed by personnel who are responsible for the institution's entire technology infrastructure. These units frequently offer noncredit workshops and help sessions. In addition, many of the departments in larger universities will have their own separate technology labs and centers where you can work and get assistance. It won't surprise you to find that much of the help provided to students comes from fellow students, who are often ahead of their faculty in these skills. Some campuses also provide such assistance in residence halls, where there might even be a "computing assistant" in addition to the resident assistant.

Discipline-Based Courses Many academic majors will include specialized courses in discipline-based research methods. You will find these listed in your campus catalog or bulletin. Students don't usually take these courses in their first year, but check them

out. If you are interested in credit courses dealing with technology, check out the courses in computer science.

ONLINE ▶

Research and documenting sources: http://owl .english.purdue.edu/owl/resource/584/02. This Purdue University link is an excellent resource for documenting sources, both print and electronic.

MY INSTITUTION'S RESOURCES ▶

_____

_____

_____

_____

_____

_____

_____

_____

_____

_____

_____

_____

_____

_____

_____

Applying What You've LEARNED . . .

Now that you have read and discussed this chapter, consider how you can apply what you have learned to your academic and personal life. The following prompts will help you reflect on chapter material and its relevance to you both now and in the future.

1. It is important to get comfortable with all of the resources in your campus library. Find out where your library keeps archived newspapers on microfiche. Search for a newspaper (such as the *New York Times*) that was published on the day you were born. What was the major headline that day? What movies were playing? What was happening in world news?

2. Using information literacy skills in college is a no-brainer, but think beyond your college experience. How will improving your information literacy skills help you once you are out of college? Think of a career that you are interested in, and describe how you might use those skills in that career.

One-Minute PAPER . . .

Did the material in this chapter make you think about libraries and research in a new light? What did you find to be the most useful information in this chapter? What would you like to learn more about?

Building Your PORTFOLIO . . .

IN THE KNOW

Reviewing multiple sources of information can help you get the whole story. This is especially important when using the Internet as a research tool. While the Internet is becoming a primary source of worldwide news, there is no overarching quality control system for information posted on the Internet. Regardless of where you are gathering your information, you need to read with a discerning eye to make sure the source is credible.

1. Choose a national current event. Carefully read about it
   a. On your favorite news Web site (e.g., http://www.cnn.com).
   b. In a traditional national newspaper (e.g., the *New York Times, Wall Street Journal, Christian Science Monitor*, or *USA Today*). Your campus library or local community library will have these national newspapers or you can find them on the Web.

2. In a Word document, compare and contrast the differences in the way the event was portrayed by the two sources.

- Is the author's name or another source provided?
- Are there clues that the author(s) are taking a biased stand in reporting? If so, describe these clues.
- Whom do you think the authors were writing for (intended audience)? For example, were they writing for any reader, or for people of a certain age or educational level?

- Were the facts presented the same way by both the Internet source and the print source? Explain your answer.

- Did one source cover more details than the other? If so, explain your answer.

- Were the writer's information sources listed? If so, what were those sources?

3. Save your responses in your portfolio on your personal computer or flash drive. Use this process as a tool to make sure you use valid resources the next time you are doing research for a project or a paper.

11 Appreciating Diversity

In this chapter you will explore

- The value of living in a diverse nation
- The concepts of culture, ethnicity, race, age, sexual orientation, physical ability, and gender as they relate to diversity
- The value of gaining knowledge about various groups
- The role colleges play in promoting diversity
- How to identify and cope with discrimination and prejudice on campus

At the core of this country's value system is the belief that the United States of America is a place where all people are welcome. This principle has created a richly diverse society that emphasizes the importance of retaining individual cultural identity while living among others. Ethnic and cultural communities throughout the United States are preserving components of their particular heritage as they join other cultures to create a nation that is more diverse than any other in the world. Throughout our history, as this country has moved toward the Constitution's goal of achieving "a more perfect union," diversity has been both a source of conflict and a national strength. The 2008 presidential campaign marked the first time in history that a woman, Hillary Rodham Clinton, nearly became the presidential nominee of a major political party, and the first time an African-American, Barack Obama, was elected as president of the United States.

A college or university serves as a microcosm of the real world—a world that requires us all to work, live, and socialize with people from various ethnic and cultural groups. In few settings do members of ethnic and cultural groups interact in such close proximity to one another as they do on a college campus. Whether you are attending a four-year university or a community college, you will be exposed to new experiences and opportunities, all of which can enhance learning and a deeper sense of understanding.

Through self-assessment, discovery, and open-mindedness, you can begin to understand your perspectives on diversity. This work, although difficult at times, will intensify your educational experiences, personal growth, and development. Thinking critically about your personal values and belief systems will allow you to have a greater sense of belonging and to make a positive contribution to our multicultural society.

YOUR TURN ▶

If you broadly define the term *diversity* as differences in race, gender, ethnicity, religion, political preference, and the like, is your college or university more or less diverse than your high school?

Understanding Diversity and the Source of Our Beliefs

Diversity is the variation in social and cultural identities among people living together. **Multiculturalism** is the active process of acknowledging and respecting social groups, cultures, religions, races, ethnicities, attitudes, and opinions. As your journey through higher education unfolds, you will find yourself immersed in this mixture of identities. Regardless of the size of the institution, going to college brings together people who have differing backgrounds and experiences but similar goals and aspirations. Each person brings to campus a unique combination of life story, upbringing, value system, view of the world, and set of judgments. Familiarizing yourself with such differ-

ences can greatly enhance your experiences in the classes you will take, the organizations you will join, and the relationships you will cultivate. For many students college is the first time they have been exposed to so much diversity. Learning experiences and challenges await you both in and out of the classroom. College provides opportunities to learn not only about others but also about yourself.

Many of our beliefs grow out of personal experience and reinforcement. If you have had a negative experience or endured a series of incidents involving members of a particular group, you're more likely to develop **stereotypes**, or negative judgments, about people in that group. Or maybe you have heard repeatedly that everyone associated with a particular group behaves in a certain way, and you might have bought into that stereotype without even thinking about it. Children who grow up in an environment in which dislike and distrust of certain types of people are openly expressed might subscribe to those very judgments even if they have had no direct interaction with those being judged.

In college you might encounter beliefs about diversity that run counter to your basic values. When your friendships with others are affected by differing values, tolerance is generally a good goal. Talking about diversity with someone else whose beliefs seem to be in conflict with your own can be very rewarding. Your goal in this kind of discussion is not to reach agreement, but to enhance your understanding of why people see diversity differently—why some seem to flee from it and others allow experiences with diversity to enrich their college experience.

Before coming to college, you might never have coexisted with most of the groups you now see on campus. Your home community might not have been very diverse, although possibly it seemed so before you reached campus. In college you have the opportunity to learn from many kinds of people.

From your roommate in the residence hall to your lab partner in your biology class to the members of your sociology study group, your college experience will be enriched if you allow yourself to be open to the possibility of learning from members of all cultural groups.

YOUR TURN ▶

Write about any specific lessons you learned in your family about the expectations you should have of diverse groups.

Forms of Diversity

When you think about diversity, you might first think of differences in race or ethnicity. While it is true that those are two forms of diversity, there are many other types of diversity that you will most likely experience in college and in the workplace, including age, religion, physical ability, gender, and sexual orientation.

ETHNICITY, CULTURE, RACE, AND RELIGION

Often, the terms *ethnicity* and *culture* are used interchangeably, although their definitions are quite distinct. Throughout this chapter we will use these two words together and in isolation. Before we start using the terms, it's a good idea to learn their definitions so that you're clear on what they actually mean.

Ethnicity refers to the identity that is assigned to a specific group of people who are historically connected by a common national origin or language. For example, let's look at one of the largest ethnic groups: Latinos. Latin America encompasses over thirty countries within North, Central, and South America, all of which share the Spanish language. A notable exception is Brazil. However, although the national language is Portuguese, Brazilians are considered Latinos (both Spanish and Portuguese are languages that evolved from Latin). The countries also share many traditions and beliefs, with some variations. However, we shouldn't generalize. Not every Latino who speaks Spanish is of Mexican descent, and not every Latino speaks Spanish. Acknowledging that differences exist within ethnic groups is a big step in becoming ethnically aware.

Culture is defined as those aspects of a group of people that are passed on and/or learned. Traditions, food, language, clothing styles, artistic expression, and beliefs are all part of culture. Certainly, ethnic groups are also cultural groups: They share a language, foods, traditions, art, and clothing, which are passed from one generation to the next. But numerous other, nonethnic cultural groups can fit this concept of culture, too. Think of the hip-hop community, in which a common style of dress, specific terminology, and distinct forms of musical and artistic expression also constitute a culture but not an ethnicity.

Although we don't use the term **race** much in this chapter, it's important to understand this word as it is commonly used in everyday language. Race is often used to refer to biological characteristics that are shared by groups of people, including skin tone, hair texture and color, and facial features.

Making generalizations about someone's racial group affiliation is risky. Even people who share some biological features—such as similar eye shape or dark skin—might be ethnically very distinct. For instance, people of Asian descent are not necessarily ethnically and culturally alike, since Asia is a vast region encompassing such disparate places as Mongolia, India, and Japan. Likewise, people of African descent come from very different backgrounds; the African continent is home to fifty-three countries and hundreds of different languages, and Africans are genetically very diverse. More and more individuals today, including President Obama, often describe themselves as multiracial. You might meet fellow students whose families include parents, grandparents, and great-grandparents of several different racial groups.

All of us come into the world with our own unique characteristics—aspects of our physical appearance and personalities that make us who we are. But people around the world have one attribute in common: We want to be respected even if we are different from others in some ways. Whatever the color of your skin or hair, whatever your life experiences or cultural background, you will want others to treat you fairly and acknowledge and value your contribution to your communities and the world. And, of course, others will want the same from you.

Diversity of **religion** has been central to the American experience since our colonial origins. In fact, many settlers of the original thirteen colonies came to North America to escape religious persecution. Religious diversity might or might not have been obvious in your hometown or neighborhood, but unless you are attending an institution that enrolls only students of one religious sect, you will find religious diversity to be part of your college experience. Religious denominations might sponsor campus centers or organizations, and students' religious affiliations might determine their dress, attitudes, or avoidance of certain behaviors. While you are in college, your openness to religious diversity will add to your understanding of the many ways in which people are different from one another.

AGE

Although many students enter college around age 18, others choose to enter or return in their thirties and beyond. In the fall of 2006, over 37 percent of American college students were 25 years of age or older. Age diversity in the classroom gives everyone the opportunity to learn from others who have different life experiences. All kinds of factors determine when students enter higher education for the first time or stop and then reenter. Therefore there is no such thing as "the norm" in considering the age of college students. If you are attending a college that has a large number of students who are older (or younger) than you, strive to see this as an advantage for learning. A campus where younger and older students learn together can be much more interesting than a campus where everyone is about the same age.

YOUR TURN ▶

Other than your grandparents, do you know people who are significantly older than you? If so, what has been the nature of your interaction and your relationship? If not, how might you meet some older people on campus or in your community?

LEARNING AND PHYSICAL ABILITIES

Although the majority of students have reasonably average learning and physical abilities, the numbers of students with physical and learning disabilities are rising on most college campuses, as are the services that are available to them. Physical disabilities can include deafness, blindness, paralysis, or a mental disorder. Also, many students have some form of learning disability (see Chapter 4) that makes college work a challenge.

People who have physical and learning disabilities want to be treated just as you would treat anyone else—with respect. If a student with a disability is in your class, treat him or her as you would any student; your overzealousness to help might be seen as an expression of pity.

If you have, or think you might have, a learning disability, consult your campus learning center for a diagnosis and advice on compensating for learning problems. Most campuses have a special office to serve students with both physical and learning disabilities.

GENDER

A basic example of diversity is gender. But other than the obvious physical differences, are men and women really that different? Or do we believe they are because of our own biases?

While you're in college, make friends with people of both genders, avoid stereotyping what is "appropriate" for one group or another, and don't limit your own interests. In today's world, there is almost no activity or profession that isn't open to everyone, regardless of gender. If your college or university has a Gender Studies department, consider taking a course in this area. Gender studies courses are generally interdisciplinary and look at the subject matter from the perspective of gender. Such a course could open up new ways of thinking about many aspects of your world.

YOUR TURN ▶

Can you remember any time in your life when you gave up a dream because you thought it was "inappropriate" for someone of your gender? Can you remember a time when you assumed you wouldn't be good at an activity, a sport, or a course because of your gender? What advice could you give to other students about not letting their gender narrow their range of life options?

SEXUAL ORIENTATION

In college you will likely meet students, staff members, and professors who are homosexual or bisexual. Because most colleges and universities openly accept gay, lesbian, bisexual, or transgendered people, many individuals who were in the closet in high school will come out in the collegiate environment. The subject of sexual orientation is highly personal and often emotionally charged, but whatever your own personal sexual orientation, it is important that you respect all individuals with whom you come in contact. Most colleges and universities have campus codes or standards of behavior that do not permit acts of harassment or discrimination based on race, ethnicity, gender, or sexual orientation.

Seeking Diversity on Campus

Acknowledging the importance of diversity to education, colleges and universities have begun to take the concepts of diversity and apply them to student learning opportunities. We see this in efforts by colleges to embrace an **inclusive curriculum**. Today, you can find courses with a diversity focus in many departments of your college or university, such as Black Studies, Asian Studies, Latino or Hispanic Studies, Women's Studies, Gay and Lesbian Studies, and Religious Studies. Many of the courses in these departments meet graduation requirements. The college setting is ideal for promoting education about diversity because it allows students and faculty of varying backgrounds to come together for the common purpose of learning and critical thinking.

According to Gloria Ameny-Dixon, education about diversity can do the following:

- Increase problem-solving skills through different perspectives applied to reaching solutions
- Increase positive relationships through the achievement of common goals, respect, appreciation, and commitment to equality
- Decrease stereotyping and prejudice through contact and interaction with diverse individuals
- Promote the development of a more in-depth view of the world[1]

Be it religious affiliation, sexual orientation, gender, ethnicity, age, culture, or ability, your campus provides the opportunity to interact with and learn alongside a kaleidoscope of individuals.

[1]Gloria M. Ameny-Dixon, "Why Multicultural Education Is More Important in Higher Education Now Than Ever: A Global Perspective." McNeese State University (http://www.nationalforum.com).

THE CURRICULUM

College students have led the movement for a curriculum that reflects disenfranchised groups such as women, people of color, the elderly, the disabled, gays, lesbians, bisexuals, and the transgendered. By protesting, walking out of classes, and staging sit-ins at the offices of campus officials, students have demanded the hiring of more faculty members from different ethnic groups, the creation of Ethnic Studies departments, and a variety of initiatives designed to support diverse students academically and socially. These initiatives have increased academic access for students from ethnic and cultural groups and have helped them stay in school. They exist today in the form of multicultural centers, women's resource centers, enabling services, and numerous academic support programs. The movement for **multiculturalism** in education has continued to gain momentum since it began during the civil rights era of the 1960s. By expressing their discontent over the lack of access and representation in many of society's niches, including higher education, ethnic and cultural groups have achieved acknowledgment of their presence on campus.

In almost all colleges and universities, you will be required to take some general education courses. The purpose of these courses is to expose you to a wide range of topics and issues so that you can develop and learn to express your own views. We hope you will include a course or two with a multicultural basis in your schedule. Such courses can provide you with new perspectives and an understanding of issues that affect your fellow students and community members—and affect you, too, possibly in ways you had not considered. And just as your college or university campus is diverse, so, too, is the workforce you will be entering. A multicultural education can improve the quality of your entire life.

STUDENT-RUN ORGANIZATIONS

Student-run organizations can provide multiple avenues to express ideas, pursue interests, and cultivate relationships. According to our definition of culture, all student-run organizations are culturally based and provide an outlet for the promotion and celebration of a culture. Let's take, for instance, two very different student groups, a Muslim Student Union and an Animation Club, and apply the components of culture to them. Both groups promote a belief system that is common among their members: The first is based on religious beliefs, and the second is based on ideas about what constitutes animation as an art form. Both have aspects that can be taught and passed on: the teachings of the Muslim faith and the rules and techniques used in drawing. Both groups utilize language that is specific to the belief system of the group. Most campus organizations bring like-minded students together and are open to anyone who wants to become involved.

To promote learning and discovery not only inside the classroom but outside as well, colleges and universities provide programming that highlights ethnic and cultural celebrations, such as Chinese New Year and Kwanzaa; gender-related topics, such as Take Back the Night; and a broad range of entertainment, including concerts and art exhibits. These events

Seeking Diversity on Campus   **191**

expose you to new and exciting ideas and viewpoints, enhancing your education and challenging your current views.

Most college students, especially first-year students, are seeking their own niche and their own identity. Many have found that becoming involved in campus organizations eases the transition and helps them make connections with their fellow students.

FRATERNITIES AND SORORITIES

Fraternities and sororities provide a quick connection to a large number of individuals—a link to the social pipeline, camaraderie, and support. Fraternities and sororities differ in their philosophies and commitment to philanthropy. Some are committed to community service; others are more socially oriented. Fraternities and sororities created by and for specific ethnic groups have existed for years and were developed by students of color who felt the need for campus groups that allowed them to connect to their communities and cultures. Nu Alpha Kappa Fraternity, Alpha Rho Lambda Sorority, Omega Psi Phi Fraternity, Alpha Kappa Alpha Sorority, Lambda Phi Epsilon Fraternity, and Sigma Omicron Pi Sorority are just some of the many ethnically based fraternities and sororities that exist across the country. Such organizations have provided many students with a means to become familiar with their campus and to gain friendships and support while promoting their culture and ethnicity.

EVERYONE iS AFFECTED BY SEXUAL ViOLENCE!

COMMUNITIES UNiTE
TAKE BACK THE NiGHT

Tuesday April 17th
Beaumont Field, MSU's Campus

10am–6pm Silent Silhouettes Display
10am–6pm Clothesline Project & Resource Tables
2–4pm Making Posters for the March
4–5:45pm Speak Out
5:30–7pm Men's Forum
6–7pm Candlelight Vigil – Women's Space
7:15–8pm Pre-March Rally with Nandi Crosby††
8–9pm March
9pm Post March Rally @ East Lansing 54-B District Court

CAREER/MAJOR GROUPS

You can explore diversity through your major and career interests as well. Groups that focus on a specific field of study can be great assets as you explore your interests. Are you interested in helping diverse groups interact more effectively? Consider majoring in sociology or social work. Do you want to learn more about human behavior? Study psychology. If you join a club that is affiliated with the major that interests you, not only will you find out more about the major, but you can also make contacts in the field that could lead to career options. Many of these clubs participate in challenges and contests with similar groups from other colleges and contribute to campus activities through exhibitions and events. The Psychology Club; the Math, Engineering, and Science Association; and the Association of Student Filmmakers are examples of such groups.

POLITICAL/ACTIVIST ORGANIZATIONS

Adding to the diversity mix on campuses are organizations devoted to specific political affiliations and causes. Campus Republicans, Young Democrats, Amnesty International, Native Students in Social Action, and other groups provide students with a platform to express their political views and share their causes with others. Contributing to the diversity of ideas, organizations provide debating events and forums to address current issues and events.

SPECIAL-INTEREST GROUPS

Perhaps the largest subgroup of student organizations is the special-interest category, which encompasses everything from recreational interests to hobbies. On your campus you might find special-interest clubs such as the Brazilian Jujitsu Club, the Kite Flyers' Club, the Flamenco Club, and the Video Gamers' Society. Students can cultivate an interest in bird watching or indulge their curiosity about ballroom dance without ever leaving campus. Many of these clubs will sponsor campus events highlighting their specific interests and talents so that you can check them out. If a club for your special interest is not available, create one yourself.

Discrimination, Prejudice, and Insensitivity on College Campuses

You might feel uncomfortable when asked about your views of diversity. We all have **biases** against certain groups or value systems. Yet it is what we do with our individual beliefs that separates the average person from the racist, the bigot, and the extremist.

Unfortunately, some individuals opt not to seek education for the common good but instead respond negatively to groups that differ from their own. Documented acts of **discrimination** and **prejudice** on campuses span the country. You might be shocked to hear that these acts of violence, intimidation, and stupidity occur on campuses, when the assumption is that college students are "supposed to be above that."

RAISING AWARENESS

At a midwestern university, students arrived on campus to find racial slurs and demeaning images aimed at various ethnic groups spray-painted on the walls of the Multicultural Center. In the wake of the terrorist attack on the World Trade Center and the Pentagon in September 2001, many students of Middle Eastern descent were subjected to both violence and intimidation because of their ancestry.

While actions like these are deliberate and hateful, others occur out of a lack of common sense. Consider a campus party to celebrate Cinco de Mayo. Party organizers asked everyone to wear sombreros. On arrival, guests encountered a mock-up of a border patrol station on the front lawn and were required to crawl under or climb over a section of chain-link fencing. Student groups voiced their disapproval over such insensitivity, which resulted in campus probationary measures for the organization that had thrown the party. At a Halloween party at a large university, members of a campus organization decided to dress in Ku Klux Klan outfits while other members dressed as slaves and wore black shoe polish on their faces. The group then simulated slave hangings during the party. When photos of the events surfaced, the university suspended the group from campus, and the community demanded that the group be banned indefinitely.

For a number of years stereotypes that are used to identify school sports teams and their supporters have disturbed ethnic and cultural groups such as Native Americans. Mascots that incorporate a bow and arrow, a tomahawk, feathers, and war paint have raised awareness about the promotion and acceptance of stereotypes associated with the concept of the "savage Indian." Some schools have responded by altering the images while retaining the mascot. Other schools have changed their mascots altogether.

YOUR TURN ▶

Have you ever witnessed or been a victim of harassment because of your gender, race, regional identity, religion, or ethnic group? What can colleges and universities do to reduce the incidence of harassment?

Colleges and universities are working to ensure that a welcoming and inclusive campus environment awaits all students, both current and prospective. Campus resources and centers focus on providing acknowledgment of and support to the diverse student population. Campus administrations have established policies against any and all forms of discriminatory actions, racism, and insensitivity, and many campuses have adopted zero-tolerance policies that prohibit verbal and nonverbal harassment, intimidation, and violence. Find out what resources are available on your campus to protect you and other students from discriminatory and racist behavior and what steps your college or university takes to promote the understanding of diversity and multiculturalism. If you have been a victim of a racist, insensitive, or discriminatory act, report it to the proper authorities.

WHAT YOU CAN DO TO FIGHT HATE ON CAMPUS

Hate crimes, regardless of where they occur, should be taken very seriously. A hate crime is any prejudicial activity and can include physical assault, vandalism, and intimidation. One of the most common forms of hate crime on campus is graffiti that expresses racial, ethnic, and cultural slurs.

Whatever form these crimes might take on your campus, it is important to examine your thoughts and feelings about their occurrence. The most important question to ask yourself is: Will you do something about it, or do you think it is someone else's problem? If you or a group to which you belong is the target of the hate crime, you might feel compelled to take a stand and speak out against the incident. But what if the target is not a group you associate with?

Will you feel strongly enough to express your discontent with the actions that are taken? Or will you feel that it is the problem only of the targeted group?

Many students, whether or not they were directly targeted in a hate crime, find strength in unity, forming action committees and making it clear that hate crimes will not be ignored or tolerated. In most cases, instead of dividing students, hate crimes bring students together to work toward denouncing hate. It is important not to respond to prejudice and hate crimes with violence. It is more effective to unite with fellow students, faculty, staff, campus police, and administrators to address the issue and educate the greater campus community.

How can you get involved? Work with existing campus services such as the campus police and the Multicultural Center as well as the faculty and administration to plan and host educational opportunities, such as training sessions, workshops, and symposiums centered on diversity, sensitivity, and multiculturalism. Organize an antidiscrimination event on campus in which campus and community leaders address the issues and provide solutions. Join prevention programs to come up with ideas to battle hate crimes on campus or in the community. Finally, look into the antidiscrimination measures your college is employing and decide whether you think they need updating or revising.

Wired WINDOW

USING THE WEB TO HELP EXPLORE YOUR BIASES

We all harbor biases against certain groups or value systems; however, first-year college students have rarely examined these biases. Not only is it difficult to accept that you do have biases, but it is often considered inappropriate to discuss biases openly. As you expand your knowledge about other ethnicities, cultures, and belief systems, it's a good idea to explore your own biases so that you can be more understanding and accepting of differences. Because you might not be comfortable discussing your biases in public (such as during a class or a campus discussion), you can opt to explore them on your own. One great Web site to help you explore biases that you might not even know that you hold is the Harvard Implicit Project (https://www.implicit.harvard.edu/implicit). Follow the link to the "Demonstration" tests. On the demonstration tests page, you can choose to assess your implicit associations based on diversity issues such as ethnicity, culture, sexuality, and age. Please keep in mind that you might not be consciously aware of or agree with the results. Although the Implicit Association Tests are not an absolute assessment, they are a good way to gauge your biases and to begin to explore them in a safe environment.

Thinking Critically

Pick one of the Implicit Association Tests and take it. What do you think about your results? Were you surprised? How can you continue to explore your biases now that you have this information? What is the next step you will take? Review your campus's diversity and multicultural resources. Which resource would help you enhance your awareness of your own feelings about culture, ethnicity, and sexual orientation?

Just because you or your particular group has not been targeted in a hate crime doesn't mean that you should do nothing. Commit to becoming involved in making your campus a safe place for students with diverse views, lifestyles, languages, politics, religions, and interests to come together and learn. If nothing happens to make it clear that hate crimes on campus will not be tolerated, it's anyone's guess as to who will be the next target.

Challenge Yourself to Experience Diversity

During his inaugural address, President Obama reiterated the value of diversity:

> For we know that our patchwork heritage is a strength, not a weakness. We are a nation of Christians and Muslims, Jews and Hindus—and non-believers. We are shaped by every language and culture, drawn from every end of this earth; and because we have tasted the bitter swill of civil war and segregation, and emerged from that dark chapter stronger and more united, we cannot help but believe that the old hatreds shall someday pass; that the lines of tribe shall soon dissolve; that as the world grows smaller, our common humanity shall reveal itself; and that America must play its role in ushering in a new era of peace.

Diversity enriches us all. Allowing yourself to become more culturally aware and more open to differing viewpoints will help you become a truly educated person. Understanding the value of working with others and the im-

portance of an open mind will enhance your educational and career goals and provide gratifying experiences, both on and off campus. Making the decision to become active in your multicultural education will require you to be active and sometimes to step out of your comfort zone. There are many ways to become more culturally aware, including a variety of opportunities on your campus. Look into what cultural programming is being offered throughout the school year. From concerts to films, from guest speakers to information tables, you might not have to go far to gain additional insight into the value of diversity.

Challenge yourself to learn about various groups in and around your community, at both school and home. These two settings might differ ethnically and culturally, giving you an opportunity to develop the skills you need to function in and adjust to a variety of settings. Attend events and celebrations outside of your regular groups. Whether they are in the general community or on campus, this is a good way to see and hear traditions that are specific to the groups being represented. Exposing yourself to new experiences through events and celebrations can be gratifying. You can also become active in your own learning by making time for travel. Seeing the world and its people can be an uplifting experience. Finally, when in doubt, ask. If you do this in a tactful, genuine way, most people will be happy to share information about their viewpoints, traditions, and history. It is only through allowing ourselves to grow that we really learn.

Where to go FOR HELP . . .

ON CAMPUS ▶

Most colleges and university campuses take an active role in promoting diversity. In the effort to ensure a welcoming and supportive environment for all students, institutions have established offices, centers, and resources to provide students with educational opportunities, academic guidance, and support networks. Look into the availability of the following resources on your campus, and visit one or more: Office of Student Affairs; Office of Diversity; Multicultural Centers; Women's and Men's Centers; Lesbian, Gay, Bisexual, and Transgendered Student Alliances; Centers for Students with Disabilities; and academic support programs for under-represented groups.

ONLINE ▶

Student Now Diversity Resources: http://www.studentnow.com/collegelist/diversity.html. A list of campus diversity resources.

Diversity Web: http://www.diversityweb.org. More resources related to diversity on campus.

Tolerance.org: http://www.tolerance.org. This Web site, a project of the Southern Poverty Law Center, provides numerous resources for dealing with discrimination and prejudice both on and off campus.

MY INSTITUTION'S RESOURCES ▶

_____

_____

_____

_____

_____

_____

_____

_____

_____

_____

_____

_____

_____

_____

_____

_____

_____

_____

Applying What You've LEARNED . . .

Now that you have read and discussed this chapter, consider how you can apply what you have learned to your academic and personal life. The following prompts will help you reflect on the chapter material and its relevance to you both now and in the future.

1. Use your print or online campus course catalog to identify courses that focus on topics of multiculturalism and diversity. Why do you think academic departments have included these issues in the curriculum? How would studying diversity and multiculturalism help you prepare for different academic fields?

2. Reflecting on our personal identities and values is a step to increase self-awareness. Read and answer the following questions to the best of your ability:

   How do you identify yourself ethnically and culturally?

   How do you express yourself according to this identity?

   Are there practices or beliefs in your culture to which you have difficulty subscribing? If so, what are they? Why do you have difficulty accepting these beliefs?

   What aspects of your identity do you truly enjoy?

One-Minute PAPER . . .

One aspect of a liberal arts education is learning about differences in cultures, ethnicities, and other groups. Were there any ideas in this chapter that influenced your personal opinions, viewpoints, or values? Was there anything that you disagreed with or found unsettling?

Building Your PORTFOLIO . . .

IT'S A SMALL WORLD AFTER ALL!

The concepts of diversity, ethnicity, culture, and multiculturalism have been explored in this chapter. Reading about these controversial topics is one thing, but really stepping into someone else's shoes is another. Study abroad and student exchange programs are excellent (and enjoyable) ways of adding new perspectives to your college experience. What better way of learning about other parts of the world than by immersing yourself in a foreign culture, language, and people?

Consider the possibilities:

1. Visit your institution's International Programs/Study Abroad office, or, if you are at a college that does not have a study abroad program, search for study abroad opportunities on the Web. *Tip:* Look for the Center for Global Education (http://www.lmu.edu/globaled/index.html), the Council on International Education Exchange (http://www.ciee.org/study.aspx), or the International Partnership for Service Learning (http://www.ispl.org).

Using a major or career that you have selected or are interested in, think about how you would like to spend a summer, semester, or year abroad to learn more about or gain experience in your major field.

2. On the basis of your research, create a PowerPoint presentation to share with your class outlining the opportunities to study abroad or participate in an exchange program.

- Describe the steps students need to take at your campus to include a study abroad trip in their college plan (e.g., whom to contact, financial aid, the best time to study abroad, how to earn course credit).
- Describe the benefits of study abroad (e.g., observing different cultures, building a good résumé).
- Include photos of the country or countries you would like to visit.
- Include information about your current or intended major and career and how a study abroad or exchange trip would fit into your plans.
- Reference web links you found useful in preparing your presentation.

3. Save your presentation in your portfolio on your personal computer or flash drive.

12 Managing Your Money

In this chapter you will explore

- How to create a budget that works for you
- How to obtain and keep financial aid
- What kinds of student loans are best
- How to use and manage credit cards
- Why you should plan for your financial future

Like it

or not, we can't ignore the importance of money. Money is often symbolically and realistically the key ingredient to independence and, some people conclude, even to a sense of freedom. You probably know of instances in which money divided a family or a relationship or seemed to drive someone's life in a direction that person would not have taken otherwise. Money can also affect your specific academic goals, causing you to select or reject certain academic majors or degree plans.

Although your primary goal in college should be a strong academic record, money or the lack of it can make it easier or more difficult to complete your degree. Educators recognize that not understanding personal finances can hinder a student's progress, and mandatory personal finance classes are now being added in high schools and are available as options at some colleges. The purpose of this chapter is to provide basic information and suggestions so that money will not be a barrier to your success in college. Think of this chapter as a summary of needed financial skills; if you want more information, consider taking a personal finance class at your college or in your community.

YOUR TURN ▶

So far, how well or poorly are you managing your money in college? Why is it difficult or easy?

Living on a Budget

Face it: College is expensive, and most students have limited financial resources. Not only is tuition a major cost, but day-to-day expenses can add up quickly. No matter what your financial situation, a budget for college is a must. While a budget might not completely eliminate debt after graduation, it can help you become realistic about your finances so that you can have a basis for future life planning.

A budget is a spending plan that tracks all sources of income (student loan disbursements, money from parents, etc.) and expenses (rent, tuition, etc.) during a set period of time (weekly, monthly, etc.). Creating and following a budget will allow you to pay your bills on time, cut costs, put some money away for emergencies, and finish college with as little debt as possible.

CREATING A BUDGET

A budget will condition you to live within your means, put money into savings, and possibly invest down the road. Here are a few tips to help you get started.

Step 1. Gather Basic Information. To create an effective budget, you need to learn more about your income and your spending behaviors.

First, determine how much money is coming in and when. Sources of income might include a job, your savings, gifts from relatives, student loans, scholarship dollars, or grants. Write them all down, making note of how often you receive each type of income (weekly paychecks, quarterly loan disbursements, one-time gifts, and so forth) and how much money you can expect each time.

To determine where your money is going and when, track your spending for a week or two (or, even better, a full month) by recording every bill you pay and every purchase you make. It might surprise you to learn how much money you spend on coffee, bagels, and other incidentals. This information will help you to better understand your spending behaviors and where you might be able to cut costs in the future.

Step 2. Build a Plan. Use the information you gathered in Step 1 to set up three columns: one for income, one for anticipated expenses, and one for actual expenses. Table 12.1 is an example of such a plan. Knowing when your money is coming in will help you decide how to structure your budget. For example, if most of your income comes in on a monthly basis, you'll want to create a monthly budget. If you are paid every other week, a biweekly budget might work better.

Be sure to recognize which expenses are fixed and which are variable. A *fixed expense* is one that will cost you the same amount every time you pay it. For example, your rent is a fixed expense because you owe your landlord the same amount each month. A variable expense is one that may change. Your textbooks are a variable expense because the number and cost of them will be different each term.

Although you will know, more or less, how much your fixed expenses will be during each budget period, you might need to estimate your variable expenses in your anticipated expenses column. Use past bills, checking account statements, and spending behaviors from your tracking in Step 1 to create an educated guess for your anticipated expenses in the variable categories. When you are in doubt, it is always better to overestimate your expenses to avoid shortfalls at the end of your budget period.

TABLE 12.1 ▶ Sample Budget

Cost Category	Expected Cost	Actual Cost
Rent	$ 500	$ 500
Electric	$ 50	$ 47
Gas (heat)	$ 75	$ 75
Cell phone	$ 45	$ 50
Water	$ 15	$ 12
Gasoline	$ 40	$ 45
Groceries	$ 150	$ 135
Dining out	$ 50	$ 40
Books	$ 200	$ 170
Miscellaneous	$ 100	$ 120
Total	$1,225	$1,194

Step 3. Do a Test Run. Use your budget plan from Step 2 for a few weeks and see how things go, recording your actual expenses as you pay them. Don't be surprised to see differences between your anticipated and actual expense columns; budgeting is not an exact science, and you will likely never see a perfect match between these two columns. It might be wise to add a "miscellaneous" category for those unexpected and added expenses throughout the budget period.

Step 4. Make Adjustments. Although your budget might never be perfect, you can strive to improve it. Are there areas in which you spent much more or much less than expected? Do you need to reallocate funds to better meet the needs of your current situation? Be realistic and thoughtful in how you spend your money, and use your budget to help meet your goals, such as planning for a trip or getting a new pair of jeans.

Whatever you do, don't give up if your bottom line doesn't end up the way you expected it would. Budgeting is a lot like dieting; you might slip up and eat a pizza (or spend too much buying one), but all is not lost. If you stay focused and flexible, your budget can lead you to financial stability and independence.

CUTTING COSTS

Once you have put together a working budget, have tried it out, and have adjusted it, you're likely to discover that your expenses still exceed your income. Don't panic. Simply begin to look for ways to reduce those expenses. Here are some tips for saving money in college:

- **Recognize the difference between your *needs* and your *wants*.** A *need* is something you must have. For example, tuition and textbooks are considered *needs*. On the other hand, your *wants* are goods, services, or experiences that you wish to purchase but could reasonably live without. For example, concert tickets and mochas are *wants*. Your budget should always provide for your *needs* first.

- **Share expenses.** Having a roommate (or several) can be one of the easiest ways to cut costs on a regular basis. In exchange for giving up a little bit of privacy, you'll save hundreds of dollars on rent, utilities, and food. Make sure, however, that you work out a plan for sharing expenses equally and that everyone accepts his or her responsibilities. For instance, remember that if only your name is on the cable account, you (and only you) are legally responsible for that bill. You'll need to collect money from your roommates so that you can pay the bill in full and on time.

- **Consider the pros and cons of living on campus.** Depending on your school's location, off-campus housing might be less expensive than paying for a room and a meal plan on campus. However, be aware that while you might save some cash, you will give up a great deal of convenience by moving out of your campus residence. You almost certainly won't be able to roll out of bed ten minutes before class, and you will have to prepare your own meals. At the same time, living on campus makes it easier to make friends and develop a sense of connection to your college or university. Before you make the decision about where to live, weigh the advantages and disadvantages of each option, and then choose.

- **Use low-cost transportation.** If you live close to campus, consider whether or not you need to keep a car on campus. Take advantage of lower-cost options such as public transportation or biking to class to save money on gasoline and parking. If you live farther away, check to see whether your institution hosts a ride-sharing program for commuter students, or carpool with someone in your area.

- **Seek out discount entertainment options.** Take advantage of discounted or free programming through your college. Most institutions use a portion of their student fees to provide affordable entertainment options such as discounted or free tickets to concerts, movie theaters, sporting events, or other special events.

- **Embrace second-hand goods.** Use online resources such as Craigslist and thrift stores such as Goodwill to expand your wardrobe, purchase extras such as games and sports equipment, or furnish and decorate your room or apartment. You'll save money, and you won't mind as much when someone spills a drink on your "new" couch.

- **Avoid unnecessary fees.** Making late payments on credit cards and other bills can lead to expensive fees and can lower your credit score (which in turn will raise your interest rates). You might want to set up online, automatic payments to avoid making this costly mistake.

Wired WINDOW

SAVE A MINT

You might have heard the saying "You have to spend money to make money." If you were to review the pricing of online and desktop programs for tracking your budget and spending, you might conclude that this statement is true. But there are low-cost options and a few good free money management software packages. For instance, Quicken (http://www.quicken.intuit.com) offers a free Web site where you can track your finances and create a budget. Another highly reviewed Web site is Mint.com, which automatically tracks your spending and creates reports based on categories that it recognizes. You can enter the information for all of your accounts, and Mint will sift through the transactions and show you where you are spending your money. The entire process takes less than ten minutes. Mint also automatically creates a budget for you on the basis of the information that it filters from your account. You might worry about the security of your information on Mint.com; however, Mint is a read-only site that does not store your login

information. That means that in the unlikely event that someone gets into your account, they can't move money around or withdraw it. Additionally, surfing on Mint is accomplished through a secure web protocol called https (Hypertext Transfer Protocol-Secure) that encrypts the information you send and receive. Always make sure that you are using an https Web site and that the Web site security certificate is valid when you are conducting your financial affairs online.

Thinking Critically

Sign up for Mint.com and have Mint distill your accounts to show your spending by category. What did you discover about the ways in which you spend your money? Were you surprised that you spent more (or less) on a certain category than you had guessed? Will you make any changes to the ways in which you spend your money because of what you found? If so, what changes will you make?

Getting Financial Aid

Very few students can pay the costs of college tuition, fees, books, room and board, bills, and random expenses without some kind of help. Luckily, several sources of financial aid, including some you might not know about, are available to help cover your costs. With a combination of research, diligence, and luck, some students even manage to enroll and succeed in college with little or no financial support from their families because of the financial aid they receive.

TYPES OF AID

Financial aid seems complex because it can come from so many different sources. Each source may have different rules about how to receive the money and how not to lose it. The financial aid staff at your college can help you find the way to get the largest amount of money that doesn't need to be repaid, the lowest interest rate on loans, and work possibilities that fit your academic program. Whether or not your family can help you pay for college, you should not overlook this valuable campus resource. The financial aid office and its Web site are the best places to begin looking for all types of assistance. Other organizations that can help students to find the right college and money to help them attend are located across the United States. Many of these organizations are members of the National College Access Network or participate in a national effort called Know How to Go. Check their Web sites at http://www.collegeaccess.org/accessprogram directory and http://www.knowhow2go.org. Very few students complete college without some type of financial assistance, and it is rare for students to cover all college expenses with only scholarships. The majority of students pay for college through a combination of various types of financial assistance: scholarships, grants, loans, and paid employment. Financial aid professionals refer to this combination as a "package."

While scholarships and grants are unquestionably the best forms of aid because they do not have to be repaid, the federal government, states, and colleges offer many other forms of assistance, such as loans, work-study opportunities, and cooperative education. You might also be able to obtain funds from your employer, a local organization, or a private group.

- **Need-based scholarships** are based on both a talent and financial need. "Talent" can be past accomplishments in the arts or athletics, your potential for future accomplishments, or even where you are from. Some colleges and universities want to admit students from other states or countries. "Need" in this context means the cost of college minus a federal determination of what you and your family can afford to contribute toward those costs. Your institution might provide scholarships from its own resources or from individual donors. Donors themselves sometimes stipulate characteristics of scholarship recipients, such as age or academic major.

- **Merit scholarships** are based on talent as defined above but do not require you to demonstrate financial need. It can be challenging to match your talent with merit scholarships. Most of them come through colleges and are part of the admissions and financial aid processes, usually described on the college's Web site. Web-based scholarship search services are another good source to explore. Be certain the Web site you use is free, will keep your information confidential unless you release your name, and will send you a notice (usually through e-mail) when a new scholarship that matches your qualifications is posted. Also be sure to ask your employer, your family's employers, and social, community or religious organizations about any available scholarships.

- **Grants** are based on financial need but, like scholarships, do not have to be repaid. Grants are awarded by the federal government and state government and by institutions themselves. Students meet academic qualifications for grants by being admitted to the college and maintaining grades that are acceptable to the grant provider.

- **Work-study** jobs are reserved for students with financial need. Students receive work-study notices as part of the overall financial aid notice and then can sign up to be interviewed for work-study jobs. Although some work-study jobs can be relatively menial, the best options provide experience related to your academic studies while allowing you to earn money for college. The salary is based on the skill required for a particular position and the hours involved. Keep in mind that you will be expected to accomplish specific tasks while on duty, although some employers might permit you to study during any down-time.

- **Cooperative (co-op) education** allows you to alternate a term of study (a semester or quarter) with a term of paid work. Engineering co-op opportunities are among the most common, and the number of co-op programs in health care fields is growing. Colleges make information about co-ops available through admissions and academic departments.

QUALIFYING FOR AID

Most financial assistance requires some form of application. The application used most often is the Free Application for Federal Student Aid (FAFSA). Every student should complete the FAFSA by the earliest deadline of the colleges you are considering. Additional forms, such as the College Board's Profile form and scholarship applications, might also be required and will be listed in colleges' financial aid or admissions materials or by organizations that offer scholarships.

The following box outlines the steps you must take to qualify for most scholarships and grants, especially those sponsored by federal or state governments.

The amount of financial aid you receive will depend on the cost of your academic program and what you or your family can pay as determined by FAFSA. Cost includes average expenses for tuition and fees, books and supplies, room and board, transportation, and personal expenses. The financial aid office will subtract from the cost the amount you and your family are expected to pay. In some cases that amount can be as little as zero. Financial aid is designed to make up as much of the balance or "need" as possible.

STEPS TO QUALIFY FOR FINANCIAL AID

1. Enroll half-time or more in a certificate or degree program at one of the more than 4,500 institutions that are certified to distribute federal financial aid. A few aid programs are available for less than half-time study; check with your department or college to see what your options are.

2. Complete the FAFSA. The first FAFSA you file is intimidating, especially if you rush to complete it right before the deadline. Completing the FAFSA in subsequent years is easier because you only need to update items that have changed. To make the process easier, get your personal identification number (PIN) a few weeks before the deadline. This PIN will be the same one you'll use throughout your college career. Try to do the form in sections rather than tackling all of it at once. Most of the information is basic: name, address, driver's license number, and things you will know or have in your billfold. For most undergraduates the financial section will require your own and your parents' information from tax materials. If you are at least 24 years of age, married, or a veteran or have dependents of your own, your tax information and that for your spouse will be needed.

3. If your school or award-granting organization requires it, complete the College Board Profile form. Review your college's admission information, or ask a financial aid advisor to determine if this applies to you.

4. Identify any additional applications that are required. These are usually scholarship applications with personal statements or short essays. The organizations, including colleges, that are giving the money will provide instructions about what is required. Most have Web sites with complete information.

5. Follow all instructions carefully, and submit each application on time. Financial aid is awarded from a fixed pool of funds. When money has been awarded, there is usually none left for those who file late.

6. Complete the classes for which you were given financial aid with at least a minimum grade point average as defined by your academic department or college or the organization that provided you the scholarship.

HOW TO AVOID LOSING YOUR FUNDING

If you earn average or better grades, complete your courses each term, and finish your program or degree on time, you should have no trouble maintaining your financial aid. It's a good idea to check with the financial aid office before you drop classes to make sure you will not lose any aid.

Some types of aid, especially scholarships, require that you maintain full-time enrollment and make satisfactory academic progress. Dropping or failing a class might jeopardize all or part of your financial aid unless you are enrolled in more credits than the minimum required for financial aid. Full-time financial aid is often defined as twelve credit hours per term. If you initially enrolled in fifteen credit hours and dropped one three-hour course, your aid should not change. Even so, talk with a financial aid counselor before making the decision to drop a course, just to be sure.

Remember that although the financial aid office is there to serve you, you must be your own advocate. The following tips should help:

- File for financial aid every year. Even if you don't think you will receive aid for a certain year, you must file annually in case you become eligible in the future.

- Meet all filing deadlines. Students who do not meet filing deadlines risk losing aid from one year to the next.

- Talk with a financial aid officer immediately if you or your family experiences a significant loss (such as loss of a job or death of a parent or spouse). Don't wait for the next filing period; you might be eligible for funds for the current year.

- Inquire every year about criteria-based aid. Many colleges and universities have grants and scholarships for students who meet specific criteria. These might include grants for minority students, grants for students in specific academic majors, and grants for students of single parents. Sometimes a donor will give money to the school's scholarship fund for students who meet certain other criteria, even county or state of residence. Determine whether any of these fit your circumstances.

- Inquire about campus jobs throughout the year, as these jobs are not available just at the beginning of the term. If you do not have a job and want or need to work, keep asking.

- Consider asking for a reassessment of your eligibility for aid. If you have reviewed your financial aid package and think that your circumstances deserve additional consideration, you can ask the financial aid office to reassess your eligibility. The office is not always required to do so, but the request might be worth your effort.

Achieving a Balance Between Working and Borrowing

After determining your budget, deciding what you can pay from savings (if any), and taking your scholarships and grants into consideration, you might still need additional income. Each term or year, you should decide how much you can work while maintaining good grades and how much you should borrow from student loans.

ADVANTAGES AND DISADVANTAGES OF WORKING

Paid employment while you are in college can be important for reasons other than money. Having a job in a field related to your major can help you develop a credential for graduate school and make you more employable later because it shows you have the capability to manage several priorities at the same time. Work can help you determine whether a career is what you will really want after you complete your education. And students who work a moderate amount (fifteen hours per week) typically get better grades than students who do not work at all.

On the other hand, it's almost impossible to get great grades if you work full-time while trying to be a full-time student. Some students prefer not to take a job during their first year in college while they're making adjustments to a new academic environment. You might find that you're able to work some terms while you are a student but not others. And family obligations or challenging classes can sometimes make the added burden of work impractical or impossible.

The majority of students today find that a combination of working and borrowing is the best way to gain experience, finance college, and complete their educational goals on time.

STUDENT LOANS

Although you should be careful not to borrow yourself into a lifetime of debt, avoiding loans altogether could delay your graduation and your progress up the career ladder. For most students, some level of borrowing is both necessary and prudent.

The following list provides information about the most common types of student loans. The list reflects the order in which you should apply for and accept loans to get the lowest interest rates and best repayment terms.

- **Subsidized federal student loans** are backed by the government, with interest paid on your behalf while you are enrolled in undergraduate, graduate, or professional school. These loans require at least half-time enrollment and a submitted FAFSA application (see page 208).
- **Unsubsidized federal student loans** may require that you make interest payments while you are enrolled. If not, the interest is added to the amount you owe, called "capitalization."
- **Parent Loan for Undergraduate Students (PLUS) loans** are applied for and owed by parents but disbursed directly to students. Interest is usually higher than that on federal student loans but lower than that on private loans. Parents who apply must provide information on the FAFSA.
- **Private student loans** are offered through banks and credit unions. Private loans often have stricter credit requirements and higher interest rates than federal loans do, and interest payments on private loans begin immediately. Student loans are a very important source of money for college, but like paid employment, loans should be considered carefully. Loans for costs such as books and tuition are good investments. Loans for a more lavish lifestyle are likely to weigh you down in the future. As one wise person put it, if by borrowing you live like a wealthy graduate while you're a student, you'll live like a student after you graduate. Student loans can be a good way to begin using credit wisely, a skill you are likely to need throughout your life.

Managing Credit Wisely

When you graduate, you will leave your institution with two significant numbers. The first is your grade point average (GPA), which represents the level of academic success you attained while in college. The second, your credit score, is a numerical representation of your fiscal responsibility. Although this second number might be less familiar to you, it could be the deciding factor that determines whether you get your dream job, regardless of your GPA. And twenty years from now, you're likely to have forgotten your GPA, while your credit score will be more important than ever.

Your credit score is derived from a credit report that contains information about accounts in your name. These accounts include credit cards, student loans, utility bills, cell phones, and car loans, to name a few. This credit score can determine whether or not you will qualify for a loan (car, home, student, etc.), what interest rates you will pay, how much your car insurance will cost, and your chances of being hired by some organizations. Even if none of these things is in your immediate future, now is the time to start thinking about your credit score.

While using credit cards responsibly is a good way to build credit, acquiring a credit card has become much more difficult for college students. In May of 2009, President Obama signed legislation that prohibits college students under the age of 21 from obtaining a credit card unless they can prove they are able to make the payments or the credit card application is co-signed by a parent or guardian.

UNDERSTANDING CREDIT

Even if you can prove you have the means to repay credit card debt, it is important for you to thoroughly understand how credit cards work and how they can both help and hurt you. Simply put, a credit card allows you to buy something now and pay for it later. Each month you will receive a statement listing all purchases you made using your credit card during the previous thirty days. The statement will request a payment toward your balance and will set a payment due date. Your payment options will vary: You can pay your entire balance, pay a specified amount of the balance, or pay only a minimum payment, which may be as low as $10.

But beware: If you make only a minimum payment, the remaining balance on your card will be charged a finance fee, or interest charge, causing your balance to increase before your next bill arrives even if you don't make any more purchases. Paying the minimum payment is almost never a good strategy and can add years to your repayment time. In fact, if you continue to pay only $10 per month toward a $500 credit card balance, it will take you more than seven years to pay it off! And assuming an 18 percent interest rate, you'll pay an extra $431 in interest—almost doubling the total amount you'll pay.

Avoid making late payments. Paying your bill even one day late can result in a finance charge of up to $30; it can also raise the interest rate not only on that card but also on any other credit accounts you have. If you decide to use a credit card to build credit, you might want to set up online, automatic payments to avoid incurring expensive late fees. Remember that the payment due date is the date the payment should be received by the credit card lender, not the date you send it.

┌─ **YOUR TURN ▶** ─────────────────────────────
Do you have your own credit card or one that you own jointly with your parents? If not, what are your reasons for not getting one? If you do have a card, do you feel you're in control of the way you use it? Why or why not? If you don't have a card, do you think you are ready for one? Why or why not?
└───

If you decide to apply for a credit card while you're in college, remember that credit cards should be used to build credit and for emergencies. They should not be used to fund a lifestyle you cannot otherwise afford or to buy wants (see the section on budgeting earlier in this chapter). On the other hand, if you use your credit card just once a month and pay the balance as soon as the bill arrives, you will be on your way to a strong credit score in just a few years.

FREQUENTLY ASKED QUESTIONS ABOUT CREDIT CARDS

Here are some answers to the most common questions college students have about credit cards:

- **I have a credit card with my name on it, but it is actually my parents' account number. Is this card building credit for me?** No. You are considered an authorized user on the account, but your parents are the primary account holders. To build credit, you must be the primary account holder or at least a joint account holder.

- **I choose the "credit" option every time I use my debit card. Is this building credit for me?** No. Using the credit function of your debit card is more like an electronic check because it is still taking money directly out of your checking account. Even if your debit card has a major credit card (Visa, MasterCard, etc.) logo on it, it is not building credit for you.

- **I have a few store credit cards (Target, Kohl's, Best Buy, etc.). Are these accounts included on my credit report?** Yes. Although they will affect your credit score, they do not carry as much weight as major credit cards (Visa, MasterCard, etc.). It is okay to have a few store credit cards, but a major credit card will do more to help you build credit.

- **Where can I apply for a major credit card?** A good place to begin is your bank or credit union. Remember that you will have to prove your ability to make payments in order to obtain a card.

- **If one credit card will help me build credit, will several build my credit even more?** Research shows that there is no benefit to having more than two major credit cards. And even if you're able to pay the required monthly amounts, having too many accounts open can make you appear risky to the credit bureaus determining your credit score.

CREDIT CARD DO'S AND DON'TS

- **Do** use your credit card to help you build credit by making small charges and paying them off each month.
- **Don't** use your credit card to bridge the gap between the lifestyle you would like to have and the one you can actually afford.
- **Do** keep an eye on your credit report by visiting the free Web site www.AnnualCreditReport.com at least once a year.
- **Do** have a credit card for emergencies if possible, even if your parents co-sign for it.
- **Don't** use your credit card to pay for spring break. This is *not* an emergency!

- **What if I forget and make a late payment? Is my credit score ruined?**
  Your credit report reflects at least the past seven years of activity but puts
  the most emphasis on the most recent two years. In other words, the farther you get from your mistakes, the less impact they will have on your
  credit score. There is no quick fix for improving a credit score, so beware
  of advertisements that say otherwise.

DEBIT CARDS

Although you might wish to use a credit card for emergencies and to establish
a good credit rating, you might also look into the possibility of applying for a
debit card (also called a checkcard). The big advantage of a debit card is that
you don't always have to carry cash and thus don't run the risk of losing it.
And since the amount of your purchases will be limited to the funds in your
account, a debit card is a good form of constraint on your spending. The only
real disadvantage is that a debit card provides direct access to your checking
account, so it's very important that you keep your card in a safe place and
away from your personal identification number (PIN). The safest way to protect your account is to commit your PIN to memory. If you lose your debit
card or credit card, notify your bank immediately.

Planning for the Future

It's never too early to begin thinking about financing your life after graduation. Here are some tips that could open future opportunities and help you
avoid future problems.

- Plan now for your next step, whether that's additional education or
  work. Get to know faculty members by using their office hours to learn
  about their specific areas of study and ask their advice about your career.
  Faculty members mention frequently that they wish more students came
  to talk with them, instead of just meeting them when a problem occurs.
- Keep your address current with the registrar even when you have finished
  your degree or program and especially if you stop classes for a term. This
  is doubly important if you have student loans so you do not get a negative
  report on your credit rating because you missed information about your
  loan.
- Make a point of establishing a savings account and adding to it regularly,
  even if you can manage only a few dollars a month. The sooner you start,
  the greater your returns will be.

Your education is the most productive investment you can make for your
future and that of your family. Research shows that completion of programs
or degrees after high school increases earnings, opens up career options, leads
to greater satisfaction in work, results in more engaged citizenship such as
voting and community service, and greatly increases the probability that your
children will go on to college. College is a big investment of both time and
money, but it's an investment of proven worth.

Where to go FOR HELP . . .

ON CAMPUS ▶

Your Institution's Financial Aid Office
Professionals in this office will help you understand financial aid opportunities and how to apply for scholarships.

Local United Way Office Many communities have credit counseling agencies within the local United Way.

Campus Programs Be on the lookout for special campus programs on money management. These programs are often offered in residence halls or through the division of student affairs.

Business School or College Faculty or staff members within a school or college of business or a division of continuing education sometimes offer a course in personal finance. Check your college catalog or Web site, or call the school, college, or division office.

Counseling Center If money problems are related to compulsive shopping or gambling, your institution's counseling center can provide help.

ONLINE ▶

Budget Wizard: http://www.cashcourse.org. The National Endowment for Financial Education (NEFE) offers this free, secure, budgeting tool.

Free Application for Federal Student Aid: http://www.fafsa.ed.gov. The online form allows you to set up an account, complete the application electronically, save your work, and monitor the progress of your application.

FastWeb: http://www.FastWeb.com. Register for this free scholarship search service and discover sources of educational funding you never knew existed.

Bankrate: http://www.bankrate.com. This free site provides unbiased information about the interest rates, fees, and penalties associated with major credit cards and private loans. It also provides calculators that let you determine the long-term costs of different kinds of borrowing.

OTHER ▶

Knox, Susan. *Financial Basics: A Money-Management Guide for Students*. Columbus: Ohio State University Press, 2004.

MY INSTITUTION'S RESOURCES ▶

_____
_____
_____
_____
_____
_____
_____
_____
_____
_____
_____
_____
_____

12 Applying What You've LEARNED . . .

Now that you have read and discussed this chapter, consider how you can apply what you have learned to your academic and personal life. The following prompts will help you reflect on chapter material and its relevance to you both now and in the future.

1. Sometimes it is hard to plan for the future. Why not start small? Describe at least two things you can do each week to save money. For example, using public transportation when possible can help reduce the expense of owning a car.

2. Money can be a difficult subject to talk about, and sometimes it seems easier just not to worry about it. Ask yourself some hard questions. Do you spend money without much thought? Do you have a lot of debt and not much to show for it? Describe what you want *your* financial picture to look like.

One-Minute PAPER . . .

This chapter covers a lot of information about financing your college experience and managing your money. Planning ahead is an important part of managing your finances. What did you find to be the most useful information in this chapter? Did anything that was covered leave you with more questions than answers? If so, what?

Building Your PORTFOLIO . . .

CREDIT CARDS: A SLIPPERY SLOPE

Remember the saying "There is no free lunch"? That is a good maxim to keep in mind as you consider adding credit cards to your financial picture. College students are often targeted by credit card companies through an offer of a free T-shirt or other novelty if they sign up for a new card. While it might seem harmless at the time, signing up for multiple credit cards can have you in financial trouble—and fast!

A big factor in effectively managing your credit card debt is being aware of the terms and conditions that apply to each account you have.

1. If you already have credit cards (including gas cards and store credit cards such as a Gap or Sears card), find your most recent billing statements. If you do not have a credit card, use an Internet search engine to search for "credit cards for college students." You will find several Internet offers specifically for college students. Find the terms and conditions for one of the offers.

2. Next, to understand the fees associated with your credit accounts, create an Excel spreadsheet with the following headers (see example below):

- Card Issuer and Card Type
- Credit Limit
- APR (Annual Percentage Rate)
- Default APR (a default APR may be used when you fail to make the minimum payment on your credit card account or exceed your credit limit by a certain amount. The default APR is always higher than the stated APR for the credit account.)

- Due On
- Late Fee
- Over Credit Limit Fee

3. List each credit card you have and enter the associated fees.

Card Issuer & Card Type	Credit Limit	APR	Default APR	Due On	Late Fee	Over Credit Limit Fee
Example: Bank of America Student Visa	*$500*	*18.25% variable*	*32.25%*	*28th day of each month*	*$29*	*$39*
Card 1.						
Card 2.						
Card 3.						

4. Save the file to your local computer or flash drive.

5. Update the file any time you open or close a credit account.

Understanding the terms and conditions of every credit card account you have can help you avoid paying extremely high interest rates and damaging your credit history.

EPILOGUE

It Ain't Over 'Til It's Over

The great baseball player Yogi Berra is often quoted as having said, "It ain't over 'til it's over!" So here you are at the end of the course. This course is over—or is it? One thing is for sure: College isn't over for you and what you learned in this course isn't over. But finishing this course has to feel good. Because there has been so much research done on students like you, we can confidently tell you that successful completion of this course is a good predictor for overall success in college.

When you finish any of your courses in college, it is a good time to reflect, step back, and ask yourself some thoughtful questions like:

- What did I learn in this course?
- Can I apply what I learned to other courses?
- Will I use what I learned both in and out of class?
- What did I learn that I am most likely to remember?
- Do I want to stay in touch with this professor?
- Did I improve my basic skills?
- How do I feel about what I accomplished?
- Did I do better than I thought I would?
- What did I do that helped me progress, and how can I repeat those kinds of successful efforts in other courses?
- What challenges do I still face?

Whether you are finishing this course at the end of your first term in college or at the end of your first year in college, there are many success strategies that you learned in this course that will continue to help you as you move through the rest of your college experience.

SOME PARTING SUGGESTIONS

Keep in Touch with Professors We suggest that you consider keeping in touch with the professor of this course. Educators who volunteer to teach a college success course or first-year seminar really do care about students and enjoy staying in touch with them over time and noting their progress. You will also want to stay in touch with your other professors. Later in college you may need to ask them to write letters of reference for you as you seek employment or admission to graduate school. When a professor becomes part of your larger support group, this is a form of networking.

Using Campus Resources You should also keep using the campus's services and resources that you learned about in this course such as the learning center or career center. Remember, these services are most heavily utilized by the best students, and you want to be one of those. Those students continue to seek help. It's a lifelong behavioral pattern of successful people.

Practice Study Strategies in All Your Courses It's important for you to keep on practicing the success strategies that were presented in this book. Usually, you don't learn these in just one term. And, if you don't keep practicing them, you get rusty. Using these strategies is like learning anything else in life such as riding a bike. Practice is absolutely essential. But we also realize that you may not yet have been ready to attempt some of the strategies we endorsed in this book. So maybe the next term, or the next year will be a better time to revisit some of these ideas. We also suggest that you hang on to all your books so you can revisit them. We know that students like to resell their books. And if you do resell them, you could get library copies at some point in the future. But your books could be valuable resources for you when you might need to revisit course topics. There may also be friends or family members who'll be coming to college. You could share these materials with them.

Planning Your Summer We would also like to suggest that you begin thinking about what you are going to do this summer. We realize that students may have learned in high school that summer school was usually for students who slacked off during the year. But in college, nothing could be further from the truth. We now know from national research on college students' progress, that continuous enrollment is a good thing; it keeps students in the swing of things, they don't fall out of practice, and they are more likely to keep on going and going—and graduate.

An alternative to summer school is to do something in the summer that is connected to your education—or sponsored by your college, like an internship, practicum, or study abroad. Continuing your learning in summer maintains your fast pace of uninterrupted development and doesn't allow you to backtrack and get out of practice. Also, students who take the initiative to attend summer school or who have held summer jobs or internships will often be more attractive to future employers.

Planning Your Remaining Time in College As you end this course, we suggest that you once again think seriously about your major. That decision is important because eventually you have to get a degree in something. And you want to feel confident and comfortable about your major. And, even more important, your chosen major is connected to that all-important idea that we stressed in the first chapter of this book: Purpose—that is your purpose for being in this college at this time in your life. One of the ways that United States colleges are different from higher education institutions in the rest of the world is the opportunity to change majors. So this is something we encourage you to revisit now. This course may have given you some new insights into yourself and what might really motivate you now and in the future.

Now is also a good time to ask yourself about your academic advisor. Are you getting what you need from this important relationship? If not, don't hesitate to request a change.

It's possible that you haven't used the career center yet, even though you learned about it in this course. Now, as this course is coming to a close would be a great time to pay a visit to the career center to learn about possible internships, summer employment, and additional help if you haven't decided on a major.

Ending a course like this is a good time to take stock of your accomplishments this term. By all means, you should pat yourself on the back. But you also may want to take a hard look at those things that didn't go so well. Learn from your mistakes and apply what you learn to future successes.

Let's circle back to that concept of purpose. Here at the end of the term, how is the *fit* between you and this college, between you and your major? Is this campus meeting your expectations and your needs? Are you getting a clearer idea of why you are here as opposed to why some other people in your life may want you to be here? Even if you're still unsure, we hope you'll give yourself more time to get adjusted to this college thing, to get more comfortable, to find a sense of *fit*, and to accomplish some things for yourself that you can be really proud of.

We wrote this book to help students like you. Much of what we know about what students need in order to be successful, we learned from our students. Thanks for giving us the chance to help you as you began *Your College Experience*. You've already come a long way from where you started, and there are many great college experiences ahead. So practice the strategies we tried to teach you in this book and remember, if millions of students before you have made it, you can, too.

Sincerely,

John N. Gardner
A. Jerome Jewler
Betsy O. Barefoot

GLOSSARY

Abstract   A paragraph-length summary of the methods and major findings of an article in a scholarly journal.

Academic freedom   The virtually unlimited freedom of speech and inquiry granted to professors to further the advancement of knowledge, as long as human lives, rights, and privacy are not violated.

Active learning   Learning by participation, such as listening critically, discussing what you are learning, and writing about it.

Adaptability   The ability to adjust your thinking and behavior when faced with new or unexpected situations.

Annotate   Add critical or explanatory margin notes on the page as you read.

Argument   Reason and evidence brought together in logical support of a claim.

Aural learner   A person who prefers to learn by listening to information. One of the preferences described by the VARK Learning Styles Inventory.

Autonomy   Self-direction or independence. College students usually have more autonomy than they did in high school.

Bias   A leaning toward a particular point of view. Also, a negative preconceived opinion of certain peoples or value systems that can manifest either in attitude or in acts of discrimination.

Biorhythms   The internal mechanisms that drive our daily patterns of physical, emotional, and mental activity.

Boolean operators   The words "AND," "OR," and "NOT." They are added to specific terms when searching in databases and search engines to help yield more relevant matches.

Budget   A spending plan that tracks all sources of income and expenses during a specific period of time.

Chunking   A previewing method that involves making a list of terms and definitions from the reading, then dividing the terms into smaller clusters of five, seven, or nine, to more effectively learn the material.

Citation   A source or author of certain material. When browsing the Internet for sources, use only material that has citations crediting the author, where it came from, and who posted it.

Co-curricular experiences   Learning that occurs outside of the classroom, through on-campus clubs and groups, co-op programs, internships, or other means.

Co-op programs   Programs offered at many institutions that allow students the opportunity to work in their field of study while enrolled in college. Co-op programs offer valuable experience and an excellent preview of what work in the chosen field is actually like. Also called cooperative education.

Cognitive restructuring   A technique of applying positive thinking and giving oneself encouraging messages rather than self-defeating negative ones.

Content skills   Cognitive, intellectual, or "hard" skills, acquired as one gains mastery in an academic field. These include writing proficiency, computer literacy, and foreign language skills.

Cornell format   A method for organizing notes in which one side of the notebook page is designated for note-taking during class, and the other as a "recall" column where main ideas and important details for tests are jotted down as soon after class as feasible.

Credit score   A numerical representation of your level of fiscal responsibility, derived from a credit report that contains information about all accounts in your name. This score can determine your loan qualification, interest rates, insurance rates, and sometimes employability.

Critical thinking   Thoughtful consideration of the information, ideas, observations, and arguments that you encounter; in essence, a search for truth.

Culture   The aspects of a group of people that are passed on and/or learned. Traditions, food, language, clothing styles, artistic expression, and beliefs are all part of culture.

Deep learning   Understanding the "why" and "how" behind the details.

Discipline   An area of academic study, such as sociology, anthropology, and engineering.

Discrimination   The act of treating people differently because of their race, ethnicity, gender, socioeconomic class, or other identifying characteristics, rather than on their merit.

Diversity   Variation of social and cultural identities among people living together.

Dyslexia   A widespread developmental learning disorder that can affect the ability to read, spell, or write.

Emotional intelligence (EI)   The ability to recognize, understand, use, and manage moods, feelings, and attitudes.

Empathy   Recognition and understanding of another person's feelings, situation, or point of view.

Ethnicity   An affiliation assigned to a specific group of people historically connected by a common national heritage or language.

Examples   Stories, illustrations, hypothetical events, and specific cases that give support to an idea.

Explanatory writing   Writing that is "published," meaning that others can read it.

Exploratory writing   Writing that helps you first discover what you want to say. It is private and is used only as a series of steps toward a published work.

Extraverts   Individuals who are outgoing, gregarious, and talkative. They are good communicators who are quick to act and lead. One of the personality preferences described by the Myers-Briggs Type Indicator.

Feeling types   Individuals who are warm, empathetic, compassionate, and interested in the happiness of others as well as themselves. They need and value harmony and kindness. One of the personality preferences described by the Myers-Briggs Type Indicator.

Financial aid   Monetary sources to help pay for college. Financial aid can come in the form of scholarships, grants, loans, work-study, and cooperative education.

Freewriting   Writing that is temporarily unencumbered by mechanical processes, such as punctuation, grammar, spelling, context, and so forth.

Grade Point Average (GPA)   A student's average grade, calculated by dividing the grades received by the number of credits earned. The GPA represents the level of academic success attained while in college.

Humanities   Branches of knowledge that investigate human beings, their culture, and their self-expression. They include the study of philosophy, religion, literature, music, and art.

Idioms   Peculiar phrases that cannot be understood from the individual meanings of the words. For example, "cost an arm and a leg" is a familiar American idiom.

Inclusive curriculum   A curriculum that offers courses that introduce students to diverse people, worldviews, and approaches. Gender studies, religious studies, and ethnic and cultural studies are some areas included in an inclusive curriculum.

Information Age   Our current times, characterized by the primary role of information in our economy and our lives, the need for information retrieval and information management skills, and the explosion of available information.

Information literacy   The ability to find, interpret, and use information to meet your needs.

Interdisciplinary   Involving two or more academic fields of study, such as history and religion. Encouraging an interdisciplinary approach to teaching can offer a better understanding of modern society.

Interpersonal   Relating to the interaction between yourself and other individuals. Friendships, professional networks, and family connections are interpersonal relationships that can be mutually beneficial.

Intrapersonal   Relating to how well you know and like yourself, as well as how effectively you can do the things you need to do to stay happy. Knowing yourself is necessary in order to understand others.

Introverts   Individuals who like quiet and privacy and who tend to think a lot and reflect carefully about a problem before taking action. One of the personality preferences described by the Myers-Briggs Type Indicator.

Intuitive types   Individuals who are fascinated by possibilities, the meaning behind the facts, and the connections between concepts. They are often original, creative, and nontraditional. One of the personality preferences described by the Myers-Briggs Type Indicator.

Judging types   Individuals who approach the world in a planned, orderly, and organized way. They strive for order and control, making decisions relatively quickly and easily so they can create and implement plans. One of the personality preferences described by the Myers-Briggs Type Indicator.

Keyword   A method of searching a topic by using a word related to the topic.

Kinesthetic learner   A person who prefers to learn something through experience and practice, rather than by listening or reading about it. One of the preferences described by the VARK Learning Styles Inventory.

Learning disabilities   Disorders, such as dyslexia, that affect people's ability to either interpret what they see and hear or to connect information across different areas of the brain.

Learning styles   Particular ways of learning, unique to each individual. For example, one person prefers reading to understand how something works, another prefers being "hands-on."

Long-term memory   The type of memory that is used to retain information and can be described in three ways: procedural, semantic, and episodic.

Mapping   A preview strategy of drawing a wheel or branching structure to show relationships between main ideas and secondary ideas and how different concepts and terms fit together and help you make connections to what you already know about the subject.

Marking   An active reading strategy of making marks in the text by underlining, highlighting, and writing margin notes or annotations.

Mind map   A review sheet with words and visual elements that jog the memory to help you recall information more easily.

Multiculturalism   The active process of acknowledging and respecting the diverse social groups, cultures, religions, races, ethnicities, attitudes, and opinions within a community.

Multitasking   Performing many tasks at the same time, such as eating dinner, typing a paper, and making phone calls.

Perceiving types   Individuals who are flexible and can comfortably adapt to change. They tend to delay decisions to keep their options open to gather more information. One of the personality preferences described by the Myers-Briggs Type Indicator.

Plagiarism   The act of taking another person's ideas or work and presenting it as your own. This gross academic misconduct can result in suspension or expulsion, and even the revocation of the violator's college degree.

Prejudice   A preconceived judgment or opinion of someone based not on facts or knowledge; for example, prejudging someone based entirely on his or her skin color.

Prewriting   Preparing to write by filling your mind with information from other sources; generally considered the first stage of exploratory writing.

Primary sources   The original research or documentation on a topic, usually referenced either at the end of a chapter or the back of the book.

Procrastination   Putting off doing a task or an assignment.

Race   A term that refers to biological characteristics shared by groups of people, including skin tone, hair texture and color, and facial features.

Racism   Prejudice directed at a racial group, which often stems from one group's fear of losing power and privilege to another.

Read/Write learner   A person who prefers to learn information displayed as words. One of the preferences described by the VARK Learning Styles Inventory.

Sensing types   Individuals who are practical, factual, realistic, and down-to-earth. Relatively traditional and conventional, they can be very precise, steady, patient, and effective with routine and details. One of the personality preferences described by the Myers-Briggs Type Indicator.

Service learning   Unpaid volunteer service that is embedded in courses across the curriculum.

Short-term memory   How many items you are able to perceive at one time. Memory that disappears in less than 30 seconds (sometimes faster) unless the items are moved to long-term memory.

Social responsibility   The establishment of a personal link with a group or community and cooperation with other members toward shared goals.

Sorting   Sifting through available information and selecting what is most relevant.

Statistics   Numerical data used to support ideas in a speech or written work.

Stereotype   An oversimplified set of assumptions about another person or group.

Supplemental Instruction (SI)   Classes that provide further opportunity to discuss the information presented in lectures.

Syllabus   Formal statement of course requirements and procedures or a course outline provided by instructors on the first day of class to all students.

Synthesis   The process of combining separate information and ideas to formulate a more complete understanding.

Testimony   Evidence in support of something. Quoting outside experts and paraphrasing credible sources are examples of testimony.

Thesis statement   A short statement that clearly defines the purpose of the paper.

Thinking types   Individuals who are logical, rational, and analytical. They reason well and tend to be critical and objective without being swayed by their own or other people's feelings. One of the personality preferences described by the Myers-Briggs Type Indicator.

Transferable skills   General skills that apply to or transfer to a variety of settings. Examples include solid oral and listening abilities, leadership skills, critical thinking, and problem solving.

Visual learner   A person who prefers to learn by reading words on a printed page or by looking at pictures, charts, graphs, symbols, video, and other visual means. One of the preferences described by the VARK Learning Styles Inventory.

Work-study award   A form of federal financial aid that covers a portion of college costs in return for on-campus employment.

CREDITS

INDEX

Note: Figures and tables are denoted by *f* and *t*, respectively.